Wolfgang Puck's
Modern French Cooking
for the American Kitchen

This book is published
by special arrangement
with
Eric Lasher and Maureen Lasher.

Wolfgang Puck's

MODERN
FRENCH
COOKING

for the American Kitchen

by Wolfgang Puck

Foreword by Raymond Thuilier

BOSTON HOUGHTON MIFFLIN COMPANY

The introductory material for this book was written in collaboration
with Barbara Lazaroff.

———————————

For information about permission to reproduce selections
from this book, write to Permissions, Houghton Mifflin
Company, 215 Park Avenue South, New York, New York 10003.

Library of Congress Cataloging in Publication Data

Puck, Wolfgang.
    Wolfgang Puck's Modern French cooking for the American kitchen.
    Includes Index.
    1. Cookery, French. I. Title.
TX719.P83   641.5944   81-6506
ISBN 0-395-93520-2 (pbk.)   AACR2

Printed in the United States of America

CRW 16 15 14 13 12 11 10

Book design by Edith Allard, Designworks, Inc.
Illustrations by Joanna Bodenweber

To my grandmother Christine, who nourished my love of
cooking as well as my stomach

and

To the guests at Ma Maison, who inspired my finest culinary performances

Acknowledgments

Judy Gethers, director of Ma Cuisine, is affectionately and deservedly known as the "Ma" of Ma Maison and Ma Cuisine. She was indispensable in the organizing and continuity of this book. If Judy had not urged me along, this book might never have become a reality.

A toast to Joan Hoien, an accomplished cook in her own right, who meticulously tested these recipes, again and again, with great skill, devotion, and imagination.

My thanks and some fresh air for Cecilia DeCastro, who spent many long hours of organizing, typing, and retyping, and never failed to bring a little sunshine indoors.

And for my former partner and good friend, Patrick Terrail, a lifetime supply of carnations for his ever-dapper lapel, and my deepest appreciation for providing the stage on which I have acted out all of my culinary fantasies.

Foreword

by Raymond Thuilier

Wolfgang Puck is a chef with a sense of the harmony and balance of cuisine and, even more, an imagination that leads him to seek new culinary heights to satisfy those who appreciate gourmet cooking. He is aware that cooking is not only an important skill but a science, and that the skill demands moral, physical, and intellectual qualities to which one must give one's best in order to attempt to achieve perfection.

I know first hand that Wolfgang has all the qualities of a great chef, for at a young age he was next to me at the stove of Baumanière. He has a lust to learn, always to know more. Cooking is his joy, his *raison d'être*, the mistress to whom he daily gives the best of his talent.

There is a story of Ningon, a young apprentice at the turn of the century, and what he was told by the chef who was his teacher: "Listen, my boy, of all the professions in the world you have chosen the best. It is certainly laborious and infinitely arduous for him who devotes himself to it, but what exquisite delight it procures! You will be rewarded handsomely for your efforts — not only by the incomparable satisfaction that you will experience from the success of a dish you have prepared, but first and foremost from the glow you will see on the faces of your guests. Truly 'la Cuisine' merits that one become her slave!"

Wolf, like Ningon, has taken these words to heart. Ningon went on to make his mark as a man of both great culture and immense culinary talent. Wolf, too, has risen to success and is today the best ambassador of "la Cuisine."

"A NOVELTY THAT CREATES A FUROR! A RESTAURANT!"
This was a headline in 1765 when an establishment that
resembled a restaurant first opened in Paris. The storefront
sign read, "Come all, you whose stomach cries hunger;
come and I will restore it." This was the birth of the first
restaurant.

Ma Maison was certainly not the first restaurant in Los
Angeles, but for me it was a first — my own restaurant
and the culmination of a dream. I wish I could make you
believe that a restaurant is the creation of one man, but
that's just not so. Just as Boulanger opened that first restaurant in 1765 with *his* partner, I opened mine in 1973.

At the Palais-Royal in 1782, Beauvillier was the first
restaurateur to dress in tails and kiss his customers' hands.
When he had special guests, he would slip out of the dining
room and ask his chef what he should plan for his distin-
guished visitors. For advice on a special menu, I would go
to Wolfgang Puck; he creates dishes the way Picasso created
new trends in art. He is a great artist in the kitchen; his
stove is his palette.

If Escoffier is remembered as "Chef of kings and king of
Chefs," Wolfgang Puck is "Chef to the stars and a star of
Chefs." I would not have Ma Maison were it not for him.
In my career, I have met very few chefs who have as much
love for their art form.

May these recipes, developed from the kitchens of Ma
Maison and Ma Cuisine, end up on your dining room table
to "restore your hunger" as they have done for our devoted
patrons over the years.

Patrick Terrail
Ma Maison
September 1981

Contents

Introduction

Cooking is creation; a collaboration of the cook, his ingredients, and, for me, a great deal of love. Fine food flows from the heart. Mastery of the craft is achieved through practice, experience, and feeling. My book is not meant to impress the professional chef or overwhelm the amateur cook; rather, I hope it will be used as an inspiration and a comprehensive tool for a style of cooking that I feel is very much in keeping with the spirit of the times. Many of the classic French recipes are now outdated. Years back, sauces were often used to mask the flavors of food that was not particularly fresh. At that time refrigeration, transportation, and storage were primitive. I strongly believe that food should maintain a simplicity and purity of taste. Sauces should be used to subtly enhance the flavor of a dish, not overpower it.

America is currently in the midst of a food revolution not unlike the revolution that occurred in France in the 1960s with the development of *nouvelle cuisine.* In 1967, the highly respected Gault-Millau cuisine journal announced: "La Nouvelle Cuisine Française Is Born!" Gourmets, critics, and young chefs alike were becoming aware of a new "attitude" concerning food preparation, most elegantly demonstrated by such innovators as Paul Bocuse, Jean and Pierre Troisgros, Michel Guérard, Roger Vergé (and today Fred Girardet). Visibly absent from their cuisine were the heavy masking sauces, the complicated garnitures. As a result of the positive attention and welcomed arrival of the "new attitude," young chefs felt encouraged and began to discard old principles, experimenting to create what pleased their palates. Similarly, young American chefs are beginning to experiment — drawing upon traditional techniques and concepts but feeling freer to decide what to incorporate into their own individual style. We are witnessing a growing interest in food and food-related items (magazines, cookbooks, cooking shows). Of particular importance is the proliferation of schools specializing in the training of men and women in all areas of the culinary arts. American chefs are no longer intimidated by

European *haute cuisine* and are now among some of the most innovative and exciting talents in the field.

In the United States there is a growing concern with proper nutrition and fitness. More of us are coming to appreciate the importance of fresh, undercooked vegetables and fish and to realize that we don't have to give up "gourmet food" to eat in a reasonably healthy manner. It is a misconception to believe that any French-influenced cooking style is fattening and unhealthy. Many people who have never eaten in some of the newer French restaurants such as Ma Maison are surprised at the light consistency and delicate flavor of the food we prepare, particularly the sauces. I greatly favor simplifying food preparation; by undercooking fish and vegetables, thus preserving their natural juices, flavor, and texture, less elaborate preparation is needed to achieve an appealing, exciting taste sensation. Also, less butter is used, and since cooking time is reduced, the butter does not undergo the unhealthy chemical change that characterizes burned oils and deep-fried foods. By reducing a sauce to its optimum point of consistency and concentration of flavor, it is possible to add only a small amount to a dish and still greatly enhance the food, rather than smother it. I prefer smaller portions of a variety of dishes at one meal rather than the presentation of one enormous portion of meat with a heavy side dish of overcooked vegetables. I place great emphasis on the importance of beautiful, creative presentations employing varying food textures and colors. For me, an artful presentation is as appetizing as the taste of the food. With this in mind, I occasionally add a fresh-picked flower to the serving plate.

Along with our fine food products, there are increasing numbers of expertly grown wines developing in America — particularly the California Chardonnays and Cabernet Sauvignons. A Frenchman from Bordeaux is unlikely to import a wine from Italy; likewise, Americans shouldn't feel their domestic food and wine is second-rate. For that reason, many of my suggested wines are Californian. Good wine benefits and accents good food. Through careful selection and combination, a union can be achieved between them that allows for a flow of taste — a continuation of flavor, rather than a conflict. A rich Zinfandel would completely overwhelm a delicate fish or crustacean, whereas a hearty full-bodied Cabernet Sauvignon can stand up to a *tournedo* with marrow in red wine sauce. Ma Maison serves increasingly less hard liquor than it did in the past, and I feel this is an expression of a growing interest in the complementary nature of good food and good wine.

A good cook flows with the seasons. Since salmon is freshest from spring to fall, in January why not choose to prepare sole instead? Why plan to make a cherry tart in November when pears are at their most divine? In the summer, if you crave duck and my recipe uses pears, why not substitute peaches, which are at their peak of sweetness?

Each recipe in this book has been tested by a person who enjoys cooking but is not a professional chef. Additionally, many dishes were prepared and sampled in the classes of our Los Angeles cooking school, Ma Cuisine. The direct contact I have had with my students over the years has greatly aided in the clarification and simplification of these recipes. I have grown with my students. Their suggestions regarding specifics of techniques, direction, and exact measurements have been incorporated in this book.

I have never been protective of my recipes or my techniques. In many ways, I view a recipe as merely a framework or foundation for the creation of a dish. A given dish will never be the same twice, no matter how many people prepare it or how many times the same person recreates it. That is not to say guidelines are not helpful. Distinctive style is likely to develop soon enough, since we each bring our own unique feelings to cooking, but first becoming familiar with the techniques is essential. Even innately talented chefs must constantly practice much of what they have learned. They may bend the rules, but the rules remain. It is difficult to begin to improvise on a recipe until you master the basic techniques.

An early experience of mine is a vivid reminder that attention to detail is vital. As a boy I decided to bake a surprise birthday cake for my grandmother Christine, a woman who played a great part in raising me and also inspired much of my interest in cooking. I was so excited with the prospect of baking my first cake — especially since it was one for Grandma — that I didn't carefully read the recipe. I immediately ran out of room in my first mixing bowl, and soon had filled all the bowls and pans I could find. When Grandma discovered me in my dilemma, she instinctively remained silent. The controlled look on her face, however, suggested to me that something was awry.

When she left the room I started to throw portions away. Apparently, the recipe was not for one cake, but for six, as is the baking style in hotels and restaurants accommodating many people. Needless to say, the cake was not perfect, although Grandma miraculously salvaged it. It is wonderful to improvise, but don't forget to read all recipes carefully and heed important instructions!

The final review of a dish occurs at the table. It is necessary, however, to "audition" each creation during and at the point of its completion. For although the recipes in this book specify the quantity of each ingredient needed, as well as the techniques, vegetables differ slightly in size, herbs possess varying strengths, and cooking time and heat distribution are controllable but not always exact. Therefore, no matter how many times you repeat the same recipe you will find a subtly different personality each time. Cooking is the science of combining ingredients, the mastering of techniques, and the artist's emotion — or simply, "a matter of taste." You must adjust or substitute your seasonings accordingly, experiment, improvise, and above all, be true to your own personal tastes, your moods, and the moment.

These recipes reflect both the simple days of my childhood and the fifteen years of training and guidance I received in many fine kitchens in France. They are composed of memories of my grandmother standing lovingly over a pot of fresh vegetable soup, and passages of M. Thuilier, a man who inspired not only my craft but my being.

Raymond Thuilier — winemaker, lecturer, painter, writer, mayor of the small French town of Les Baux, chef and owner of the three-star restaurant L'Oustau de Baumanière — is truly a Renaissance man. His robust and poetic approach to all aspects of his life touched and deeply influenced me. Perhaps there are more technically excellent chefs (he did not decide he wanted to cook until the age of fifty), but for me, none greater exemplifies a love of life, creation, and constant growth. I believe I always had within me the ability to excel, but Thuilier's support allowed me the confidence to express myself and accept responsibility. Most of all, he offered me the freedom to grow.

You, too, I hope, will express yourself and believe in your capabilities. If you are giving an important party, it is sometimes better to present five recipes that you have mastered, rather than struggle with twenty that are new to you. It is also important to remember that what you serve will be affected not only by its preparation but also by its appearance. Use your plate as a canvas, paint a picture with what fills it.

Cooking is my *kinderspiel* — my child's play. You can make it yours, too. And while you're cooking, don't forget to share and laugh. Laugh a great deal, and with much love — it enhances the flavor of food.

Voilà!
Wolfgang Puck

Suggested Kitchen Equipment

Definitions

Cooking Techniques

Suggested Kitchen Equipment

There are individuals who undergo a complete metamorphosis from rational consumer to unrestrainable "buy-aholics" the moment any salesperson inquires, "May I help you?" If you are of this mold — and also love to cook — beware of the new "culinary candy stores."

I have been cooking professionally for more than sixteen years, and my *batterie de cuisine* is extensive. Surprisingly, I still delight at all the pots, pans, knives, gadgets, and "oddities" that can be found in cook stores. When in Paris, I frequently spend an entire day in the professional culinary shops near the district of Les Halles.

The purpose of this section is to familiarize you with some special items you may require, or find helpful, when preparing these recipes. A number of my recipes call for the use of a food processor, blender, mixer, or meat grinder; if you are fortunate to already have them, they will award you more time, less effort, and in many cases finer results, but the recipes in which they are used can also be made in the more traditional manner.

Without these "extras," you can fare quite well in the kitchen with just a few simple, top-quality items. A must is a set of durable, sharp knives. Carbon steel is preferred because the blades stay sharper longer and are easy to resharpen on stone or steel. However, the acidity of certain fruits and vegetables discolors carbon knives, and in turn these knives can cause the cut edges to blacken. For these two food categories, and for those of you who do not immediately wash and dry your utensils, I recommend high-carbon stainless steel.

At home I have a beautiful set of rather expensive copper pots. Copper is wonderful because it conducts heat so evenly. Nonetheless, these pots are mostly aesthetic indulgences on my part, and not really essential. Professionally I use many Teflon pans, which are easy to clean and do not absorb odors or retain tastes. I use large pots with multi-ply bottoms for stocks. These pots are composed largely of stainless steel, but they have a coating of copper on the bottom, over which is a layer of stainless steel to protect the more malleable copper. I never cook fish stock in a meat stockpot — that's a personal rule that needn't be followed if you use stainless steel; but if you cook with cast iron it can make a significant difference. Also, when cleaning a cast-iron sauté pan never use water (the pan will rust); wipe it out with a paper towel, scrape it with salt, and wipe clean again. I am not fond of white aluminum pots either; they ionize in boiling water, react with acids, and emit aluminum particles into the food. I use Calphalon anodized aluminum pots, which do not impart the odor or taste of their metal to food. You only need a few pots. The more you own, the more you tend to use, and, unhappily, the more you have to clean!

You will find that high-quality equipment can make a difference. It is a good idea to first develop your own style and then discover what you really require and can comfortably afford.

3 sauté pans (8, 10, and 15 inches)
3 saucepans (1½, 2½, and 4 quarts)
2 stockpots (6- or 8-quart and 12-quart)
2 covered round or oval casseroles (4 and 8 quarts)
2 nonstick skillets (6 and 10 inches)
2 roasting pans (10 by 14 and 12 by 20 inches)
1 springform pan (9 inches)
1 quiche pan (10 or 11 inches by 1½ inches)
3 nonstick baking sheets (14 by 18 inches, 11 by 14 inches, and 12 by 16 inches)
1 loaf pan (9 by 5 by 3 inches)
1 6-cup pâté mold
1 6- or 8-cup soufflé dish
1 steamer with rack
1 colander
3 stainless steel mixing bowls (small, medium, and large)
1 12- or 14-inch balloon wire whisk
2 small wire whisks
3 or 4 wooden spoons of various sizes
2 rubber spatulas
1 flexible long-bladed metal spatula
2 ladles (small and large)
1 large slotted kitchen spoon
1 long-handled kitchen fork
1 metal tongs

3 glass measuring cups for liquids (1-cup, 2-cup, and 1-quart capacities)
1 set metal measuring cups, for dry ingredients
1 set measuring spoons
1 14- or 16-inch plastic-lined pastry bag with assorted tips
2 pastry brushes
1 rolling pin
2 cutting boards
1 set aluminum beans
Parchment paper
Kitchen string
1 vegetable peeler
1 *tamis* or strainer
1 *chinois* or fine conical sieve
1 candy thermometer
4 knives (3½-inch paring; 8-inch chef's; 10-inch slicing; boning)
1 sharpening tool for knives
2 pepper mills (one containing black peppercorns, the other white)
1 timer
1 scale
1 grater
1 food mill
1 food processor
1 blender
1 electric mixer
8 ½-cup ramekins, timbales, or custard cups

Definitions

Every art, craft, and science has its own personal language. In fact, they have two, an official language and "dialects" or slang. This is true of the culinary arts as well. This chapter defines "official" expressions you will need in order to understand and effectively use this book. If they are not already, these phrases and terms will shortly become a part of your everyday cooking vocabulary; in no time you are certain to sound like a native of *la cuisine*.

AL DENTE Italian phrase used to describe the cooking of vegetables or pasta to the slightly crisp stage. The French word for *al dente* is *croquant,* which means crisp and crunchy.

BAIN-MARIE To cook food in a *bain-marie* is to cook it over simmering water (on top of the stove) or in a hot-water bath (in the oven). The first method requires an ordinary double boiler or you can improvise with a saucepan and heat-proof bowl; this is used for such things as melting chocolate, scrambling eggs, preparing chocolate mousse, and keeping sauces (especially egg-based ones) warm. With the second method, a *bain-marie* can be created by half-filling a roasting pan with simmering water and then placing the dishes to be cooked in the water.

BEURRE NOISETTE Butter that has been cooked until it turns light brown.

BEURRE MANIÉ A mixture of one part butter and one part flour, kneaded and used as a thickening agent for soups and sauces.

BOUQUET GARNI A small bundle of aromatic herbs (usually celery leaves, parsley, thyme, peppercorns, and a bay leaf) tied together with string or in a small piece of cheesecloth and added to stocks or stews to enhance the flavor. In this book the above-listed ingredients are used unless the recipe specifies otherwise. The bouquet garni is always removed before the dish is served.

CORNICHONS Sour gherkins preserved in vinegar, salt, and spices. They are commercially available in jars.

CRÈME FRAÎCHE A naturally fermented cream used in the preparation of many French dishes, *crème fraîche* is available in some specialty food stores. A suitable substitute can be made at home. Combine 1 cup heavy cream with ½ cup sour cream *or* 2 teaspoons buttermilk. Stir the mixture over very low heat until it is just lukewarm. Pour into a clean jar and let sit at room temperature until set. This may take a few hours or overnight. Cover the *crème fraîche* and refrigerate; use as needed. It will keep up to 1 week.

DEGLAZE After meat has been sautéed or roasted, the pan is degreased and liquid (stock, wine, water, or cream) is added. The browned particles are scraped up and incorporated into the liquid as it cooks. This is an important step in the preparation of all meat sauces, since the glaze becomes part of the sauce.

DEMI-GLACE AND GLACE *Demi-glace* is the result of cooking a stock until it is reduced by half; *glace* is the result of cooking it to a syrup.

DUXELLES A mixture of finely chopped mushrooms, shallots, and seasonings sautéed in butter with cream until the liquid is evaporated. For a recipe, see the Vegetable chapter.

FINES HERBES A mixture of fresh, finely chopped parsley, tarragon, chives, and chervil. I do not recommend using dried herbs; fresh herbs release flavor much more quickly, which is very important because so many of my dishes require a minimal amount of cooking.

FLEURONS Crescent-shaped puff pastry pieces cut with a special cutter. The rolled-out pastry should be ¹/₁₆ inch thick, and the *fleurons* are baked in a 400° oven for 10 to 12 minutes. They are used as decorations.

FORCEMEAT OR FARCE A mixture of finely chopped and highly seasoned meat, fish, or vegetables used in pâtés, galantines, and molds, or served alone.

GRATINÉE OR AU GRATIN Terms used to describe dishes that have been sprinkled with butter, bread crumbs, and/or cheese and baked or broiled until brown.

HERBES DE PROVENCE A combination of chopped herbs (such as thyme, laurel, rosemary, sage, savory, fennel, and marjoram) used in home kitchens in the south of France and available dried in specialty food shops. French cooks generally use these herbs in a dried form.

MOUSSE OR MOUSSELINE The name given to a purée of vegetables, meat, or fish lightened by the addition of whipped cream.

NAP To lightly cover food with a sauce so that the outlines of the food are preserved.

NOISETTE A small individual portion of meat, particularly a small round slice cut from the fillet or rib of lamb.

EN PAPILLOTE A method of cooking in which food (fish, for example) is enclosed in a sheet of oiled parchment paper or aluminum foil and baked until the paper or foil swells as a result of the heat.

GREEN AND PINK PEPPERCORNS Green peppercorns come from Madagascar. They are available in cans; the best ones are preserved in water and salt, rather than vinegar. Pink peppercorns grow on the West Coast of the United States as a wild berry. They are commercially available freeze-dried in jars. They should be soaked in port for 24 hours before using.

PETITS FOURS Petits fours are bite-sized pastries served with coffee at the end of an elegant meal. Some petits fours included in this book are candied grapefruit peel, palmiers, ladyfingers, and marjolaine cut to size.

REDUCE To cook a liquid, decreasing its volume with evaporation, in order to concentrate its flavor and make a thicker consistency.

ROUX A cooked mixture of butter and flour used as a thickening agent in some sauces.

SHERRY WINE VINEGAR Vinegar made from sherry, as opposed to red or white wine. Good red wine vinegar with a dash of sherry may be substituted.

SWEAT To cook food until it is translucent and glossy, without affecting its color.

Cooking Techniques

It is the "doing" that creates and tunes one's skills. I have attempted to make these descriptions and illustrations clear and thorough, but you are your own best teacher and your own best student. You must constantly hone your techniques through repetition. If you enjoy cooking, this will not be difficult, but it will not always be thoroughly pleasant. Try to remember that great chefs, like masters of any profession or craft, never stop learning. They are always, happily and luckily, apprentices.

ADDING BUTTER TO SAUCES The butter should be at room temperature. For better control, add the butter with your hands, letting a small amount at a time slip into the sauce, whisking all the while as the butter is incorporated. If the sauce gets too hot, remove the saucepan from the flame and continue adding the butter. The sauce should get neither too hot nor too cold.

CLARIFYING BUTTER Melt the butter over low heat and skim the foam that forms on top. Spoon the clear liquid under the foam into another container and discard the milky residue. Food sautéed in clarified butter can be sautéed at a higher temperature than with fresh butter.

BONING A CHICKEN LEG Using a boning knife, separate the thigh bone from the meat (1) and cut the thigh bone free (2). Cut the leg bone from the meat in the same manner and break off the end of the leg bone with the back of a heavy knife (3). Sever the bone completely from the meat (4) and the leg is ready to stuff (5).

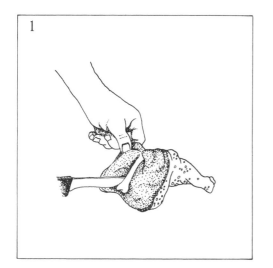

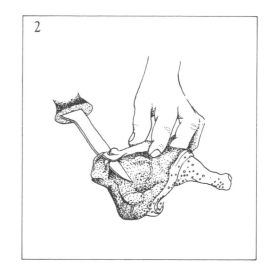

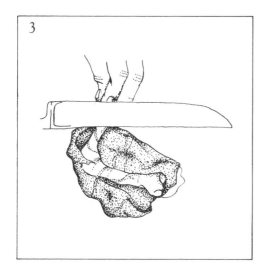

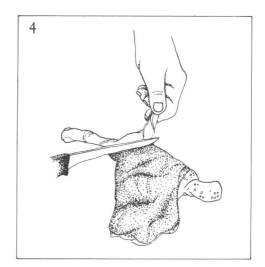

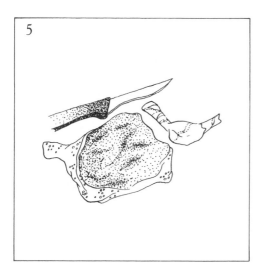

CUTTING A CHICKEN INTO EIGHT PIECES Several of my
recipes call for cutting a chicken into eight pieces. Here
is how it is done: Cut off the wing tips (1). Cut off the
legs (2 and 3). Remove the meat from the breast, cutting
¾ of an inch away from the breastbone (4 and 5). Separate
the back from the breast (6) and cut the breast into two
pieces (7). Cut each leg into two pieces at the joint (8).
You now have eight pieces of chicken ready to cook (9)
and several others that can be used for stock or soup (10).

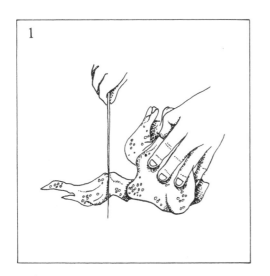

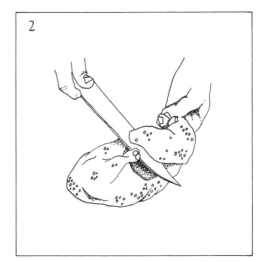

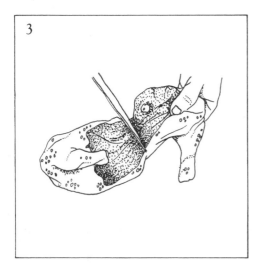

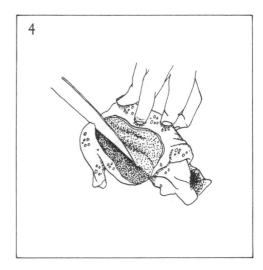

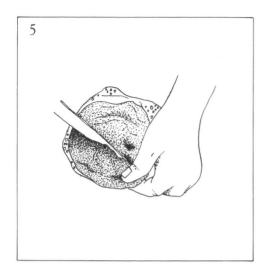

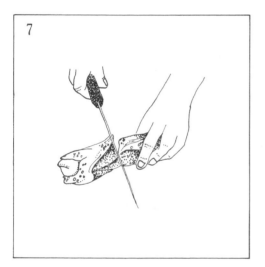

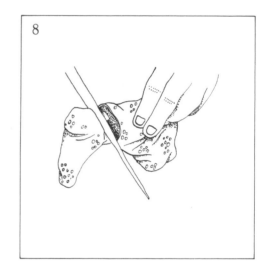

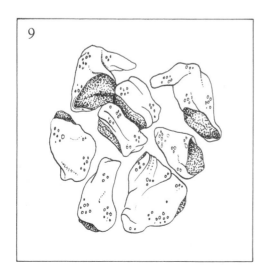

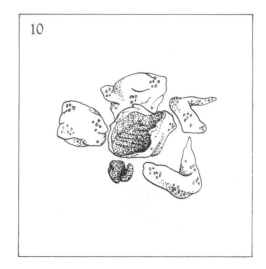

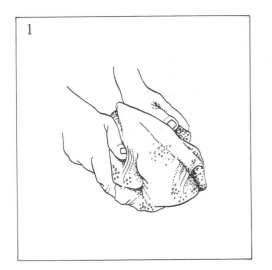

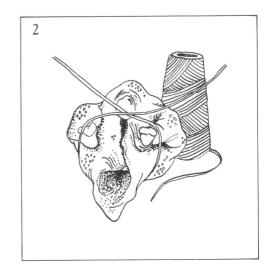

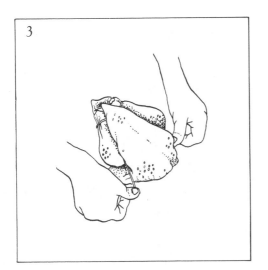

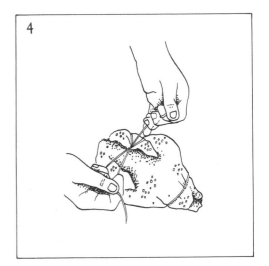

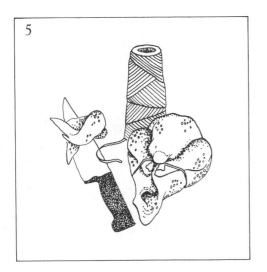

TRUSSING A CHICKEN Begin with a piece of kitchen string about twice the length of your forearm. Remove the wing tips and then grasp the legs and push them toward the cutting board or other work surface (1). Tie the string around the back and legs (2). Move the string toward the wings (3) and then turn the chicken over and make a knot (4). Turn the chicken right side up (5), and it is ready to cook.

WHIPPING CREAM TO THE CHANTILLY STAGE Whip heavy cream in a bowl using a whisk or an electric beater until the cream has the consistency of a soft mousse. It will rest upon itself when dropped from the beater or whisk, and will not form peaks. It may be sweetened or flavored to taste.

BEATING EGG WHITES When beating egg whites it is best to use eggs that are at least three days old. Have the eggs at room temperature. Place the whites in a perfectly clean bowl and, using a balloon-shaped wire whisk, beat gently until the whites form firm peaks when the whisk is lifted from the bowl. The purpose is to incorporate as much air as possible into the beaten whites. An electric beater may be used in place of the whisk. Beaten egg whites should be used immediately.

BEATING EGG YOLKS TO A RIBBON To reach this point, sugar is gradually added to egg yolks while the yolks are being beaten with a wire whisk or electric beater; the beating continues until the mixture thickens and turns pale yellow. When dropped from the lifted beater, the mixture will form a slowly dissolving ribbon on the surface. It is important not to beat beyond this stage, as that could cause the mixture to become granular.

ROLLING OUT PASTRY The rolling pin and the pastry should both be chilled to facilitate the rolling. (A plain rolling pin without handles is best, as it helps you roll the pastry more evenly.) The pastry should be rolled as quickly as possible to prevent the dough from becoming soft and difficult to handle. Refer to individual recipes for additional tips.

TESTING THICKNESS OF SAUCES AND SOUPS Stir a spoon through the sauce or soup, and then lift it out of the liquid. It should be thick enough to leave a film on the surface of the spoon. When you run a finger across this film, it should leave a clean streak.

CUTTING AND CHOPPING There are several classic shapes and sizes that food is cut into according to its role in a recipe. Perhaps the most familiar is *julienne*. To cut a potato, for example, into julienne, first cut it into $1/16$-inch-thick slices (1a) and then cut the slices into matchsticks $1/16$ inch thick and about 2 inches long (1b). Form *batonettes* in the same manner, but slice the potato (or other food) ⅛ inch thick (2a), and then cut the slices into ⅛-inch-thick strips 2 inches long (2b). A *brunoise* (3) is formed by cutting julienne strips into tiny cubes. A *mirepoix* (4), used to enhance the flavor of stocks and sauces, consists of carrots, celery, and onions cut into ¾-inch cubes. Breasts of poultry and pieces of meat are sometimes cut into *aiguillettes,* which are thin slices cut lengthwise, with the grain. *Chiffonade* is the term that describes plant leaves, including lettuces and herbs, cut into fine strips or ribbons and used in salads or as a garnish for soup.

As an attractive addition to some recipes, vegetables, or pieces of them, are sometimes cut into oval shapes. Before you attempt to do this, practice by moving a small sharp knife over the surface of an egg, which is very similar to the desired shape (5). Take, for example, a potato, and cut off both ends (6). Holding the potato between your thumb and index finger, cut from top to bottom, removing

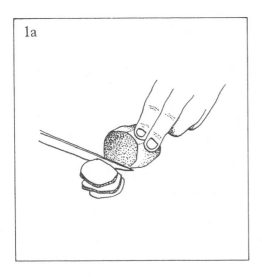

1a

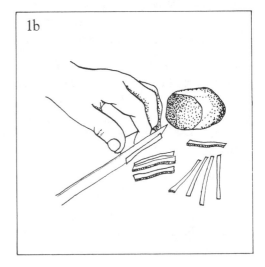

1b

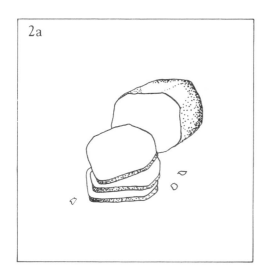

2a

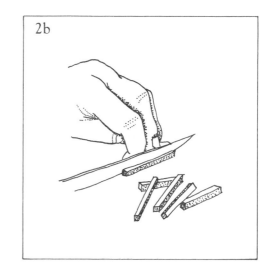

2b

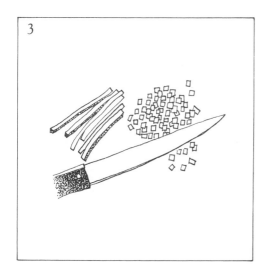

3

4

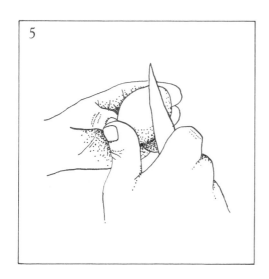

5

6

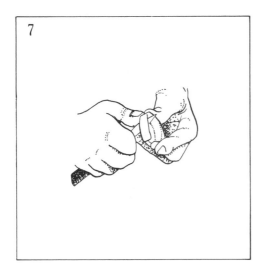

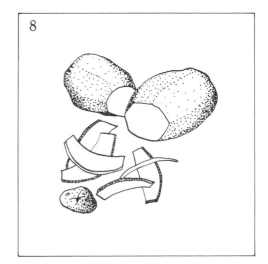

the peel and a small amount of potato as well (7). Besides potatoes (8), pieces of cucumber and turnip are frequently shaped in this manner.

FILLETING SOLE AND SIMILAR FLAT FISH Use a long, flexible knife (1). Insert the blade in the flesh near the head (2), cut along the spine toward the tail (3), and carefully remove the fillet (4). Turn the fish around and proceed in the same manner (5), but this time work from the tail to the head (6). Remove the fillets from the other side of the fish in exactly the same manner, and you then have four fillets ready to cook (7).

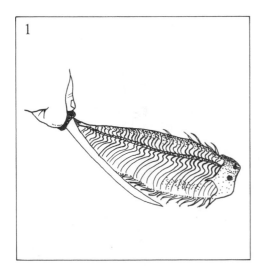

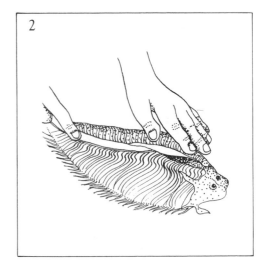

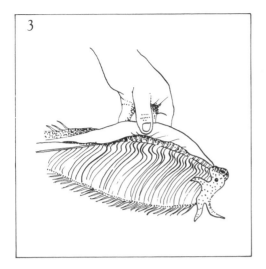

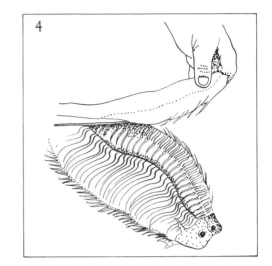

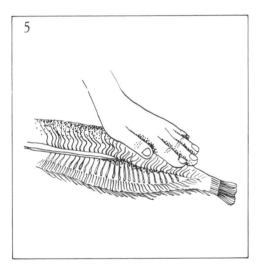

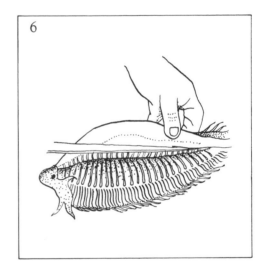

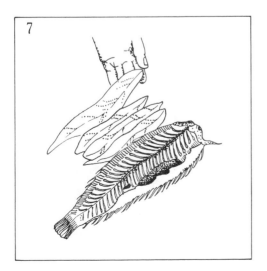

FILLETING A SALMON OR OTHER LARGE WHOLE FISH
Begin with a whole salmon (1) that has been cleaned by
the fishmonger. Cut off the head (2) and then cut the fish
lengthwise (3) along the uppermost back portion until
bones are visible. Guiding the point of the knife along the
backbone, separate the fillet from the bone (4). Once this
is done, the fillet is ready to skin (5). Grasp the tail end
of the fillet with one hand and, with the knife lying almost
flat in relation to the cutting board, slip the knife between
the skin and the fillet. Keeping the blade of the knife
against the skin, and holding the skin firmly (6), gradually
remove the skin with a pulling motion (7). Once the fillet
has been skinned (8), use a pair of tweezers to pull out any
remaining bones (9).

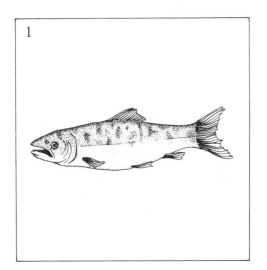

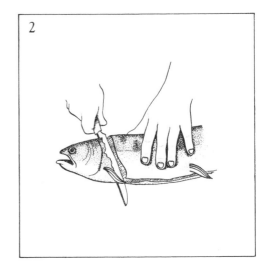

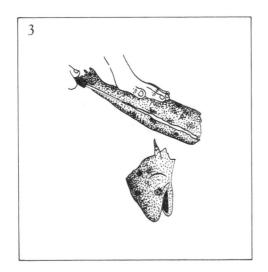

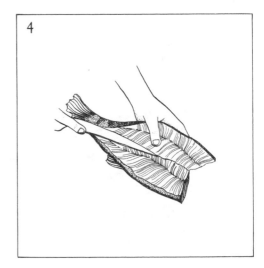

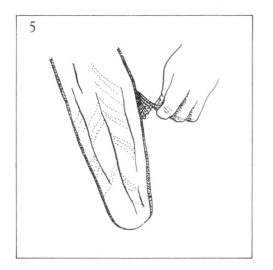

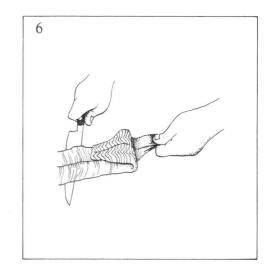

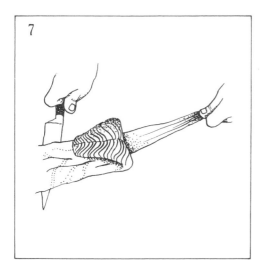

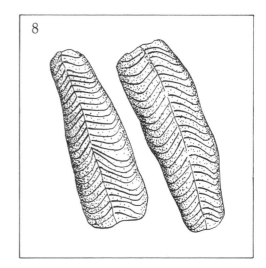

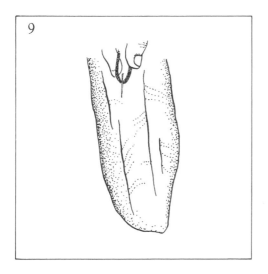

SKIMMING FAT FROM STOCKS AND SAUCES The fat will rise to the surface of a stock or sauce if the cooking is stopped temporarily. The fat then can be skimmed off by moving a small ladle in a circular motion just under the surface of the liquid. Discard the skimmed-off fat.

TESTING A MOUSSE FOR TASTE Poach a spoonful of the mousse in salted simmering water for 4 or 5 minutes. Remove the mousse from the water and taste. Correct the seasoning as necessary.

KILLING A LIVE LOBSTER Plunge the lobster, head first, into boiling water and leave it there for 3 minutes. This method will kill the lobster immediately. After 3 minutes, remove the lobster and proceed with the given recipe.

Warm and Cold Appetizers

Timbales of Chicken with Truffles

Cold Chicken and Vegetable Mousseline with Fresh
Tomato Sauce

Zucchini Flowers Filled with Shrimp Mousse

Mousseline of Whitefish with Oysters and Truffle Butter

Smoked Fish Mousse

Fish Terrine

Country-Style Pâté

Duck Terrine with Hazelnuts and Green Peppercorns

Oysters in Lettuce Bundles

Salmon Françoise

Shrimp with Mustard

Salmon Soufflé

Bass and Salmon with Avocado

Pasta with Truffles

Croissants with Lobster or Crab

Quiche

Sausage Wrapped in Brioche with Truffle Butter

Asparagus in Puff Pastry

Salmon Napoleon

Spinach and Brains Between Layers of Puff Pastry

Scallops in Puff Pastry

Crêpes Surprise

Artichokes à la Greque

Mousseline of Broccoli with Mushroom Sauce

As a schoolboy, when I had the opportunity to visit a magnificent castle in Vienna, I was overwhelmed by the palatial entrance hall and surprised by how many of the more often used rooms paled in comparison. I learned that kings doted upon grand hallways because they were aware that the first impression was often the most salient.

It was a memorable lesson that extends to my kitchen. An appetizer should be given earnest thought and care because it provides your guests with their first impression and sets the tone for the rest of the meal.

Appetizers should be served in small portions to stimulate (not satiate) the appetite, and to prepare your guests for the next course. Portion size is determined by the number of courses to be offered, and the nature of the dish. A rich soup, for example, is better appreciated in moderate portions when many courses are planned. Many of these appetizers can be served in larger portions as luncheon or late-supper entrées.

If you are presenting more than one appetizer, warm ones are generally served after the cold. Time of year is also a consideration. Chilled soups are delightfully refreshing on a warm summer evening, whereas pasta, which can be enjoyed year-round, imparts a particularly cozy feeling on a brisk fall day. The seasonal availability of ingredients is another concern.

When deciding what appetizer to select, consider the meal as a whole. If you are serving only one appetizer, and have decided on a fowl or meat dish for the entrée, a fish appetizer provides contrast and variety.

Innovate: By including these recipes in your menu planning, you can change the mood of a too-familiar meal. Strive for consistently good quality, but never be too predictable, and you will delight your friends from the start.

Timbales of Chicken with Truffles

Timbales de Volaille aux Truffes

I serve this mostly as an appetizer, but the mousseline can also be used as a stuffing for chicken breasts or legs.

To make the mousseline:
1. Be sure all the ingredients are very cold. This is *important.*
2. Cut chicken into 1-inch pieces. Remove all traces of fat and tendons.
3. In a food processor, combine the chicken, tarragon, parsley, truffle juice, egg, salt, and pepper. Process until the mixture is a very smooth purée. Transfer to a cold mixing bowl and chill over ice or refrigerate.
4. Preheat oven to 325°.
5. Lightly whip the heavy cream. Set the chicken purée over ice and fold in the cream. Test the mousseline in simmering water (see page 20). Taste and correct seasoning. Refrigerate until needed.
6. Generously butter six or eight ½-cup timbales. Half-fill each timbale with mousseline and layer with *duxelles*. Top with the remaining mousseline. Cover with buttered foil, buttered side down.
7. Bake in a *bain-marie* for 30 to 40 minutes, or until the mousseline springs back when lightly pressed.

To make the sauce:
1. In a medium saucepan, combine the wine, shallot, chicken stock, and truffle juice. Cook, over high heat, until only ½ cup remains.
2. Add the cream and reduce until slightly thickened.
3. Whisk in the butter, one small piece at a time. Strain sauce and stir in truffles. Season to taste with salt, pepper, and lemon juice.

PRESENTATION: Unmold timbales onto warm plates. Spoon sauce over mousselines.

SUGGESTED WINE: A California Riesling

TO SERVE 6 OR 8

Mousseline:

¾ pound boneless, skinless chicken breasts
1 tablespoon chopped fresh tarragon
2 tablespoons minced fresh parsley
6 tablespoons truffle juice
1 egg
1 teaspoon salt
½ teaspoon freshly ground white pepper
1 cup heavy cream
½ cup duxelles (page 174)

Sauce:

½ cup dry white wine
1 shallot, minced
½ cup chicken stock (page 65) or brown veal stock (page 66)
¼ cup truffle juice
½ cup heavy cream
¼ pound unsalted butter, cut into small pieces
1 tablespoon minced truffle or truffle peelings
Salt
Freshly ground pepper
Lemon juice

Cold Chicken and Vegetable Mousseline with Fresh Tomato Sauce
Mousseline de Volaille Portugaise

This makes a wonderful appetizer on a hot summer day and is much lighter than the usual pâté or terrine.

TO SERVE 8

1 recipe chicken mousseline (page 25) without duxelles
1 teaspoon salt
½ teaspoon freshly ground white pepper
1 medium zucchini, cut lengthwise into ¼-inch pieces
2 small carrots, cut into ½-inch pieces
½ pound spinach, chopped
4 medium mushrooms, sliced
½ cup cauliflower florets
1 large tomato, peeled and seeded
Fresh tomato vinaigrette (page 101)

1. Prepare the chicken mousseline and add the additional salt and pepper.
2. Blanch vegetables (zucchini, carrots, spinach, mushrooms, and cauliflower), in separate batches, in boiling, salted water until they are tender. Chill. Cut tomato into strips and add to blanched vegetables.
3. Generously butter a 6-cup loaf pan. Cut waxed paper to fit the bottom of the pan and generously butter the paper.
4. Preheat oven to 325°.
5. *To make layers:* Spread one third of the chicken mousseline over the bottom of the loaf pan; arrange half of the vegetables as desired; top with one third of the mousseline and the remaining half of the vegetables; and cover with the remaining third of the mousseline. Cover with buttered foil, buttered side down.
6. Set loaf pan in a *bain-marie* and bake 40 to 50 minutes, or until the mousseline springs back when lightly pressed.
7. Chill at least 24 hours.

PRESENTATION: Unmold the mousseline. Coat each plate with fresh tomato vinaigrette and place a slice of the mousseline on the sauce.

SUGGESTED WINE: A slightly chilled Beaujolais

Zucchini Flowers Filled with Shrimp Mousse

Fleurs de Courgettes à la Mousse de Crevettes

Like many other vegetables, zucchini is at its best when young. To serve it with the flower is not only delicious but innovative. You may have to ask your greengrocer to special-order these for you.

1. From the plain end of the zucchini, make three or four thin lengthwise slices (as though to make a fan), stopping just about ¼ inch from the flower.
2. Make sure all the mousse ingredients are very cold. In a food processor, prepare the mousse by combining shrimp, egg, salt, white pepper, cayenne pepper, and port. Process until puréed. With the motor running, pour 1 cup cream through the feed tube and process just until cream is incorporated. Poach a small amount in simmering water (see page 20). Correct seasoning to taste. Press through a fine sieve and chill until ready to use.
3. Using a pastry bag fitted with a number 6 plain tip, pipe mousse into each flower, filling it to the top. It will take about 1 ounce of mousse per flower. Chill until ready to use.
4. In a heavy saucepan, bring vermouth, fish stock, tomatoes, and shallots to a boil. Add zucchini and simmer slowly for 10 to 12 minutes. *Do not boil.*
5. Transfer zucchini to a plate and keep warm. Over high heat, reduce the sauce by half. Pour it into a blender and purée. Return to saucepan and add remaining cup of cream. Reduce until sauce thickens slightly. Strain.
6. Whisk in the butter, one small piece at a time. Season to taste with salt, white pepper, cayenne pepper, and lemon juice.

PRESENTATION: Pour sauce onto six hot serving plates. Arrange two zucchini fans on each plate and sprinkle with a *chiffonade* of basil.

SUGGESTED WINE: A Chardonnay from the Santa Inez Valley

SPECIAL EQUIPMENT:
Pastry bag and number 6 tip

TO SERVE 6

12 zucchini, with flowers attached
¾ pound fresh shrimp, peeled
1 egg
1 teaspoon salt
½ teaspoon freshly ground white pepper
½ teaspoon cayenne pepper
1 tablespoon port
2 cups heavy cream
1 cup dry white vermouth
2 cups fish stock (page 65)
½ cup peeled, seeded, and chopped tomatoes
2 shallots, peeled
6 ounces unsalted butter, cut into small pieces
Extra salt, freshly ground white pepper, and cayenne pepper for the sauce
Lemon juice
6 fresh basil leaves

Mousseline of Whitefish with Oysters and Truffle Butter
Mousse de Féra aux Huîtres et Beurre aux Truffes

With the advent of the food processor, this has become a rather simple, though still extravagant, dish to prepare. The truffle butter adds color and bite to the taste.

TO SERVE 6 OR 8

Mousseline:

12 fresh oysters
4 shallots, minced
¼ pound plus 1
  tablespoon unsalted
  butter at room
  temperature
1 pound whitefish, cut
  into 1½-inch pieces
2 eggs
1½ teaspoons salt
1 teaspoon freshly
  ground pepper
1½ cups heavy cream,
  lightly whipped
Extra butter for the
  molds

Brown Sauce:

½ cup brown veal stock
  (page 66)
2 ounces truffle peelings
  or minced truffles
½ cup dry sherry
8 ounces unsalted butter,
  cut into small pieces
Salt and freshly ground
  pepper

1. Open the oysters, remove them from their shells, and reserve the liquid, pouring it into a small saucepan. Add the oysters and poach them for 2 or 3 minutes over medium heat. Transfer the contents of the saucepan to a bowl and allow to cool at room temperature.
2. Over medium heat, sauté the shallots in the 1 tablespoon butter until they are translucent. Set aside to cool.
3. *To make the mousseline:* Purée the whitefish in a food processor. Add the eggs, ¼ pound butter cut in pieces, reserved shallots, salt, and pepper and process until the mixture is homogeneous. Transfer the mixture to a bowl and place over ice. Fold in the cream. To test, poach a small amount in simmering water (see page 20). Correct seasoning to taste.
4. Preheat oven to 400°.
5. Butter six or eight individual ½-cup soufflé molds. Half-fill each mold with the mousseline. Add one or two oysters to each mold, and cover with the remaining mousseline.
6. Place the molds in a *bain-marie* and cover with buttered foil, buttered side down. Bring the *bain-marie* to a boil over high heat on top of the stove. Transfer it immediately to the hot oven and bake for 15 minutes, or until the mousselines are firm to the touch.

To make the sauce:
1. Combine the stock, truffles, and sherry in a saucepan. Cook over high heat until the liquid becomes syrupy.
2. Add the butter, one small piece at a time. Whisk in each piece of butter thoroughly before adding the next piece.
3. Season with salt and pepper to taste.

PRESENTATION: Unmold mousselines onto hot plates and nap with sauce. Serve with *fleurons* (page 6) if desired.

SUGGESTED WINE: A Chardonnay or Chénin blanc

SPECIAL EQUIPMENT: Oyster knife

Smoked Fish Mousse

Mousse de Poisson Fumé

Chilling overnight gives this mousse the desired firm consistency. Lox may be substituted for the smoked salmon, but if you use lox don't add the salt.

TO MAKE 2½ CUPS

1. In a food procesor, purée the sturgeon. Strain through a *tamis* or a fine sieve into a medium bowl and keep cold.
2. In a food processor, purée the smoked salmon. Strain through a *tamis* or a fine sieve into a separate bowl and keep cold.
3. Season each fish purée with salt, pepper, and lemon juice to taste.
4. Fold half the cream into the salmon and half into the sturgeon.
5. In the bottom of a 3-cup serving dish, spread the sturgeon purée. Sprinkle with half the caviar and top with the salmon purée. Sprinkle remaining caviar over all. Chill overnight.

4 ounces sturgeon, cut in 1-inch pieces
4 ounces smoked salmon, cut in 1-inch pieces
½ teaspoon salt
½ teaspoon freshly ground pepper
Juice of half a lemon
1 cup heavy cream, whipped
2 ounces red or black caviar

PRESENTATION: Serve from the dish. Do not unmold.

SUGGESTED WINE: Champagne or a dry white wine

Fish Terrine

Terrine de Poisson

This pâté is rich enough to serve in small portions as an appetizer, or it can be cut into larger slices for a light lunch or supper.

TO SERVE 10 OR 12 AS AN
APPETIZER; 6 OR 8 AS AN
ENTRÉE

Juice of 1 medium lemon
½ cup dry white wine
3 tablespoons chopped
  fresh tarragon
1½ teaspoons salt
1 teaspoon freshly
  ground white pepper
¾ pound salmon, boned,
  skinned, and cut into
  strips 5 inches by ¼
  inch
2 tablespoons unsalted
  butter
⅔ cup diced carrots
½ cup diced leeks
6 large asparagus spears,
  peeled
1 pound spinach,
  cleaned, with stems
  removed
1 pound sea scallops,
  unwashed
1 egg
¼ teaspoon cayenne
  pepper
2 cups heavy cream

1. In a glass bowl, combine the lemon juice, white wine, 2 tablespoons chopped tarragon, ½ teaspoon salt, and ½ teaspoon white pepper. Add the salmon and marinate for 2 hours, turning two or three times.
2. In a small saucepan, melt the butter over moderate heat. Add the carrots and leeks and sauté until tender but still crisp, about 10 minutes. Cool and reserve.
3. Cook the asparagus in boiling, salted water for 5 minutes, just until tender. Do not overcook. Drain and reserve. Cut off the bottom ends so the asparagus will lie flat in the terrine.
4. In lightly salted boiling water, cook the spinach leaves for 1 minute. Drain and reserve.
5. Preheat oven to 350°.
6. *To make the scallop mousse:* In a food processor, purée the scallops. Add the egg, the remaining 1 tablespoon chopped tarragon, 1 teaspoon salt, ½ teaspoon white pepper, and the cayenne pepper. Process until the mixture is smooth. With the motor running, pour the cream through the feed tube and process till it is well blended.
7. Transfer the mixture to a large bowl. Gently fold in the leeks and carrots. Test the mousse by poaching a teaspoonful in a small amount of simmering water (see page 20). Correct seasoning to taste. It should be slightly overseasoned.
8. Generously butter a loaf pan or pâté mold. Arrange the spinach leaves on the bottom, to a depth of about ½ inch, and up the sides of the pan, leaving an overhang. Add a 1-inch-deep layer of scallop mousse. Arrange half the asparagus over the mousse. Cover the asparagus with a thin layer of mousse. Arrange the salmon in a layer on top of the mousse and arrange the remaining asparagus over the salmon. Fill the terrine with the remaining mousse and fold the spinach leaves back over the mousse to cover.
9. Butter a piece of aluminum foil and fit it over the terrine, buttered side down. Bake in a *bain-marie* for 1 hour and 15 minutes, or until the terrine is firm to the touch. Do not allow the water to boil. Remove from oven and cool. Refrigerate for 24 hours.

PRESENTATION: Slice and serve with *mayonnaise légère* or *mayonnaise cresson* (page 102).

SUGGESTED WINE: A fruity white wine from the Napa Valley

Country-Style Pâté
Pâté de Campagne

A simple pâté that can become a more elegant and ex-travagant terrine with the addition of goose liver, truffles, pigeon breast, or duck breast. The chicken livers can be replaced by pork livers.

1. Cut the salt pork, pork shoulder, and 1 pound fatback into ½-inch cubes. Clean the chicken livers. Place with the pork in a glass or ceramic bowl.
2. In a small bowl, combine the shallot, salt, pepper, allspice, thyme, Madeira, and Cognac. Pour over the meat and stir well. Marinate for five or six days in the refrigerator.
3. Preheat oven to 350°.
4. Using the medium disk of a meat grinder, grind the meat mixture. Mix well with any remaining marinade. Reserve.
5. Slice remaining fatback into very thin slices and line a 6-cup pâté mold or terrine, leaving a slight overhang. Pat the forcemeat into the mold and place a bay leaf on top. Fold back the overhang of fatback. Cover with buttered foil, buttered side down.
6. Set the mold into a *bain-marie* and bake for 1 hour and 10 or 15 minutes. Check for doneness by inserting a skewer into the center of the pâté and leaving it for one minute; then remove the skewer and carefully touch it to your lower lip. It should feel very hot. The melted fat and juices around the pâté should be clear. Remove the pâté from the oven when done.
7. Cool to room temperature and chill for at least 24 hours.

PRESENTATION: Unmold the pâté on a serving platter. Slice a few slices and overlap them. Garnish with *cornichons* or Artichokes à la Greque (page 46).

SUGGESTED WINE: A lightly chilled Beaujolais

SPECIAL EQUIPMENT: Meat grinder, fitted with medium disk

TO SERVE 12

4 ounces salt pork
1 pound pork shoulder
1⅓ pounds pork fatback
6 chicken livers
1 shallot, minced
1 tablespoon salt
1 teaspoon freshly
  ground pepper
1 teaspoon allspice
A pinch of thyme
½ cup Madeira
¼ cup Cognac
1 bay leaf

Duck Terrine with Hazelnuts and Green Peppercorns

Terrine de Canard aux Noisettes et Poivre Vert

The hazelnuts give this country pâté its distinctive flavor. The terrine can be made as much as a week in advance.

TO SERVE 12

1 recipe country-style
pâté (page 31)
2 duck livers
1 whole duck breast
½ cup port
1 6-ounce can goose
liver pâté
½ to ¾ pound fatback,
very thinly sliced
½ cup hazelnuts, roasted
and peeled
1 tablespoon green
peppercorns

1. Prepare forcemeat from the Country-Style Pâté recipe, substituting the duck livers for the chicken livers.
2. Bone the duck breast and cut the meat into small strips. Marinate it in enough port to cover.
3. Cut the goose liver mousse into small strips. Set aside and reserve.
4. Preheat oven to 350°. Line an 8-cup terrine with the fatback.
5. Combine forcemeat with hazelnuts and peppercorns and mix well. Spread a layer ½ inch deep in the bottom of the prepared terrine. Arrange the strips of duck and goose liver mousse over the top of the forcemeat. Repeat layers one or two more times, or until all the forcemeat, duck, and goose liver mousse are used. Cover with buttered foil, buttered side down.
6. Set the terrine in a *bain-marie* and bake for 1 hour and 15 minutes, or until it tests done. Cool to room temperature and chill at least 24 hours.

PRESENTATION: Unmold the terrine on a serving platter. Slice a few slices and overlap them. Garnish with *cornichons* or Artichokes à la Greque (page 46).

SUGGESTED WINE: A lightly chilled Merlot or Zinfandel

SPECIAL EQUIPMENT:
Meat grinder, fitted with medium disk
8-cup terrine

Oysters in Lettuce Bundles
Huîtres aux Feuilles de Laitues

Warming rather than cooking will result in more tender oysters. The reduced oyster juice combined with the butter enhances the natural flavor of the oysters. The julienne of vegetables provides a contrast in texture.

1. Be sure to buy very fresh oysters. Open the oysters and remove their meat, being careful to retain the juice. Reserve the shells.
2. Strain the oyster juice and poach the oysters in it for 2 or 3 minutes. *Do not boil.*
3. Blanch the lettuce leaves in boiling, salted water. Refresh them in cold water.
4. Slice the carrot, leek, and celery into julienne. In a medium skillet, melt 2 tablespoons butter. Sauté vegetables until tender but still crisp, about 2 or 3 minutes.
5. Arrange four oyster shells on each of six oven-proof plates containing approximately ⅓ cup of rock salt to secure them. Wrap each oyster in one lettuce leaf and place in a shell. Keep warm.
6. Reduce the oyster juice until approximately ⅓ cup remains. Add lemon juice and pepper. Slowly add remaining butter, a small amount at a time.
7. Preheat oven to 450° and place plates of oysters in oven for approximately 30 seconds.

NOTE: Lightly blanched spinach leaves may be substituted for the Boston lettuce.

PRESENTATION: Spoon sauce over the oysters and sprinkle with vegetables. Serve immediately.

SUGGESTED WINE: A Riesling from California

SPECIAL EQUIPMENT:
6 oven-proof plates

TO SERVE 6

24 fresh oysters
24 Boston lettuce leaves
1 large carrot
1 medium leek
2 stalks celery
Rock salt
½ pound butter
Juice of 1 lemon
Freshly ground pepper

Salmon Françoise
Saumon Françoise

This is a recipe from restaurant L'Oasis in La Napoule, France. Don't try to prepare it for more than six or eight guests, since the salmon has to be cooked and served immediately.

TO SERVE 6

6 or more slices fresh salmon (sliced thinly in the manner of smoked salmon)
Salt and freshly ground pepper
¼ cup dry white vermouth
1 cup fish stock (page 65)
2 shallots, minced
1 cup heavy cream
¼ pound unsalted butter (cut into small pieces), plus butter for the plates
1 or 2 tablespoons finely chopped fresh herbs, such as parsley, tarragon, and chervil
4 tomatoes, peeled and seeded
12 large white mushrooms

1. Lightly butter six cold oven-proof appetizer or dinner plates. Place raw slices of salmon to cover the centers of the plates. Season with salt and pepper.
2. In a heavy saucepan, reduce vermouth, fish stock, and shallots until the mixture is syrupy.
3. Add cream and reduce again until the sauce thickens slightly. Remove from heat and whisk in the butter, one small piece at a time.
4. While the cream is reducing, preheat oven to broil. Chop herbs; cut tomatoes and mushrooms into brunoise.
5. Add the herbs and vegetables to the reduced sauce and bring to a light boil. Taste and correct seasoning. The sauce should be slightly overseasoned.
6. Cover salmon with sauce and cook under the broiler until sauce is lightly browned. It is best to have salmon slightly underdone, for it will finish cooking on the way to the table.

NOTE: Do not attempt to use frozen salmon in this recipe, as it would only break into pieces if you tried to slice it thinly.

PRESENTATION: Serve on the plates as an appetizer or main course.

SUGGESTED WINE: A young, slightly chilled St. Emilion

SPECIAL EQUIPMENT:
Very sharp chef's knife or electric knife, for slicing the salmon
6 oven-proof appetizer or dinner plates

Shrimp with Mustard

Crevettes à la Moutarde

This is the most requested appetizer at Ma Maison. The shrimp will be crisp and succulent when sautéed over very high heat.

1. Season the shrimp with salt and pepper. Using two large sauté pans, heat the oil until it begins to smoke. Over very high heat, sauté the shrimp for 6 to 7 minutes. Transfer to a warm plate, set aside, and keep warm.
2. To each sauté pan add one minced shallot and 1 tablespoon minced tarragon. Sauté for 2 to 3 minutes. Deglaze each pan with the sherry and then combine the sauce in one pan. Add the cream and reduce the sauce until it coats the back of a spoon. Whisk in the butter, one small piece at a time. Whisk in the mustard, just at the last minute. Do not let the sauce boil, or the mustard will become grainy. Correct seasoning to taste.

PRESENTATION: Arrange shrimp decoratively on serving plates, nap with sauce, and sprinkle with chives.

SUGGESTED WINE: A Fumé blanc

TO SERVE 6

6 to 8 medium shrimp per person
Salt and freshly ground pepper
4 tablespoons mild-flavored oil, such as almond or safflower
2 medium shallots, minced
1 bunch fresh tarragon, minced
½ cup dry sherry
½ cup heavy cream
½ pound unsalted butter, cut into small pieces
2 tablespoons Dijon mustard
1 tablespoon minced chives

Salmon Soufflé
Saumon Soufflé

The salmon and the fish force can be prepared earlier and the recipe completed at serving time. Instead of the mustard sauce, it can be served with a simple *beurre blanc* with herbs or a *beurre rouge*.

TO SERVE 12 AS AN APPETIZER OR 6 AS AN ENTRÉE

3 pounds salmon, skinned and boned
1 pound pike, cut into 1-inch pieces
Salt (about 2 teaspoons)
Freshly ground pepper
2 tablespoons chopped fresh herbs (tarragon, chives, and so on), plus extra for garnish
A pinch of cayenne pepper
1 egg
¼ pound unsalted butter, at room temperature
¾ cup whipping cream
2 shallots, minced
½ cup dry white wine
Sauce moutarde (page 103)

1. Cut the salmon into 6-ounce fillets for an entrée or 3-ounce fillets for an appetizer. Season with salt and pepper to taste, and 1 tablespoon chopped herbs. Set aside.
2. *To make the fish force:* Purée the pike in a blender or food processor. Add 1 teaspoon salt, pepper to taste, cayenne pepper, and 1 tablespoon chopped herbs. Add the egg through the feed tube. Then add the butter slowly, one small piece at a time. With the motor still running, add the cream. Process until just blended. Taste, and correct seasoning.
3. Preheat oven to 400°.
4. Top each salmon fillet with the fish force. Butter a shallow baking pan and sprinkle the shallots over the surface. Add the wine to the pan and place the fillets in the wine. Bake for 10 minutes. Remove from the oven and place under the broiler for 2 to 3 minutes, until golden brown.

NOTE: For a diet adaptation, use 2 lightly beaten egg whites in place of the butter, eliminate the whole egg, and substitute ¼ cup water for cream. Add as much milk to the fish purée as it will hold.

PRESENTATION: Nap heated appetizer or dinner plates with mustard sauce. Place salmon soufflés in the center and sprinkle lightly with herbs.

SUGGESTED WINE: A Chénin blanc (If using a *beurre rouge*, however, serve a red wine.)

Bass and Salmon with Avocado

Bar et Saumon Cru aux Avocats

This dish is inspired by the Japanese sashimi and the wonderful California avocado. The fish must be completely fresh.

1. Arrange fish slices on a large platter.
2. Whisk together the olive oil, lime juice, salt, and pepper or green peppercorns. Drizzle over the fish and refrigerate for 30 minutes.
3. Peel the avocados and cut them in half lengthwise. Remove the pits and cut each half into eight slices.
4. Arrange eight avocado slices on each of six plates and cover with one slice of salmon and one slice of bass. Sprinkle with fresh herbs.

PRESENTATION: Decorate with lemon slices and serve cold.

SUGGESTED WINE: A Chardonnay from Sonoma County

SPECIAL EQUIPMENT: Very sharp chef's knife or electric knife, for slicing the fish

TO SERVE 6

9 ounces bass, cut into 6 paper-thin slices (like smoked salmon)
9 ounces salmon, cut into 6 paper-thin slices (like smoked salmon)
4 tablespoons olive oil
2 tablespoons lime juice, lemon juice, or good wine vinegar
Salt
Freshly ground pepper (or substitute 1 teaspoon green peppercorns)
3 ripe avocados
1 tablespoon minced fresh tarragon or chives
3 lemons, sliced

Pasta with Truffles

Pâtes Fraîches aux Truffes

Fresh noodles are a *must,* as they serve to accentuate the subtle, exquisite flavor of the truffles. Because of the richness of this dish, small portions should be sufficient.

TO SERVE 6

1 recipe pasta dough
  (page 208)
2 medium carrots, peeled
1 leek, white part only
2 stalks celery, with
  strings removed
1 tablespoon unsalted
  butter
1 whole truffle
3 slices prosciutto
¼ cup truffle juice
½ cup heavy cream
Salt
Freshly ground pepper

1. Cut the pasta into thin strips and let it dry for 30 minutes.
2. Cut the carrots, leek, and celery into fine julienne. Over moderate heat, sauté the vegetables in the butter until tender but still crisp.
3. Cut the truffle and prosciutto into julienne.
4. Deglaze the pan with truffle juice. Add the truffle, prosciutto, and cream and bring to a boil, then remove from heat. *Do not* reduce the sauce or it will separate.
5. Bring a large pot of salted water to a boil. Cook the pasta for 2 or 3 mintues, until *al dente.* Drain and refresh under cold running water. Add the pasta to the vegetable-and-cream mixture. Season to taste with salt and pepper and heat through. Serve immediately (this is very important; if the noodles are not consumed right away, all your effort in making fresh pasta will be worthless).

SUGGESTED WINE: A Merlot

Croissants with Lobster or Crab

Croissants d'Homard ou Crabe

The croissants are a change from the usual *feuilletée*. If you do not make them yourself, be sure to buy them from a good pastry shop.

1. After killing the lobsters (see page 20), break them apart, separating the claws and tails from the bodies.
2. Heat a large heavy saucepan, add the olive oil, and, over high heat, sauté the lobster pieces until red. Add the carrot, celery, tomatoes, garlic, shallots, tarragon, and thyme to the saucepan. Continue to sauté for another 3 or 4 minutes. Flame with Cognac and immediately deglaze with white wine.
3. Add tomato paste and partially cover with water. Season with pinches of salt, pepper, and cayenne pepper. Add the bay leaf. Over medium heat, boil for 15 minutes. When cooked, remove the lobster claws and tails. Reserve.
4. In a small saucepan, reduce the cream until only ½ cup remains. Add it to the sauce and reduce until slightly thickened. Strain through a very fine strainer, taste, and correct seasoning.
5. Shell claws and tails and slice into bite-size pieces. Add to the sauce and keep warm.
6. Preheat oven to 400°.
7. Prepare the *beurre blanc* and keep it warm.
8. Slice the croissants in half horizontally, and warm them in the hot oven for 3 minutes.

NOTE: The ingredients and procedure through step 3 are the base for any shellfish soup. Crayfish can also be prepared in this way.

PRESENTATION: Nap half of each warm plate with lobster sauce and the other half with *beurre blanc*. Sprinkle chives over the *beurre blanc*. Place the bottom half of a croissant in the center of each plate and arrange the lobster slices on top. Moisten the lobster meat with a spoonful of the lobster sauce and cover with the remaining croissant half.

SUGGESTED WINE: A vintage Chardonnay

SPECIAL EQUIPMENT: *Chinois* or very fine strainer

TO SERVE 6

3 live lobsters, 1 to 1½ pounds each (or substitute the same amount of crab)
3 tablespoons olive oil
1 carrot, sliced
2 stalks celery, sliced
3 medium tomatoes, chopped
5 cloves garlic, minced
5 shallots, minced
3 sprigs fresh tarragon, minced
A pinch of dry thyme
3 tablespoons Cognac
2 cups dry white wine
⅓ cup tomato paste
Salt
Freshly ground pepper
Cayenne pepper
1 bay leaf
1½ cups heavy cream
1 recipe beurre blanc (page 106)
6 croissants (page 205)
2 teaspoons minced chives

Quiche

This is a classic quiche recipe. Bacon and ham can be replaced by smoked salmon and onions or lightly poached shrimp or scallops. To prepare a vegetarian quiche, any combination of cooked and well-drained vegetables can be used.

TO SERVE 8

1 pound puff pastry
(page 200)
1 egg yolk, lightly
beaten, for egg wash
½ pound bacon
6 ounces cooked ham,
diced
¼ cup finely chopped
chives
½ cup (3 ounces)
Gruyère cheese,
coarsely grated
7 large eggs
3 cups heavy cream or
half heavy cream and
half milk
⅛ teaspoon nutmeg
½ teaspoon freshly
ground white pepper

1. Preheat oven to 350°.
2. Line a buttered 10- or 11-inch quiche pan with puff pastry, but do not trim edges. Line the pastry with aluminium foil or parchment paper. Fill with aluminum beans (or dried beans) and bake for 20 minutes. Take from oven and remove beans. Brush the bottom of the crust with egg wash and return quiche pan to oven for 10 minutes.
3. Meanwhile, dice the bacon and cook until crisp. Drain it on paper towels and sprinkle into the baked shell. Add ham, chives, and cheese.
4. In a large bowl, combine eggs with remaining ingredients until blended. Pour into shell. Trim edges of shell.
5. Bake in a 350° oven for 50 minutes, or until the quiche has puffed and browned.

NOTE: Quiche may be refrigerated and then reheated, but never freeze a quiche. Freezing makes quiches soggy.

PRESENTATION: Cut the quiche into wedges and serve on warmed plates.

SUGGESTED WINE: Any good dry white wine

Sausage Wrapped in Brioche with Truffle Butter

Saucisson en Brioche au Beurre Truffe

Brioche with sausage and truffles is a delicacy originating in Lyon, France. The sauce may be prepared without truffles.

1. Using a fork, prick sausage casing all over. In a saucepan, combine the sausage, wine, celery, thyme, peppercorns, bay leaf, and enough cold water to cover. Bring to a boil, reduce heat, and simmer for 20 minutes. Transfer sausage to a plate and allow to cool. Peel off casing and reserve sausage.
2. Roll out brioche dough to a thickness of ½ inch, large enough to enclose the sausage. Wrap the sausage and trim away any excess dough. Brush with egg wash and let rest for half an hour at room temperature.
3. Preheat oven to 400°.
4. Bake the sausage in brioche for 30 minutes or until brioche is golden brown.
5. *To make the truffle butter*: Reduce the sherry and truffles until only ½ cup remains. Add the cream and *demi-glace* and reduce again until slightly thickened. Whisk in the butter, one small piece at a time. Season with salt and pepper to taste.

PRESENTATION: Slice off the ends of the brioche and cut sausage into ½-inch slices. Nap each plate with truffle butter and top with a sausage slice.

SUGGESTED WINE: A young Cabernet Sauvignon or a Beaujolais such as a Brouilly or St. Amour

TO SERVE 6 OR 8

1 2-pound Polish sausage
1 cup dry white wine
1 stalk celery, sliced
A pinch of thyme
¼ teaspoon whole peppercorns
½ bay leaf
1 recipe brioche dough (page 206), using only 1 tablespoon sugar
1 egg, lightly beaten, for egg wash

Truffle Butter:

1 cup dry sherry
2 ounces chopped truffles or truffle peelings
3 tablespoons heavy cream
3 tablespoons brown veal stock (page 66), demi-glace
½ pound unsalted butter, cut into small pieces
Salt
Freshly ground pepper

Asparagus in Puff Pastry
Feuilletée d'Asperges

Though I serve this as an appetizer, it makes a light luncheon entrée as well.

TO SERVE 6

2 pounds large asparagus spears, peeled
1 pound puff pastry (page 200)
1 egg, lightly beaten, for egg wash
4 tablespoons heavy cream
3 tablespoons water
1 medium lemon
1 tablespoon finely minced fresh tarragon
½ pound unsalted butter, cut into small pieces
½ teaspoon salt
½ teaspoon freshly ground white pepper

1. Preheat oven to 375°.
2. Blanch the asparagus in rapidly boiling salted water for 2 minutes. They should still be very crisp. Cool rapidly by plunging into ice water.
3. Divide the puff pastry into two pieces, one a bit larger than the other. Roll out the smaller piece to a 12-inch square, approximately ⅛ inch thick, and cut into six 4-by-6-inch rectangles. Place on a baking sheet.
4. Dry the asparagus thoroughly and cut in approximately 5-inch lengths. Place three or four spears on each rectangle. Refrigerate.
5. Roll out the remaining piece of puff pastry to a 16-by-18-inch rectangle, approximately ⅛ inch thick. Cut it into six 6-by-8-inch rectangles, which should be large enough to blanket the asparagus completely.
6. Brush the egg wash around the edges of the bottom pastry and cover with the top pastry. Lightly press the edges together and trim if necessary. Brush the tops with the egg wash.
7. Bake the *feuilletées* for 25 minutes, or until golden brown.
8. *To prepare the sauce:* Combine the cream, water, juice of half the lemon, and tarragon in a saucepan. Bring to a boil and reduce the heat to low. Add the butter bit by bit, whisking in after each addition. Season the sauce to taste with additional lemon juice, salt, and white pepper.

PRESENTATION: Spoon 3 tablespoons of sauce onto the center of each plate. Carefully place a *feuilletée* on top of the sauce.

SUGGESTED WINE: A Johannisberg Riesling

Salmon Napoleon

Mille-Feuilles de Saumon

The thin slices of salmon should be cooked over high heat for seconds only, to prevent them from overcooking and becoming dry. Because the puff pastry has enough salt in it, the salmon need not be salted.

1. Roll out the puff pastry into a 14-by-18-inch rectangle and place on a baking sheet of the same size. (The pastry should be about $^1/_{10}$ inch thick.) Pierce it all over with a fork. Refrigerate for at least 2 hours.
2. Preheat oven to 450°.
3. Cut salmon into slices ⅜ inch thick and refrigerate.
4. In a heavy saucepan, combine the shallots, white wine, and fish stock. Reduce until ½ cup remains.
5. Add heavy cream and reduce till slightly thickened.
6. Season to taste with salt, pepper, and lemon juice. Keep warm.
7. Remove pastry from refrigerator and bake for 15 mintues; reduce the heat to 350° and continue baking until golden brown and cooked through, approximately 15 minutes longer.
8. Cut the pastry into three equal pieces, approximately 6 by 14 inches each.
9. Heat a sauté pan. Add the butter; sauté salmon rapidly, a few pieces at a time. Do not overcook. Keep warm.
10. *To assemble the napoleon:* On a cutting board, alternate layers of puff pastry and salmon, beginning and ending with puff pastry. With a serrated knife, trim the ends and sides to make them neat and even.
11. Slice the napoleon into six equal servings approximately 2½ inches wide.

NOTE: If the napoleon should cool off too much before serving, reheat the individual portions for 1 or 2 minutes in a 500° oven.

PRESENTATION: Nap each warm plate with sauce and top with a slice of napoleon. Sprinkle sparingly with minced parsley or chervil.

SUGGESTED WINE: A Sauvignon blanc

SPECIAL EQUIPMENT:
Very sharp chef's knife, for slicing the fish
Serrated knife

TO SERVE 6

1 pound puff pastry (page 200)
1 pound fresh salmon tail, preferably Chinook salmon
6 medium shallots, minced
2 cups dry white wine
2 cups fish stock (page 65)
1 quart heavy cream
Salt
Freshly ground pepper
Juice of half a lemon
2 tablespoons unsalted butter
1 tablespoon minced fresh parsley or chervil

Spinach and Brains Between Layers of Puff Pastry

Mille-Feuilles de Cervelle et Épinards

The components can be prepared early in the day and then assembled at serving time. Sweetbreads or scallops may be substituted for the brains.

TO SERVE 6

1 pound puff pastry (page 200)
1 pound calves' or lambs' brains, soaked overnight in water
Juice of 1 lemon
A pinch of thyme
1 branch fresh tarragon
1 bay leaf
1 teaspoon salt
½ teaspoon freshly ground pepper
1 cup dry white wine
4 tablespoons minced shallots
1 tablespoon minced fresh tarragon
3 tablespoons heavy cream
10 ounces unsalted butter
1 pound fresh spinach, thoroughly washed and stems removed
Flour
Fresh tarragon leaves

1. Preheat oven to 350°.
2. Roll out puff pastry to a thickness of ¼ inch, and line a baking sheet measuring approximately 11 by 14 inches. Prick the pastry all over with the tines of a fork and bake for 30 minutes, or until golden brown and crisp. Reserve.
3. Peel the brains and place in a saucepan with the lemon juice, thyme, branch of tarragon, bay leaf, salt, ¼ teaspoon pepper, and enough water to cover. Bring to a boil. Remove brains from the water and refresh under cold running water. Place on a towel and dry gently.
4. Combine the wine, 2 tablespoons shallots, minced tarragon, and ¼ teaspoon pepper. Reduce until only 2 tablespoons of liquid remain. Add the cream and reduce slightly. Slowly whisk in 6 tablespoons butter, one small piece at a time. Correct seasoning to taste, strain, and add the remaining 2 tablespoons shallots. Set aside and keep warm.
5. Sauté the spinach in 2 tablespoons butter until wilted. Season to taste with salt and pepper. Drain well and reserve.
6. Cut the brains into ½-inch slices, season with salt and pepper, and sprinkle lightly with flour. Sauté, over moderate heat, in the remaining 2 tablespoons butter for 2 minutes on each side, or until they feel resilient to the touch.
7. Using a very sharp knife, cut the pastry into three equal parts. Cover the first layer with the sautéed spinach, and top with the second piece of puff pastry. Cover with sautéed brains and top with the last layer of pastry. Cut into six equal portions and keep warm.

PRESENTATION: Place each filled pastry on a warm plate and nap with sauce. Garnish with a few tarragon leaves.

SUGGESTED WINE: A Gewürztraminer

SPECIAL EQUIPMENT: 11-by-14-inch baking sheet

Scallops in Puff Pastry
Feuilletée de Coquilles Saint-Jacques

The tenderness of the scallops and the crispness of the pastry, enhanced by the light butter sauce, make for a delicate dish. It can be served as an appetizer or with a light salad as a lovely luncheon entrée.

1. Slice the carrot, leek, and celery root into julienne. In a skillet, heat 1 tablespoon butter and sauté the vegetables slowly, just until tender but still crisp. Season with salt and pepper to taste. Reserve.
2. If the scallops are large, slice them in half horizontally, retaining the disklike shape. If small, leave whole.
3. In a saucepan, combine vermouth, shallot, and a dash of salt and pepper. Add scallops and bring to a boil. Boil no more than 2 minutes, less if scallops are small. Remove from heat and drain, reserving scallops and liquid.
4. Preheat oven to 400°.
5. Cook liquid till reduced by half. Add cream and continue cooking till mixture thickens, about 10 minutes.
6. Whisk remaining 6 ounces of butter into the sauce, one piece at a time. Add vegetables and scallops and stir.
7. Split each *feuilletée* in half and heat them through in the hot oven for 1 to 2 minutes.

NOTE: To make the *feuilletées*, roll out puff pastry (page 200) into a ¼-inch-thick rectangle. Cut into rectangles 4 inches by 2 inches, and place them on a baking sheet. Let rest for 1 hour in the refrigerator. Brush with an egg wash and bake in a 400° oven for 15 mintues, or until golden brown.

PRESENTATION: Place the bottom half of each *feuilletée* on a plate. Fill with scallops and sauce. Arrange the top half over the scallops.

SUGGESTED WINE: A Gewürztraminer

TO SERVE 6

6 feuilletées (see note below)
1 medium carrot, peeled
1 small leek, white part only
1 celery root (celeriac), peeled
1 tablespoon unsalted butter, plus 6 ounces cut into small pieces
Salt and freshly ground pepper
1 pound sea scallops
¾ cup dry white vermouth
1 large shallot, chopped fine
½ cup heavy cream

Crêpes Surprise

Serve these when you feel particularly rich. Only fine caviar will do. Oregon produces one of the finest.

TO SERVE ANY NUMBER

Two or three 4-inch crêpes (page 204) per person
2 teaspoons sour cream per crêpe
1 tablespoon Beluga caviar per crêpe

1. Heat crêpes.
2. Spread each one with sour cream.
3. *Carefully* spread caviar over sour cream and fold the crêpes into triangles.

NOTE: Whitefish caviar (also called golden caviar) costs much less, but is an excellent substitute.

PRESENTATION: Serve two or three crêpes per person as an appetizer, or serve crêpes on a platter as canapés.

SUGGESTED WINE: A fine champagne

Artichokes à la Greque

Artichauts à la Greque

TO SERVE 6

18 small artichokes or 10 large artichoke bottoms, quartered
2 or 3 lemons, cut in half
1 medium onion, diced
6 tablespoons olive oil
6 tomatoes, peeled, seeded, and diced
1 bell pepper, diced
1 clove garlic, peeled and minced
A pinch of thyme
1 small bay leaf
1 cup dry white wine
4 cups chicken stock (page 65)
1 teaspoon salt
½ teaspoon freshly ground pepper

Artichokes must be fresh, never canned or frozen. Serve these cold as an appetizer or as a condiment with pâtés and terrines.

1. Clean the artichokes, removing any bad leaves. Cut them in half, vertically, and rub them all over with the cut side of the lemons.
2. Over low heat, sauté the onion in olive oil until it is translucent. Add the tomatoes, bell pepper, garlic, thyme, and bay leaf.
3. Deglaze the pan with the white wine. Add the stock and bring it to a boil. Season with salt and pepper.
4. Add the artichokes to the pan and cook them for approximately 20 minutes, or until tender. Remove the artichokes and reduce sauce over high heat until most of the liquid has evaporated, about 20 minutes.
5. Place the artichokes in a bowl and pour sauce over them. Correct seasoning to taste. Refrigerate overnight.

VARIATION: Use 2 pounds whole button mushrooms in place of the artichokes. The cooking time is the same.

Mousseline of Broccoli with Mushroom Sauce

Mousseline de Brocolis aux Morilles

Since broccoli is a rather ordinary vegetable, I have combined it with the mushroom sauce to create a very sophisticated appetizer.

To make the mousseline:
1. Heavily butter six ½-cup timbales or soufflé dishes. Preheat oven to 375°.
2. Wash broccoli and plunge into heavily salted boiling water. Cook until tender, 10 to 12 minutes. Plunge into ice water to stop the cooking process.
3. Bring the heavy cream to a boil in a large saucepan. Add the broccoli, salt, pepper, lemon juice, and nutmeg. Cook until cream is absorbed, about 10 minutes.
4. Purée broccoli in a food processor. Add the eggs, one at a time, processing until blended after each addition. Taste carefully and correct the seasoning.
5. Fill the timbales and cover with buttered foil. Bake in a *bain-marie* for 25 minutes.

To make the sauce:
1. Clean the morels carefully to remove the sand. Cut into halves or quarters. Soak overnight in water to cover. Drain.
2. Heat a small heavy saucepan. Add 1 tablespoon butter, the shallot, and the morels. Sauté over medium-low heat until the liquid has evaporated.
3. Deglaze the pan with vermouth and cook until reduced by half. Add cream and reduce again until sauce is slightly thickened.
4. Remove from heat and whisk in the remaining butter, one small piece at a time. Season to taste with salt, pepper, and a little lemon juice.

PRESENTATION: Unmold the mousselines onto warm plates and surround with sauce.

SUGGESTED WINE: A Chardonnay

TO SERVE 6

Mousseline:

1 pound broccoli florets with ½ inch of stem
½ cup heavy cream
1 teaspoon salt
½ teaspoon freshly ground pepper
Juice of half a lemon
A pinch of nutmeg
4 eggs

Sauce:

3 or 4 morels per person (any mushroom may be substituted)
½ pound unsalted butter
1 shallot, minced
½ cup dry white vermouth
1 cup heavy cream
Lemon juice

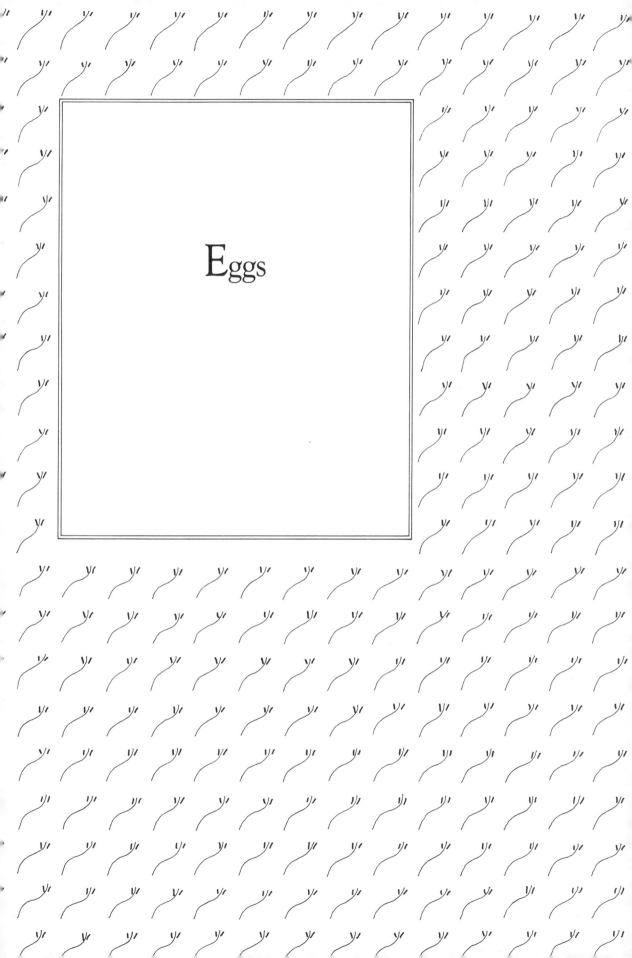

Eggs

Eggs with Salmon and Sorrel

Eggs with Crayfish or Shrimp

Poached Eggs Toupinel

Eggs Poached in Red Wine

Scrambled Eggs Garin

Eggs Surprise

Scrambled Eggs with Caviar

No cookbook is complete without a section on eggs. Because of their excellent nutritional value and their delicate flavor, eggs are held in high esteem in the most diversified of cultures. In some societies they hold symbolic value as well, and depending on regional availability, certain types of eggs have earned positions of noble distinction.

In Great Britain and the Netherlands, duck eggs are quite popular. People in some countries consider plover eggs a delicacy, and others use turtle eggs to make a soup. In China, eggs are pickled and preserved for a hundred days to produce "ancient eggs." The Japanese use the roe of the crab. And of course fish eggs, particularly sturgeon roe (caviar), are a highly prized food. The popularity of the tasty and wonderfully attractive golden caviar (whitefish roe) and salmon roe is growing rapidly.

Whether you choose to serve eggs as an appealing appetizer or satisfying entrée, simply or elegantly, the most important consideration is their careful cooking. Scrambled eggs should be creamy, poached eggs should be removed from their cooking medium when soft to the touch, and omelettes are best when cooked only to a very light golden color on the outside, producing airy, fluffy interiors.

I have chosen to include only a few special egg dishes. I think you will find them unusual and interesting to prepare and serve. Though I sometimes serve quail eggs, they are difficult to obtain and must be eaten very fresh. I have therefore limited my recipes to the hen egg, which is very popular but never common. Perhaps you will discover anew "the incredible edible egg."

Eggs with Salmon and Sorrel

Oeufs en Cocotte au Saumon et Oseille

Smoked salmon can be substituted for fresh salmon in this recipe, but omit the salt. Lining the bottom of the *bain-marie* with parchment paper keeps the water from boiling.

1. Butter two ½-cup or 4-ounce cocottes with 1 teaspoon of butter each and chill for 15 minutes.
2. Slice salmon as you would smoked salmon, into ¼-inch-thick slices, and season to taste with salt and pepper. Line the bottom and sides of each cocotte with salmon and place 1 tablespoon cream in the bottom. Chill again until ready to use.
3. Preheat oven to 400°.
4. Cut the sorrel into ¼-inch julienne. In a small sauté pan, heat the remaining teaspoon butter and sauté the sorrel for 1 minute. Add the remaining cream and reduce by half. Season to taste and keep warm.
5. Break an egg into each cocotte. Line a *bain-marie* with parchment paper and half-fill with boiling water. Place the cocottes in it and cover them with buttered aluminum foil, buttered side down. Bake for 10 to 12 minutes. Eggs must still be soft.

PRESENTATION: Nap with sorrel sauce and serve with toast fingers.

SUGGESTED WINE: A dry champagne from New York or California

SPECIAL EQUIPMENT:
2 cocottes

TO SERVE 2

3 teaspoons unsalted butter
2 ounces fresh salmon
Salt
Freshly ground pepper
3 sorrel leaves, with stems removed
6 tablespoons heavy cream
2 eggs

Eggs with Crayfish or Shrimp
Oeufs Écrevisses ou Crevettes

An unusual combination that works very well.

TO SERVE 2

12 live crayfish or 12 medium shrimp
1 tablespoon mild-flavored oil, such as almond or safflower
½ cup dry white wine
1 shallot, minced
2 medium tomatoes, peeled, seeded, and diced
1 cup plus 2 tablespoons heavy cream
Salt and freshly ground pepper
4 eggs
A pinch of thyme
2 teaspoons minced chives
2 teaspoons minced parsley
2 tablespoons unsalted butter

1. Peel the crayfish or shrimp, reserving the shells.
2. Heat the oil in a heavy sauté pan. Add the crayfish and the shells and sauté until the shells turn pink.
3. Deglaze the pan with the white wine. Add the shallot, tomatoes, and 1 cup cream, and cook over moderate heat. Remove the crayfish or shrimp as they are cooked, approximately 3 or 4 minutes.
4. Continue to reduce for 10 minutes, or until the sauce heavily coats the back of a spoon. Season to taste with salt and pepper. Strain over the crayfish or shrimp and keep warm.
5. In a mixing bowl, using a whisk, thoroughly combine the eggs, remaining 2 tablespoons cream, thyme, chives, salt, pepper, and 1 teaspoon parsley.
6. Melt 1 tablespoon butter in a sauté pan. Over low heat, cook the eggs, stirring with a whisk or spatula, until thick and creamy. Stir in the remaining 1 tablespoon butter.

PRESENTATION: Divide the eggs into two warm soup plates. Top with the crayfish or shrimp and the sauce. Sprinkle with the remaining parsley.

SUGGESTED WINE: A champagne or Chardonnay

Poached Eggs Toupinel

Oeufs Pochés Toupinel

A luxurious luncheon dish. The baked potato, mashed and stuffed back into its shell, is topped with a poached egg and glazed.

TO SERVE 6

1. Preheat oven to 450°.
2. To make covers for the baked potatoes, make a slight incision one third of the way down from the top of each potato (all the way around). On a bed of rock salt, bake the potatoes until soft. (Baking time will vary depending on the size of the potatoes.)
3. Carefully cut off the potato cover where the incision was made and reserve. Leaving a ⅛-inch layer of potato in the shell, scoop out the potato from both parts, reserving shells.
4. Purée the scooped-out potato pulp and combine with 3 tablespoons butter, *crème fraîche*, ham, mushrooms, and truffles. Refill potato shells with this purée and keep warm.
5. In a medium saucepan, bring the water and vinegar to a simmer. Carefully break each egg into a bowl and gently slide it into the simmering water. Poach 3 to 4 minutes. With a slotted spoon, transfer eggs to a warm platter and reserve.

6 small baking potatoes
Rock salt
5 tablespoons unsalted butter, at room temperature
3 tablespoons crème fraîche or heavy cream
3 slices ham, cut into julienne
3 tablespoons julienne of mushrooms
2 tablespoons julienne of truffles (optional)
1 quart water
¼ cup red wine vinegar
6 eggs
1 cup sauce Mornay (page 108), with double the amount of cheese
2 tablespoons freshly grated Swiss cheese

PRESENTATION: Top each filled potato shell with one poached egg and cover with *sauce Mornay*. Dot with the remaining 2 tablespoons butter and the grated cheese. Brown under the broiler, but do not burn! Rest the potato cover decoratively on the side of the filled potato shell.

SUGGESTED WINE: A fruity white wine or a light red wine

Eggs Poached in Red Wine

Oeufs Pochés au Beurre Rouge

This is my version of *oeufs Meurettes*. I like to use a heavy red wine like Petit Sirah or Zinfandel for the color as well as the taste.

TO SERVE 6 AS AN APPETIZER

1 recipe of pâte brisée
(page 199)
1 tablespoon unsalted
butter
½ cup fine brunoise of
carrots and leeks
1 cup mushroom
duxelles (page 174)
1⅔ cups beurre rouge
(page 106)
3 tablespoons reduced
brown veal stock (page
66)
1 branch fresh thyme,
chopped fine
Salt
Freshly ground pepper
1½ cups Petit Sirah
6 eggs

1. Preheat oven to 400°.
2. Roll out *pâte brisée* approximately ¹/₆ inch thick. Cut out six circles large enough to fit 2½- to 3-inch tartlet pans. Mold into pans, removing excess pastry. Prick the pastry with a fork.
3. Line with parchment paper and fill with aluminum (or dried) beans. Bake about 20 minutes until golden brown. Remove beans and paper and continue to bake 15 minutes longer. Turn out shells from pans and keep warm.
4. In a small skillet, melt the butter and sauté the *brunoise* of carrots and leeks until *al dente*. Set aside and reserve.
5. Prepare *duxelles* and keep warm.
6. Prepare *beurre rouge*, add brown stock, and keep warm.
7. In a medium saucepan, combine the Petit Sirah and enough water to make a depth of 2 inches. Season lightly with salt and pepper and bring to a simmer.
8. Carefully break each egg into a bowl and gently slide it into the simmering wine. Do this as quickly as possible, until all the eggs are poaching. Simmer 3 to 4 minutes and, with a slotted spoon, transfer eggs to a warm platter.
9. Spread 1 tablespoon *duxelles* at the bottom of each tart shell. Place a poached egg on top and nap with *beurre rouge*.

NOTES:
1. This recipe can be doubled (place 2 eggs in each tartlet) and served as a main dish for a light supper.
2. Leek fondue may be substituted for the mushroom *duxelles*. Leek fondue is prepared by completing through step 2 of the leek timbales recipe (page 173).
3. The pastry may be molded in an 8-inch fluted tart pan and baked until golden. Spread the *duxelles* on the bottom and arrange the poached eggs over the *duxelles*. Proceed as above.

4. If the sauce gets too thick, a tablespoon of the wine used for poaching may be added.

PRESENTATION: Lightly nap each plate with *beurre rouge* and set a filled shell in the center of the plate. Sprinkle with reserved *brunoise*.

SUGGESTED WINE: The same wine you cooked with

SPECIAL EQUIPMENT: 6 tartlet pans

Scrambled Eggs Garin

Oeufs Brouillés Garin

This recipe comes from the now-defunct Parisian restaurant Garin. Eggs should be so softly scrambled that you eat them with a spoon, not a fork.

1. Cut each slice of bread into fingers approximately 1 by 4 inches. Place on a baking sheet and, under a hot broiler, toast both sides until golden brown. Reserve.
2. Break the eggs into a large mixing bowl, reserving 2 yolks in a separate bowl. To the large mixing bowl add the *fines herbes*, salt, pepper, and 2 tablespoons butter. Combine with a whisk.
3. Combine the heavy cream and mustard with the two reserved egg yolks and mix well.
4. In a heavy sauté pan, over low heat, melt the remaining 2 tablespoons butter. Pour in the whole eggs and cook, whisking, until creamy and slightly thickened.
5. Add the egg yolk mixture and tomatoes to the slightly thickened cooked eggs and continue to whisk, stirring constantly. Perfectly scrambled eggs should be creamy with very soft curds.

PRESENTATION: Serve on lightly warmed plates garnished with toasted whole-wheat-bread fingers. Sprinkle with chopped chives.

SUGGESTED WINE: A light red or white wine

TO SERVE 6

4 to 6 slices of whole-wheat bread, with crusts removed
12 large eggs
1 tablespoon freshly chopped fines herbes
1 teaspoon salt
½ teaspoon freshly ground pepper
4 tablespoons unsalted butter, cut into small pieces
3 tablespoons heavy cream
2 or 3 tablespoons Dijon mustard
3 small tomatoes, peeled, seeded, diced, and drained
1 teaspoon chopped chives

Eggs Surprise
Oeufs en Surprise

Scrambled eggs and smoked salmon is recognized as a gourmet dish in many countries. Serving it in brioches makes this an elegant appetizer or brunch entrée.

TO SERVE 2

2 small brioches (page 206)
2 tablespoons unsalted butter
2 tablespoons minced shallots
2 ounces smoked salmon
4 eggs
2 tablespoons heavy cream
Freshly ground pepper
1 teaspoon black caviar

1. Preheat oven to 450°.
2. Cut off the tops of the brioches. Carefully scoop out the center, leaving only the shell. Reserve.
3. Heat 1 tablespoon butter in a sauté pan and sauté the shallots until translucent.
4. Cut the smoked salmon into julienne, reserving 2 small triangles of salmon for a garnish.
5. Using a whisk, combine the eggs and cream. Season with pepper and stir in the sautéed shallots.
6. Melt 2 teaspoons butter in a heavy sauté pan. Over low heat, cook the eggs, stirring constantly with a whisk or rubber spatula. When the eggs begin to thicken, stir in the julienne of salmon and continue to cook until soft and creamy.
7. Meanwhile, heat the brioches in the oven for 3 or 4 minutes.

PRESENTATION: Place each brioche case on a warm serving plate. Divide the eggs and fill each brioche. Garnish with a salmon triangle and top with a small amount of caviar. Set the brioche lids at an angle.

SUGGESTED WINE: A champagne or California Chardonnay

Scrambled Eggs with Caviar

Oeufs Brouillés au Caviar

If your budget allows, Beluga or Sevruga or American Malassol would be the ideal substitute for golden caviar. However, golden caviar (whitefish roe) is much less expensive; it gives the appearance and taste of the more expensive caviar.

1. Preheat oven to 450°.
2. Roll out the puff pastry to a rectangle ⅜ inch thick and cut out two 4-inch circles. Cut a concentric circle halfway through each circle, ½ inch from the edge. Place the rounds on a baking sheet and brush with egg wash.
3. Bake 15 to 18 minutes, reduce the temperature to 350°, and bake 20 minutes longer, or until golden brown.
4. Remove the lid created by the cut concentric circle. Pull out any "doughy" uncooked pastry.
5. Whisk together the eggs, heavy cream, and pepper until thoroughly combined.
6. In a sauté pan, over low heat, melt 1 tablespoon butter. Pour in the eggs and cook until they begin to thicken; keep the eggs moving with a whisk or spatula.
7. Stir in the chives and cook until thick and creamy. Add half the caviar.
8. Remove from the heat and stir in the remaining butter. Add white pepper to taste.
9. Meanwhile, reheat the pastry cases.

PRESENTATION: Spoon eggs into each pastry case. Garnish with the remaining caviar. Set pastry lids at an angle.

SUGGESTED WINE: A champagne or Chardonnay

TO SERVE 2

3 ounces puff pastry (page 200)
1 egg, lightly beaten, for egg wash
4 eggs
2 tablespoons heavy cream
Freshly ground white pepper to taste
2 tablespoons unsalted butter
1 tablespoon minced chives
2 tablespoons golden caviar

Stocks and Soups

Chicken Stock

Fish Stock

Court Bouillon

Brown Veal Stock

Duck Stock

Cream of Chicken Soup

Mushroom Soup

Cold Cream of Sorrel Soup

Watercress Soup

Lobster Bisque

Mussel Soup

Crayfish Soup

Onion Soup

Vegetable Soup with Sweet Basil

Duck Soup and Cheese Ravioli

Cold Avocado Soup

Cold Tomato-Vegetable Soup

"The stockpot should never be treated as a rubbish bin" is the amusing and intelligent suggestion of playwright and amateur food authority Tom Stoppard. My own feeling, precisely. It is possible to be somewhat casual about the amounts and kinds of ingredients that go into the stockpot, but freshness and quality are just as important in stock making as they are in all other aspects of cooking.

Stocks are produced by simmering, in water, ingredients such as meat, bones, fish, fowl, game, and vegetables, for an extended period of time to extract the essence of their flavor. Many of the recipes in this book require a brown stock (made with veal or beef), or a duck, chicken, or fish stock. I reduce these stocks and bind them with a small amount of butter. I never use flour or starch to thicken a stock, which accounts for the light consistency of my sauces. Besides being the foundation of many soups, stocks are the heart of many sauces.

Because stocks are essential for so many recipes, they should be prepared in large quantities, reduced, and then stored in the refrigerator or freezer, to be available at a moment's notice.

It is generally accepted that the measure of a good cook is his or her sauces. Although soups are considered simple fare, I'm of the belief that sometimes the simplest dishes require the most care. If I were to judge a good home kitchen, I would start with the soup.

Chicken Stock
Fond de Volaille

One of the most useful stocks in your kitchen, chicken stock will enhance your sauces and soups.

1. Clean the vegetables and cut them into 1-inch pieces. Place in a stockpot with the chicken, salt, peppercorns, thyme, bay leaf, and water.
2. Bring to a boil and skim as necessary. Cook for 30 minutes or until chicken is tender.
3. Remove whole chicken or bones and wings, and strain the stock into a clean bowl or stockpot. Skim to completely remove fat.
4. For a *glace*, reduce to about 2½ or 3 cups.

TO MAKE 1 GALLON

2 leeks
2 carrots
2 stalks celery
1 2½- to 3-pound chicken or chicken bones and wings
½ teaspoon salt
½ teaspoon whole peppercorns
A pinch of thyme
1 bay leaf
4 quarts water

Fish Stock
Fumet de Poisson

Fish stock is essential for many fish preparations, especially as the base for a light butter sauce.

1. In a saucepan, over medium heat, sauté the fish bones, carrot, onion, shallot, and celery in the olive oil for 10 minutes.
2. Deglaze the pan with white wine. Add the bouquet garni and enough water to cover. Bring to a boil and cook for 25 minutes. Remove from the heat and strain.

TO MAKE 1 QUART

2 pounds fish bones, cut into pieces (use any saltwater fish except salmon)
1 carrot, sliced
½ onion, sliced
1 shallot, sliced
½ stalk celery, sliced
2 tablespoons olive oil
2 cups dry white wine
1 bouquet garni
Water

Court Bouillon

TO MAKE APPROXIMATELY 2 QUARTS

2 medium carrots
2 stalks celery
1 leek
1 sprig of fresh thyme or
  a pinch of dried thyme
1 bay leaf
1 teaspoon salt
½ teaspoon freshly
  ground pepper
2 quarts water
2 cups dry white wine

Court bouillon is excellent for poaching fish for the health- and weight-conscious. I also like to use it as the liquid for steaming fish.

1. Slice carrots, celery, and leek into ¼-inch pieces. Place in the bottom of a saucepan.
2. Add the remaining ingredients and bring to a boil. Boil for 20 minutes. Use as needed.

Brown Veal Stock

Fond Brun de Veau

TO MAKE ½ GALLON STOCK, 1 QUART DEMI-GLACE, OR 1 CUP GLACE

10 pounds veal bones,
  cut into 2-inch pieces
  (beef bones may be
  substituted)
2 onions, quartered
2 carrots, chopped
2 stalks celery, chopped
1 leek, chopped
2 tomatoes, quartered
1 bouquet garni
1 gallon water
  (approximately)

A good brown stock is essential to a fine sauce. The browning of the bones gives the stock its wonderfully dark color.

1. Preheat oven to 450°.
2. Arrange the bones in a large roasting pan and brown on all sides, turning as often as necessary. Transfer the bones to a large stockpot. Add the vegetables and bouquet garni. Discard the fat from the roasting pan. On the stove top, deglaze the pan with 1 cup water, scraping up any particles that stick to the bottom of the pan. Add to the stockpot and pour in enough water to cover by 2 inches.
3. Bring to a boil. Then reduce heat so that the liquid continues to simmer. Skim foam as it accumulates.
4. Continue to simmer for at least 6 hours, skimming and degreasing as necessary. Add more water as necessary to keep the bones and vegetables covered at all times.
5. After 6 hours, strain off the liquid into a clean pot. Degrease and skim if necessary. Reduce over moderate heat until 2 quarts remain.
6. Cool and store in covered containers, or continue to reduce to 1 quart (*demi-glace*) or to a syrup (*glace*).

Duck Stock

Fond de Canard

For this stock you can use bones from cooked or uncooked ducks.

1. Preheat oven to 500°.
2. Place the duck bones, onion, and celery in a roasting pan and roast until the bones are a dark golden brown, about 30 minutes. Turn the bones once or twice as they cook.
3. Transfer the duck bones and vegetables to a 6-quart stockpot. Deglaze the roasting pan with the white wine and pour it into the stockpot. Add the tomatoes, thyme, bay leaf, peppercorns, and enough water to cover all the ingredients by 1 inch. Bring the stock to a boil, reduce the heat, and simmer for 3 hours. Skim off the foam and fat as it rises to the top.
4. Strain into a clean pot or saucepan and carefully skim away any remaining fat.
5. Over high heat, reduce the stock until only half remains.

TO MAKE 1 QUART

2 duck carcasses, roughly chopped
1 unpeeled onion, quartered
1 stalk celery, coarsely sliced
1½ cups dry white wine
2 ripe tomatoes, quartered
¼ teaspoon dried thyme or 1 branch fresh thyme
½ bay leaf
½ teaspoon whole peppercorns
Water

Cream of Chicken Soup

Crème de Volaille

Chicken backs and necks may be substituted for the chicken half with equally good results.

1. In a 6-quart stockpot, combine chicken, leek, carrot, celery, salt, pepper, thyme, bay leaf, and water. Bring to a boil and let boil gently for 30 minutes. Skim foam and fat from stock as necessary.
2. Remove chicken from the pot and set aside to cool. When cool enough to handle, cut into bite-size pieces.
3. In a 4-quart saucepan, melt the butter. Stir in the flour and cook, over a low flame, for 10 minutes. Cool.

TO SERVE 4 OR 5

Half a chicken, about 1½ pounds
1 medium leek, coarsely chopped
1 carrot, coarsely chopped
1 stalk celery, coarsely chopped

1 teaspoon salt
Freshly ground pepper to
  taste
A small pinch of thyme
1 small bay leaf
2 quarts water
2 tablespoons unsalted
  butter
2 tablespoons all-purpose
  flour
2 egg yolks
1 cup heavy cream
Juice of half a medium
  lemon

Strain the chicken stock into the same saucepan and stir thoroughly. Over a moderate flame, bring the stock to a boil and boil gently for 30 minutes.

4. Add chicken pieces to the stock.
5. Gradually whisk 2 cups of the hot soup into the combined egg yolks and cream. Return this to the soup and simmer for a few minutes. *Do not boil.* Taste, and correct seasonings with salt, pepper, and lemon juice.

PRESENTATION: Serve immediately in warm bowls.

Mushroom Soup

Crème de Champignons

As with so many of my recipes, this soup must not be overcooked. You will be delighted at how simple it is to prepare.

TO SERVE 4

1 pound firm white
  mushrooms, cleaned
1 medium lemon
1 tablespoon unsalted
  butter
2 tablespoons minced
  shallots
¼ teaspoon dried thyme
½ bay leaf
1 teaspoon salt
½ teaspoon freshly
  ground pepper
2 cups heavy cream
1½ cups chicken stock
  (page 65)
1 teaspoon cornstarch
  dissolved in 1
  tablespoon water
1 tablespoon minced
  parsley

1. Sprinkle the mushrooms with lemon juice. In a food processor, coarsely chop them.
2. Melt the butter in a heavy saucepan and lightly sauté the shallots. Add the mushrooms, thyme, and bay leaf and sauté over moderate heat for 10 minutes, or until the liquid disappears.
3. Add the salt, pepper, cream, and chicken stock and bring to a boil. Reduce the heat and simmer for 20 minutes.
4. Add the cornstarch to the soup and continue to simmer 10 minutes longer, stirring constantly.
5. Correct seasoning to taste.

PRESENTATION: Serve in warm bowls. Sprinkle with minced parsley.

Cold Cream of Sorrel Soup

Germiny Glacé

This soup may be served hot as well as cold. The tangy flavor of the sorrel and the rich chicken broth make a smooth combination.

1. Mince the sorrel. In a large saucepan, over medium heat, melt the butter and sauté the sorrel until wilted.
2. In a separate saucepan, bring the chicken stock to a boil.
3. In a large mixing bowl, combine the egg yolks and cream and beat well. Slowly whisk in the hot chicken stock.
4. Return mixture to saucepan and cook over very low heat for 10 minutes, or until the soup coats the back of a spoon. *Do not let it boil.* Strain into the wilted sorrel.
5. Cool over ice.

PRESENTATION: Serve in chilled bowls.

TO SERVE 6

8 ounces sorrel, washed, with stems removed
2 tablespoons unsalted butter
1 quart chicken stock (page 65)
8 egg yolks
½ cup heavy cream
Salt and freshly ground pepper

Watercress Soup

Potage Cressonière

The basic recipe for this country-style soup is the same as for any cream soup. Simply replace the watercress with sorrel, lettuce, spinach, or any vegetable of your choice.

1. Wash the leeks and cut them into small pieces.
2. Clean the watercress and reserve a few nice leaves.
3. In a large saucepan, sauté the watercress and leeks in 4 tablespoons butter, over medium-low heat, for 10 minutes.
4. Add the potatoes and chicken stock. Bring this to a boil and cook soup for 25 to 30 minutes, or until the potatoes are tender.
5. Purée the soup in a food processor. Strain the purée into a clean saucepan.

TO SERVE 6 OR 8

4 leeks, white part only
3 bunches watercress
6 tablespoons unsalted butter
5 medium potatoes, peeled and sliced
6 cups chicken stock (page 65)
2 cups heavy cream
1 tablespoon crème fraîche or sour cream
1 teaspoon salt
½ teaspoon freshly ground white pepper
1 teaspoon lemon juice

6. Add the cream, *crème fraîche*, and remaining butter. Heat almost to a boil.
7. Season to taste with salt, pepper, and lemon juice.

PRESENTATION: Serve hot or cold, garnished with reserved watercress leaves.

Lobster Bisque
Soupe d'Homard

It is absolutely necessary to use live lobsters to guarantee the flavor of this king of soups. Cooking the shell after the meat has been extracted enriches the soup.

TO SERVE 6 OR 8

3 live lobsters, 1 to 1¼
  pounds each
3 tablespoons olive oil
1 carrot, chopped
2 stalks celery, chopped
3 tomatoes, chopped
5 cloves garlic, chopped
5 shallots, chopped
3 sprigs fresh tarragon,
  chopped
3 tablespoons Cognac
2 cups dry white wine
2 tablespoons tomato
  paste
10 cups fish stock (page
  65), court bouillon
  (page 66), or water
Salt, freshly ground
  pepper, and cayenne
  pepper to taste
A pinch of dried thyme
1 bay leaf
2 cups heavy cream
1 tablespoon minced
  chives or parsley

1. After killing the lobsters (see page 20), break them, separating the claws and tails from the bodies.
2. Heat a 6-quart stockpot. Add the oil and sauté the lobster pieces until they are red. Remove the claws and tails as they are cooked.
3. Add the carrot, celery, tomatoes, garlic, shallots, and tarragon and continue to sauté for 10 minutes. Pour in the Cognac and ignite.
4. When the flame has subsided, deglaze with white wine, and add the tomato paste and enough fish stock, court bouillon, or water to cover. Season with salt, pepper, cayenne pepper, thyme, and bay leaf and boil gently for 15 minutes.
5. Grind the lobster legs and stomach shells with the vegetables in a food processor. Add back to the soup and reduce until thick.
6. In a small saucepan, reduce the cream by half.
7. Strain the soup and stir in the reduced cream.
8. Shell the claws and tails, cut into bite-size pieces and add to the soup.

NOTE: Add more tomato paste for extra color, if desired.

PRESENTATION: Serve in heated soup bowls and garnish with minced chives or parsley.

Mussel Soup

Soupe aux Moules

Souple aux moules is to France what clam chowder is to America. This recipe transcends geography.

1. Wash the mussels carefully, removing the sand and any beards.
2. Roughly chop ¼ pound each of the carrots, leeks, and celery. Place the vegetables in a large saucepan with the mussels, stock, and wine. Bring to a boil and cook for 5 minutes. Strain and reserve liquid and mussels separately.
3. Cut the remaining vegetables into *brunoise.* Melt the butter in a 6-quart saucepan. Add the vegetables, saffron, and thyme and cook slowly, over low heat, for 8 to 10 minutes.
4. Add the cream to the vegetable mixture and bring to a boil. Reduce slightly by cooking the mixture for 5 to 10 minutes.
5. Add the reserved liquid from the mussels and reduce slightly over high heat to concentrate the flavors.
6. Shuck the mussels and add them to the soup.
7. Season with salt, pepper, cayenne, and lemon juice to taste.

PRESENTATION: Serve in heated bowls.

TO SERVE 6

2½ pounds fresh mussels in their shells
½ pound carrots
½ pound leeks
½ pound celery
2 cups fish stock (page 65)
1 cup dry white wine
1 tablespoon unsalted butter
½ teaspoon saffron
½ teaspoon dried thyme
2 cups heavy cream
Salt
Freshly ground pepper
Cayenne pepper
Juice of half a small lemon

Crayfish Soup
Soupe d'Écrevisses

Live crayfish must be used. The tail meat may be used for
écrevisses à la nage or for Fisherman's Salad.

TO SERVE 8

¼ cup olive oil
5 dozen crayfish, heads
  separated from tails
5 carrots
3 medium leeks
5 stalks celery
6 tablespoons tomato
  paste
2 cups dry white wine
¼ cup Cognac
2 quarts court bouillon
  (page 66) or fish stock
  (page 65)
6 cloves garlic, chopped
A pinch of thyme
1 bay leaf
A pinch of cayenne
  pepper
3 cups heavy cream

1. Heat a 6-quart stockpot. Add oil and sauté crayfish
   heads until bright red.
2. In a food processor or with a knife, roughly chop 2
   carrots, 1 leek, and 2 celery stalks. Add to crayfish.
3. Stir in tomato paste and deglaze with white wine and
   Cognac. Add court bouillon, garlic, thyme, bay leaf,
   and cayenne pepper. Cook at a light boil for 1 hour.
4. Remove crayfish from the soup and purée in a food
   processor. Return purée to the stockpot and cook 30
   minutes longer, or until it has a full-bodied flavor.
5. In a separate saucepan, bring the cream to a boil and
   reduce for 10 minutes. Add the cream to the soup and
   strain through a *chinois* or fine sieve. Taste carefully and
   continue to cook to concentrate flavors if necessary.
6. Cut the remaining vegetables into *brunoise*. Sauté in
   additional olive oil or butter until they are tender but
   still have texture. And the *brunoise* to the soup, bring
   to a boil, and serve.

PRESENTATION: Serve in heated bowls.

SPECIAL EQUIPMENT:
Chinois or fine sieve

Onion Soup

Soupe à l'Oignon

Here is the perfect example of how the simplest ingredients can be used to create a very special soup. The addition of port turns hearty fare into a chef's delight. By the way, did you know that Les Halles in Paris were as famous for their onion soup as for their fine food market?

1. Thinly slice the onions.
2. Heat a 6-quart stockpot. Heat the oil and sauté the onions until golden brown.
3. Deglaze the pan with port. Add the stock, salt, pepper, and bouquet garni and simmer for 30 to 40 minutes.
4. Dry the slices of French bread in a warm oven.
5. Pour the soup into six oven-proof bowls. Top each bowl with two slices of bread and sprinkle with cheese. Brown under the broiler or salamander.

NOTE: If you wish to thicken the soup, combine 2 or 3 egg yolks with 3 tablespoons port and slowly pour soup into the egg mixture.

PRESENTATION: Serve immediately with French bread.

SPECIAL EQUIPMENT:
6 oven-proof bowls

TO SERVE 6

4 medium onions
3 tablespoons mild-flavored oil, such as almond or safflower
½ cup port
8 cups chicken stock (page 65) or brown veal stock (page 66)
Salt and freshly ground pepper to taste
1 bouquet garni (fresh thyme, bay leaf, and celery stalk tied together)
12 slices French bread, ¼ inch thick
Swiss cheese, grated or sliced

Vegetable Soup with Sweet Basil

Soupe au Pistou

The distinctive flavor of this Provençal soup can only be achieved with fresh tomatoes and fresh basil added at the last moment.

TO SERVE 6

2 small leeks, white part only
1 large potato, peeled
1 small onion
2 stalks celery
1 medium zucchini
12 green beans
2 medium carrots, peeled
6 tablespoons olive oil
3 tablespoons water
½ gallon chicken stock (page 65) (or ½ gallon water, 4 bouillon cubes, a pinch of thyme, and ½ bay leaf)
6 ripe tomatoes, peeled and seeded
4 medium garlic cloves
30 fresh basil leaves, washed and dried
Salt
½ teaspoon freshly ground pepper

1. Cut the leeks, potato, onion, celery, zucchini, green beans, and carrots into ¼-inch dice.
2. In a 6-quart stockpot, combine 3 tablespoons olive oil with 3 tablespoons water. Add the vegetables and sauté, over medium-low heat, until all the water evaporates. Do not brown the vegetables.
3. Add the stock and bring to a boil. Cook at a gentle boil for 30 minutes.
4. Meanwhile, make a purée with the tomatoes, basil leaves, garlic, and remaining 3 tablespoons olive oil. Add the purée to the cooked soup. Stir thoroughly. Do not boil again.
5. Season to taste with salt and pepper.

NOTE: We generally do not serve wine with this soup.

PRESENTATION: Serve hot or cold from a tureen or in individual bowls.

Duck Soup and Cheese Ravioli

The essence of the duck bones combined with the cheese ravioli makes this a light but hearty soup.

1. In a bowl, combine the cream cheese, olive oil, pepper, thyme, 1 tablespoon parsley, and 1 tablespoon chives.
2. Roll out half the pasta dough into a rectangle. Brush with egg wash. Using a small spoon, drop approximately ½ teaspoon cheese filling at even intervals over the surface of the dough. Roll out the remaining dough to the same size and cover the first half. Press the dough together around the filling and form squares. Cut with a knife, pastry cutter, or ravioli cutter.
3. Bring the duck stock to a boil, add the ravioli, and cook for 10 minutes, or until they are *al dente.* Add the remaining herbs during the last 2 or 3 minutes.

NOTE: A good chicken stock can be substituted for the duck stock.

PRESENTATION: Divide the ravioli among eight soup plates, add the steaming hot duck stock, and serve.

TO SERVE 8 AS AN APPETIZER

8 ounces cream cheese, softened
2 tablespoons olive oil
1 teaspoon freshly ground pepper
1 teaspoon fresh thyme
½ cup minced parsley
½ cup minced chives
1 recipe pasta dough (page 208)
1 egg, lightly beaten, for egg wash
6 cups duck stock (page 67)

Cold Avocado Soup

Crème d'Avocat Glacée

The avocados should be very ripe for the best flavor. Serve the soup in the avocado skins for a wonderful, natural appearance.

1. Cut the avocados in half. Remove the pits, and carefully scoop out the meat. Reserve the skins intact.
2. Combine avocado meat, onion, and the juice of half a lemon in a food processor and purée. Strain into a large mixing bowl.
3. Stir in the thoroughly defatted chicken stock and mix well. Add the cream. Season to taste with salt, pepper, and lemon juice. Refrigerate until serving time.

TO SERVE 6

3 large ripe avocados
1 small onion, chopped
Juice of 1 lemon
2 cups chicken stock (page 65)
1 cup heavy cream
Salt and freshly ground pepper
Watercress leaves
Red or black caviar

PRESENTATION: Set the avocado skins in individual serving bowls and fill with soup. Garnish with watercress leaves and caviar.

Cold Tomato-Vegetable Soup
Gazpacho

This is my version of the traditional Spanish summer soup.

TO SERVE 6

8 very ripe medium-size
  tomatoes
2 medium-size
  cucumbers
2 small bell peppers
1 stalk celery
1 tablespoon sherry wine
  vinegar
3 to 4 tablespoons
  tomato paste
3 tablespoons olive oil
2 teaspoons salt
½ teaspoon freshly
  ground pepper
½ teaspoon cayenne
  pepper
1 small cucumber

1. Core the tomatoes and cut them into quarters. Peel and seed the medium cucumbers, and cut them into 1-inch pieces. Core and seed the bell peppers and cut them into quarters. Slice the celery into 1-inch pieces.
2. Place all the vegetables in a stainless steel, glass, or ceramic bowl with the vinegar. Cover with plastic wrap and let the mixture sit 6 to 8 hours or overnight. Stir once or twice while it is marinating.
3. Using a food processor or grinder, process the vegetables until they are minced but still have some texture. Return to the bowl.
4. Stir in the tomato paste, olive oil, salt, pepper, and cayenne pepper. Taste and correct seasonings. If the tomatoes are not too flavorful it may be necessary to add more tomato paste. Chill until serving time.
5. Peel, seed, and slice the small cucumber.

PRESENTATION: Serve in icy cold bowls and garnish with cucumber slices.

SUGGESTED WINE: A very dry and acidic white wine

Poultry and Game

Chicken Pie with Morels

Chicken in a Salt Crust

Sautéed Chicken with Vinegar Sauce and Wild
Mushrooms

Chicken in Petit Sirah

Chicken Legs Steamed with Thyme

Chicken Breasts Stuffed with Goose Liver

Chicken with Tomato Fondue

Duck with Green Peppercorns

Duck Legs with Turnips and Green Onions or Leeks

Stuffed Breast of Duck

Duck Breast with Port Wine

Duck with Pears and Pink Peppercorn Sauce

Duck Ravioli

Duck Ravioli with Fresh Herbs

Pigeon with Pears and Red Wine

Pigeon in Puff Pastry with Artichoke Mousse

The public's loyalty to and continued gastronomic interest in the chicken is best attributed to its immense range of possible preparations and almost universal economy. Chicken, served hot or cold, can be stuffed, basted, boiled, broiled, steamed, seasoned, fermented, flavored, and garnished with almost any combination of herbs, fish, nuts, grain, fruits, vegetables, and sauces. Last year I was amused when I removed my simple cold chicken salad from the Ma Maison menu (to provide room for an alternative) and was besieged by requests for its reinstatement. There is no doubt that chicken still holds allure, even for those who can well afford other game and fowl and have sampled such items in fine restaurants all over the world.

For me, and seemingly for the French as well, duck is unquestionably the most delectable of all birds. In America, the duck is just beginning to become domesticated. Among the broadly domesticated variety, I prefer the Peking duck. Its tasty, tender meat is much leaner than many other readily available ducks. The reduced fat factor is important because I do not cook my ducks merely to burn off fat; I cook them with texture and taste in mind, and duck tastes best when done to a delicate pink color. My preferred duck presentation in two courses (the pink duck breast first, and the leg and crisp skin served in a curly endive salad afterward) is certainly not an exotic recipe, but it is one of the best loved.

Pigeon should be eaten young and very fresh, since the longer they are kept the less flavor they have. Older pigeons should be used only for stock, stewing, or pies. I have found that pigeon also retains its best flavor when cooked to a vivid pink.

When purchasing chickens, duck, or pigeons, seek out a quality meat market and pass over birds that have scaly, bruised legs (particularly chickens), which is a sign of advanced age. Sometimes age is difficult to ascertain. Pressing the end of a young pigeon breast should reveal supple bones; this technique can be used for many other birds as well.

I have chosen this group of recipes for their unique taste combinations, originality, and artful, impressive presentations. These recipes can easily be adapted for pheasant, quail, partridge, and other fowl and game that the adventurous among you might procure in the wild.

Chicken Pie with Morels

Poulet sous Croûte aux Morilles

This is the French version of the English chicken pie. When the crust is broken into, the perfume of the ingredients is inebriating.

1. Soak the morels overnight in enough water to cover. Drain and cut in half lengthwise, and wash carefully to remove all the sand.
2. Season chicken pieces with salt and pepper to taste and dust lightly with flour. Sauté in 1 tablespoon each of butter and oil and cook till golden brown on all sides.
3. Remove the chicken from the pan and pour off the fat. Add the shallots and morels, and deglaze the pan with the port. Add the cream and bring to a boil. Return the chicken to the pan and simmer, covered, for 10 minutes. The sauce should thicken slightly.
4. Whisk in the remaining 3 tablespoons butter, one small piece at a time. Season to taste with salt, pepper, and lemon juice.
5. Divide the chicken and sauce equally among four or six individual casseroles. Set aside to cool.
6. Roll out the puff pastry, keeping it at least ¼ inch thick. Cut rounds of pastry 2 inches larger than the casseroles.
7. When the chicken has cooled, brush sides of casseroles with egg wash and cover with the round pastry, pressing the edges down gently. (Do not make any holes in the pastry.) Refrigerate for 1 hour or longer.
8. Preheat oven to 400°.
9. Brush pastry with egg wash and bake for 35 minutes, or until crust is a rich golden brown. Serve immediately.

NOTE: It is important to roll the pastry to a thickness of at least ¼ inch and to chill it thoroughly before baking. Otherwise the crust will collapse into the casseroles.

PRESENTATION: Place the hot casseroles on dinner plates and bring to the table.

SUGGESTED WINE: A St. Emilion

SPECIAL EQUIPMENT: 4 or 6 individual casseroles

TO SERVE 4 OR 6

24 dried morels
2 whole chickens (2½ pounds each), cut in eighths
Salt
Freshly ground white pepper
1 tablespoon all-purpose flour
4 tablespoons unsalted butter
2 tablespoons peanut oil
2 shallots, minced
1 cup port
2 cups heavy cream
Juice of half a lemon
1 pound puff pastry (page 200)
1 egg, lightly beaten, for egg wash

Chicken in a Salt Crust

Poulet en Croûte de Sel

By enclosing the chicken hermetically with the salt dough, the tarragon is steamed and flavors the chicken perfectly.

TO SERVE 6 OR 8

2 whole chickens, 3
 pounds each
1 teaspoon freshly
 ground pepper
4 sprigs fresh tarragon
3 pounds sea salt
3 pounds all-purpose
 flour
3 cups water
 (approximately)
2 eggs, lightly beaten, for
 egg wash
Mustard vinaigrette
 (page 101)

1. Season the insides of the chickens with pepper. Place the fresh tarragon under the skin of the chicken breasts. Fix the wings akimbo.
2. Preheat oven to 350°.
3. In a large mixing bowl, combine the salt, flour, and enough water to make a stiff dough.
4. For each chicken, use half the dough recipe. Divide each half into two pieces, one slightly larger than the other. Roll out the smaller piece of dough to a thickness of ½ inch, slightly larger than the chicken. Place the dough in a shallow roasting pan and set the chicken on top.
5. Roll out the remaining half of the dough to a thickness of ½ inch, large enough to generously cover the chicken. Brush the edges with water and seal chicken completely, so no air can escape.
6. Brush the tops with egg wash and roast for 1½ to 2 hours, until the crust is golden brown.
7. Remove the chickens from the oven.

PRESENTATION: Place the chickens on serving platters. At the table, break the crusts so your guests may enjoy the wonderful aroma. Cut each chicken into quarters. Nap each plate with mustard vinaigrette and place a piece of chicken on top. Serve the remaining vinaigrette separately.

SUGGESTED WINE: A Chardonnay

Sautéed Chicken with Vinegar Sauce and Wild Mushrooms

Fricassée de Poulet au Vinaigre et Champignons Sauvages

Vinegar, as opposed to something sweet, opens the taste buds. The reduction of the vinegar combined with the flavor of the chicken and wild mushrooms gives this dish its characteristic taste.

1. Season the chicken pieces with salt and pepper. Dust lightly with flour.
2. Heat a large heavy sauté pan. Add the oil and 1 tablespoon butter. Sauté the chicken until it is golden brown on all sides and just cooked through. Remove the chicken and reserve.
3. Drain the remaining fat from the pan and heat 1 tablespoon butter. Add the shallots and tarragon and, over moderate heat, sauté for 1 minute. Deglaze the pan with the vinegar and white wine and reduce the liquid until only 3 tablespoons remain.
4. Pour in the stock and reduce it until the sauce is slightly thickened. Whisk in 8 tablespoons butter, one small piece at a time. Add the chicken and heat through. *Do not boil.*
5. In a sauté pan, heat the remaining 2 tablespoons butter and quickly sauté the mushrooms over high heat. Stir the mushrooms in with the chicken.

NOTE: Dried mushrooms that have been soaked overnight in water or quartered silver-dollar-size cultivated mushrooms may be substituted for the Japanese tree mushrooms or wild mushrooms.

PRESENTATION: Transfer the chicken to a deep serving dish or casserole. Garnish with a bit of tarragon or minced chives.

SUGGESTED WINE: A Pinot Noir

TO SERVE 6

2 chickens, 3 pounds each, cut into eighths
1 teaspoon salt
¼ teaspoon freshly ground pepper
All-purpose flour
1 tablespoon mild-flavored oil, such as almond or safflower
12 tablespoons unsalted butter
3 medium shallots, minced
1 tablespoon chopped fresh tarragon
¼ cup sherry wine vinegar or red wine vinegar
1 cup dry white wine
3 cups chicken stock (page 65) or brown veal stock (page 66)
1 pound Japanese tree mushrooms, or any edible wild mushrooms, cleaned

Chicken in Petit Sirah

Coq au Petit Sirah

Californian *coq au vin*. The use of a heavy red wine from California produces the unusual color and taste.

TO SERVE 4

A 4-pound chicken, cut
  into eighths
2 tablespoons flour
1½ teaspoons salt
1 teaspoon freshly
  ground pepper
2 tablespoons olive oil
10 slices bacon, cut into
  1-inch slices
1 medium onion, cut
  into 1-inch pieces, or
  16 small boiling onions,
  cut in half
16 button mushrooms or
  12 medium mushrooms
  cut in half
1 large carrot, cut into
  ½-inch pieces
1 stalk celery, cut into
  ½-inch pieces
3 cloves garlic, minced
½ teaspoon dried thyme
1 tablespoon minced
  fresh tarragon
½ bottle Petit Sirah
1 tablespoon flour
1 tablespoon unsalted
  butter

1. Dust the chicken pieces with the 2 tablespoons of flour and season with ½ teaspoon salt and ½ teaspoon pepper. Set aside.
2. Heat a large sauté pan and add the oil. When the oil is hot, add the chicken, skin side down, and sauté it over high heat until dark golden brown on all sides. Remove the chicken from the pan and set aside. Drain the grease.
3. In the same pan, sauté the bacon over medium heat until brown but not crisp. Remove the bacon and reserve.
4. In the bacon fat, in separate batches, sauté the onions, mushrooms, carrots, and celery. As each batch is lightly browned, transfer to a bowl. Drain the remaining fat.
5. Return the chicken pieces to the pan with the vegetables, garlic, thyme, and tarragon. Pour in the Petit Sirah and bring to a boil. Reduce the heat to low, cover the pan, and cook 25 to 30 minutes, or until the chicken and vegetables are tender.
6. Prepare *beurre manié* by combining the flour and butter until smooth.
7. Transfer the chicken to a warm platter. Over moderate heat, reduce the sauce by one third. Thicken with *buerre manié* as needed. Add the remaining 1 teaspoon salt and ½ teaspoon pepper, taste, and correct the seasoning.

NOTE: This dish may be prepared ahead of time, partially or completely, and reheated just before serving. The Petit Sirah may be replaced by a Zinfandel or a full-bodied Cabernet.

PRESENTATION: Place two chicken pieces on each hot dinner plate. Spoon sauce and vegetables over each serving.

SUGGESTED WINE: The same wine you cooked the chicken with

Chicken Legs Steamed with Thyme

Gigots de Poulet Cuit à la Vapeur de Thym

The chicken legs may be boned and stuffed the day before, so the final preparation should take about 45 minutes. Any herb of your choice may be substituted for the thyme.

1. *To make the farce:* In a heavy sauté pan, heat the olive oil. Add the mushrooms and onions and, over moderate heat, sauté for 2 minutes, or until most of the liquid evaporates. Add the sweetbreads, chicken breast, salt, and pepper, and cook 2 minutes longer. Add the port and reduce by half. Add the chicken stock, cover, and cook slowly for 30 minutes.
2. Using a slotted spoon, transfer the farce to a bowl. Reduce any remaining juice to a glaze and pour over the farce. Set aside and allow the mixture to cool.
3. Bone the chicken legs, using a small boning knife. Season the insides with salt and pepper.
4. When the farce is cool, cut it into small cubes. Stuff each leg and close, reshaping to resemble the original leg. Secure with toothpicks. Poke holes through the leg to prevent it from exploding while cooking.
5. Pour the 1 quart chicken stock into the bottom of a steamer and add the thyme. Butter the steamer rack and place the legs on the rack. Sprinkle with a few thyme leaves and steam for 25 minutes.
6. Meanwhile, cut the vegetables for garniture into *bâtonettes* and cook in salted boiling water until *al dente*.
7. *To make the sauce:* In a food processor, purée the blanched watercress with the butter. Reserve. Reduce the chicken stock until only ½ cup remains, add the cream, and reduce slightly. Stir in 1 tablespoon of the watercress purée. Strain and season with salt and pepper.

NOTE: Should you desire a stronger, meatier flavor, reduce some of the chicken stock from the steamer to a glaze and add it to the sauce according to your taste.

PRESENTATION: Nap each warm dinner plate with sauce and set a stuffed chicken leg in the center. Sprinkle with thyme leaves and surround with vegetables.

SUGGESTED WINE: A white Graves or a Sauvignon blanc

TO SERVE 4

Farce:

2 tablespoons olive oil
2 ounces silver-dollar-size mushrooms, cut in half
2 ounces minced onion
½ pound sweetbreads, soaked in cold water overnight
2 ounces chicken breast meat
Salt
Freshly ground pepper
2 tablespoons port
2 cups chicken stock (page 65)

Chicken:

4 chicken legs with thighs
Salt
Freshly ground pepper
1 quart chicken stock
3 or 4 branches fresh thyme, plus a few leaves

Garniture:

3 ounces carrot
1 ounce celery root (celeriac)
3 ounces asparagus
12 small onions

Sauce:

½ bunch blanched watercress
2 tablespoons unsalted butter
¾ cup chicken stock
¼ cup heavy cream
Salt
Freshly ground pepper

Chicken Breasts Stuffed with Goose Liver
Paupiettes de Volaille au Foie Gras

This is an elegant presentation of chicken breasts, in which the breasts are tender and juicy.

TO SERVE 6

4 large whole chicken breasts, halved
1 egg
1 tablespoon chopped fresh tarragon
1 teaspoon salt
½ teaspoon freshly ground pepper
1 cup heavy cream
2 to 3 ounces foie gras
6 tablespoons unsalted butter
2 tablespoons oil
1 shallot, minced
6 tablespoons wine vinegar
1 cup chicken stock (page 65) or brown veal stock (page 66)

1. In a food processor, combine two boned and skinned chicken breast halves with the egg, tarragon, salt, and pepper. Process until chicken mixture is puréed. With the processor on, pour the cream through the feed tube and process until blended. Chill mousse until it is needed.
2. Preheat oven to 400°.
3. Lightly flatten the six remaining boned and skinned chicken breast halves with the flat side of a chef's knife, and season them with salt and pepper. To form *paupiettes*, spread chicken mousse over each breast and top with a ribbon of foie gras, roll up, and tie with kitchen string.
4. In a heavy pan, heat 1 tablespoon each of butter and oil. Set the *paupiettes* in the hot pan and bake for 20 minutes.
5. When the *paupiettes* are done, transfer them to a warm platter and pour off the grease from the pan.
6. Over high heat, sauté the shallots in the same pan for 1 minute. Deglaze the pan with the vinegar and reduce to a glaze.
7. Add the stock and let reduce until syrupy. Whisk in the remaining 5 tablespoons butter, one piece at a time. Season with salt and pepper to taste.

PRESENTATION: Slice the chicken breasts. Strain the sauce onto hot dinner plates and top with sliced breasts.

SUGGESTED WINE: A red wine from Provence

Chicken with Tomato Fondue

Poulet à la Fondue de Tomate

A good example of *cuisine minceur,* this dish is low in calories and high in flavor.

1. Over medium heat, sauté the onion in olive oil until translucent.
2. Add the bell pepper and zucchini and sauté 5 minutes longer.
3. Add tomatoes and cook until vegetables are tender.
4. Cut chicken into eight pieces. Sauté in a nonstick skillet until golden brown. Drain grease.
5. Preheat oven to 375°.
6. Place half the vegetables in the bottom of a 1½-quart casserole. Arrange the chicken over the vegetables and top with the remaining half of the vegetables. Season with thyme, garlic, salt, and pepper. Cover and bake for 30 minutes.

PRESENTATION: Serve from the casserole, either hot or cold.

SUGGESTED WINE: A Fumé blanc

TO SERVE 4

½ large onion, sliced
½ tablespoon olive oil
1 medium bell pepper, cut into 1-inch cubes
1 medium zucchini, cut into 1-inch cubes
6 tomatoes, peeled, seeded, and quartered
A 3½-pound chicken
A pinch of thyme
2 cloves garlic, chopped
1 teaspoon salt
½ teaspoon freshly ground pepper

Duck with Green Peppercorns

Canard au Poivre Vert

In this recipe the duck breasts should be roasted and then allowed to sit for 30 minutes before slicing so the meat retains its juices.

TO SERVE 8

4 whole ducks (4 or 5
  pounds each)
4 medium shallots,
  chopped
2 cups port
2 cups duck stock (page
  67) or chicken stock
  (page 65)
1 cup heavy cream
6 tablespoons green
  peppercorns
¼ pound unsalted butter
2 teaspoons salt
1 teaspoon freshly
  ground white pepper
4 Golden Delicious
  apples

1. Separate the legs from the breasts of the ducks in the same way you would remove chicken legs. Remove the wings and necks and reserve. Roast the legs and breasts separately in a 350° oven, the legs for 90 minutes and the breasts for 40 to 45 minutes.
2. Cook the wings and necks in a large, heavy saucepan until they are golden brown (about 30 minutes). Pour off the grease and add the shallots. Over medium-low heat cook the shallots for 10 minutes longer. Deglaze the pan with the port and let it reduce until approximately 1 cup remains.
3. Add the stock, cream, and 4 tablespoons green peppercorns. Over medium heat, cook until the sauce reduces and thickens slightly.
4. Strain the sauce and taste; it should be full-bodied. If necessary, reduce it further to concentrate the flavor. Whisk in 4 tablespoons butter, 1 tablespoon at a time, and season to taste with salt and pepper.
5. While the sauce is being reduced, peel, core, and quarter the apples. Over low heat, sauté them with the remaining 4 tablespoons butter until tender, approximately 15 minutes.
6. Free the duck breasts from the bones and remove the skin and fat.

NOTE: Poached peaches or pears may be used in place of the apples.

PRESENTATION: Arrange apples on a serving platter. Slice the breasts and arrange on the platter. Separate thighs from leg bones and set both around the outside of the platter. Pour sauce over meat and sprinkle with remaining peppercorns.

SUGGESTED WINE: A Médoc or an aged Cabernet Sauvignon

Duck Legs with Turnips and Green Onions or Leeks

Civet de Canard aux Oignons et Navets

Duck legs are very gelatinous and need slower and longer cooking than duck breasts. This dish tastes even better when reheated the following day.

TO SERVE 2

1. Season the duck legs with salt and pepper. Over high heat, sauté in a heavy pan until golden brown on both sides. Discard the grease.
2. Add the shallot, garlic, thyme, bay leaf, and celery.
3. Deglaze the pan with white wine and add the duck stock, salt, and pepper. Bring to a boil, cover, and let the duck legs simmer for 50 to 60 minutes, or until tender.
4. Cut the turnip into six or eight pieces and turn into oval shapes (see page 14). Blanch for 2 minutes and refresh in ice water. Sauté in 1 tablespoon butter until tender. Set aside and keep warm until needed.
5. Trim the green onions or leeks and place in a small saucepan with water to cover. Season with a bit of salt and pepper and 1 tablespoon butter. Cover and simmer until tender when pierced with the tip of a knife, approximately 10 minutes.
6. Remove duck legs from their cooking liquid and keep warm. Strain the sauce and reduce until lightly thickened. Whisk in the remaining 6 tablespoons butter, one piece at a time. Taste and correct seasonings.

2 duck legs
Salt
Freshly ground pepper
1 shallot, chopped
1 clove garlic
A pinch of thyme
½ bay leaf
1 stalk celery, sliced
½ cup dry white wine
¾ cup duck stock (page 67)
1 medium turnip
¼ pound unsalted butter
8 green onions or 2 medium leeks
½ teaspoon minced parsley

PRESENTATION: Place a duck leg on each warm dinner plate, surround with vegetables, cover with sauce, and sprinkle very lightly with minced parsley.

SUGGESTED WINE: A red Burgundy

Stuffed Breast of Duck
Paupiettes de Canard aux Pistaches et Poivre Vert

Boning a raw duck breast or leg is a minor operation. With a little practice you will be able to remove the bone in no time at all. Since this can be done one or two days in advance, you should try it for your next special dinner party.

TO SERVE 6

3 ducks, 4 to 5 pounds each
1 egg
1 teaspoon salt
½ teaspoon freshly ground pepper
1 cup port
½ cup pistachio nuts, shelled, blanched, and peeled
½ cup pine nuts
1 tablespoon mild-flavored oil, such as almond or safflower
2 cups duck stock (page 67)
½ pound unsalted butter
2 tablespoons green peppercorns, crushed

1. Bone the ducks, leaving the wing tips attached to the breasts.
2. *To make the forcemeat:* Remove the meat from the duck legs. Using a food processor, grind the meat finely. Add the egg, salt, and pepper and continue to process just until combined. Transfer to a bowl. Stir in 3 tablespoons port and 3 tablespoons each of the pistachios and pine nuts. Refrigerate until ready to use.
3. Cut away the excess fat from the breasts and flatten them a bit with the flat side of a chef's knife. Season both sides with salt and pepper. To form *paupiettes*, spread forcemeat over each breast, roll up, and tie with kitchen string.
4. Preheat oven to 450°.
5. In a heavy sauté pan, over high heat, use oil to brown the *paupiettes.* Transfer to the oven and roast for 25 minutes.
6. Place *paupiettes* on a platter and keep warm. Pour off the grease from the pan, deglaze it with the remaining port, and reduce by half. Add the duck stock, and reduce again until slightly thickened. Whisk in the butter.
7. Remove the pan from the stove, and strain the sauce.
8. Add the remaining pine nuts, pistachios, and green peppercorns to the sauce. Adjust seasonings as necessary.

PRESENTATION: Slice the duck breasts and arrange them on heated dinner plates. (Note: It is not elegant to serve a whole stuffed breast on a plate.) Nap with sauce and serve with *galettes de pommes de terre* (page 175).

SUGGESTED WINE: A Cabernet Sauvignon

Duck Breast with Port Wine

Poitrine de Canard au Porto

The natural sweetness of port and the spiciness of the green peppercorns combine to make a perfect sauce for the duck breast.

TO SERVE 6

1. Preheat oven to 400°.
2. Reduce the duck stock until only half remains. Dissolve the cornstarch in ¼ cup port, add it to the stock, and stir thoroughly. Reserve.
3. Season duck breasts with salt and pepper, place in a roasting pan with ½ cup water, and bake for 30 to 35 minutes. The meat should remain pink. Remove from the pan and keep warm.
4. Discard all fat in the roasting pan and deglaze with the remaining port. Reduce to a glaze and add to the duck stock.
5. While the ducks are roasting, poach the pears in a mixture of the white wine, sugar, and lemon slices until tender. (This will take anywhere from 5 to 30 minutes, depending on the ripeness of the fruit.)
6. Bring the sauce to a boil and add 5 to 6 tablespoons of the poaching liquid. Continue to reduce until only 1½ cups remain. Taste and correct seasonings.
7. Remove the duck breasts from the bone. Peel off the skin and fat, and slice the breasts thinly lengthwise. Cut the pears in thin lengthwise slices.

1 quart duck stock (page 67)
1 tablespoon cornstarch
1 cup port
3 whole duck breasts
Salt
Freshly ground pepper
3 pears (or peaches), peeled, halved, and seeded
1 cup dry white wine
3 tablespoons sugar
2 slices lemon
1 tablespoon green peppercorns

PRESENTATION: Arrange slices of duck and slices of pear alternately on each warm plate, nap with sauce, and sprinkle with green peppercorns.

SUGGESTED WINE: A Cabernet Sauvignon

Duck with Pears and Pink Peppercorn Sauce

Canard aux Poires et Poivre Rose

The combination of ripe fresh pears and tangy pink peppercorns creates an exciting taste. Chicken or turkey may be substituted for the duck.

TO SERVE 6

3 whole 5-pound ducks, legs separated from breasts
Salt
Freshly ground pepper
1 carrot, peeled and chopped
2 stalks celery, chopped
1 onion, chopped
1 cup port
½ cup Madeira
2 cups brown veal stock (page 66)
6 small pears, peeled and cored
1 bottle red wine
½ cup sugar
1 teaspoon black peppercorns
1 or more tablespoons each of pink peppercorns and their juice
2 to 4 tablespoons pear brandy
½ pound unsalted butter, cut into small pieces
Curly endive
Mustard vinaigrette (page 101)

1. Preheat oven to 450°.
2. Season the ducks with salt and pepper to taste and poke holes in the skin with a fork. Roast for 35 to 40 minutes, until medium rare.
3. Remove the ducks from the oven and the roasting pan. Pour off the fat. Add the chopped vegetables to the pan and sauté them until slightly golden. Deglaze the pan with port and Madeira. Add the stock and reduce the sauce over moderate heat until it is syrupy.
4. While the sauce is reducing, place the pears in a saucepan with red wine, sugar, and black peppercorns. Poach the pears until tender but still firm.
5. Pour 2 cups of the poaching liquid into a separate saucepan and reduce with half the pink peppercorns until 1 cup liquid remains. Strain the duck stock into the pan and add the pear brandy. Slowly whisk in the butter, one small piece at a time. Adjust seasoning as necessary, strain, and keep warm.
6. Skin duck breasts and remove the meat from the bones. Slice the breasts lengthwise (with the grain).
7. Meanwhile, place the duck legs in a roasting pan and finish cooking them, at 450°, until crisp (15 to 20 minutes).
8. Sauté duck skin in sauté pan until crisp. Remove and cut into small pieces.

NOTE: Pear brandy can be replaced by Armagnac or Grand Marnier.

PRESENTATION: For the first course, arrange slices of duck breasts and one pear on six oven-proof, heated dinner plates. Place in a hot oven (450°) for 2 to 3 minutes. Remove from the oven and spoon sauce over the duck slices, reserving ½ cup. Sprinkle with the remaining pink peppercorns. When everyone is finished with the first course, remove plates and serve the second course. Coat 6 small heated plates with the remaining sauce and place one duck leg on each plate. Toss curly endive with vinaigrette, sprinkle with crisp duck skin, and serve on separate chilled plates with the duck leg.

SUGGESTED WINE: A Cabernet Sauvignon

Duck Ravioli

At last, the definitive agreement of two powerful temperaments — the French-food fanatic and the pasta "*passionado.*"

1. Separate the duck legs from the breasts. Reserve breasts for duck salad (page 186). Season legs lightly with salt and pepper.
2. Preheat oven to 450°.
3. In a heavy oven-proof sauté pan, heat 1 tablespoon oil and sauté duck legs until they are golden brown. Remove them from the pan and reserve. Add the chopped onion and sauté over medium heat until translucent. Drain off all the fat.
4. Deglaze the pan with the wine. Return onions and duck legs to pan. Add stock and bring liquid to a boil. Add the bouquet garni and mushrooms. Cover and transfer to the hot oven. Braise for 50 to 60 minutes, or until tender.
5. Transfer duck legs and mushrooms to a plate and allow to cool.
6. Over moderate heat, reduce the stock to a *demi-glace* and strain. Reserve.
7. When legs are cool, remove skins and cut duck meat into chunks. In a food processor, place the duck meat and mushrooms, 1 egg, 3 tablespoons reduced duck stock (*demi-glace*), chervil, and duck liver. Using on-and-off turns, process until the duck is finely chopped. Do not process to a purée. Taste and correct seasoning.
8. Prepare the pasta dough.

TO SERVE 6

2 whole ducks, 4 to 5 pounds each
1 teaspoon salt
½ teaspoon freshly ground pepper
2 tablespoons mild-flavored oil, such as almond or safflower
1 small onion, chopped
1 cup dry red or white wine
1 cup chicken stock (page 65), brown veal stock (page 66), or duck stock (page 67)
1 bouquet garni (page 5)
6 large mushrooms, quartered
2 eggs (1 lightly beaten, for egg wash)
1 tablespoon minced chervil or fresh parsley
1 tablespoon fresh duck or goose liver
½ recipe pasta dough (page 208)
1 recipe tomato sauce (page 109)
½ cup freshly grated Parmesan cheese
½ cup freshly grated Swiss cheese

9. Roll out half of the dough to a rectangle 12 by 25 inches. Brush with egg wash. Using a small spoon, drop approximately ½ teaspoon duck filling at even intervals over the surface of the dough. You should have 60 to 64 ravioli. Roll out the remaining dough to the same size and cover the duck mixture. Press dough together around the filling and form squares. Cut with a knife, pastry cutter, or ravioli cutter.

10. In a large quantity of boiling, salted water, with the remaining 1 tablespoon oil added, cook the ravioli until just *al dente*, approximately 5 minutes.

11. Preheat oven to 350°.

12. Transfer ravioli to a buttered gratin dish, or six individual ones, cover with tomato sauce, and sprinkle with a mixture of Parmesan and Swiss cheeses. Set in a *bain-marie* and bake for 20 minutes.

PRESENTATION: Serve from the gratin dish or place individual gratin dishes on dinner plates.

SUGGESTED WINE: A Zinfandel

SPECIAL EQUIPMENT:
Large gratin dish or 6 individual gratin dishes
Pastry or ravioli cutter

Duck Ravioli with Fresh Herbs

This is the perfect way to use leftover duck legs or breasts. An Italian-style recipe with a French flavor.

TO SERVE 6

1½ quarts duck stock (page 67)
1 recipe duck ravioli (page 93)
6 ounces unsalted butter, cut into small pieces
¾ cup minced fresh parsley
¼ cup minced fresh chives

1. Bring the duck stock to a boil. Add the ravioli and cook them for 5 to 6 minutes, until *al dente*. Strain ravioli and keep warm.

2. Reduce the duck stock slightly over moderate heat to concentrate the flavor. Whisk in butter, one small piece at a time.

3. When the butter is incorporated, stir in the minced herbs.

PRESENTATION: Divide ravioli among six soup plates. Ladle the hot duck stock over the top. Serve immediately.

SUGGESTED WINE: A Sauvignon blanc

Pigeon with Pears and Red Wine

Pigeon Salmis avec Poires au Vin Rouge

To determine whether you are buying a young pigeon, feel the breastbone. The bone should be flexible, not hard to the touch. Peaches, plums, or cherries may be substituted for the pears in this recipe.

1. Preheat oven to 400°.
2. In a saucepan, combine wine, sugar, and peppercorns. Poach the pears in this liquid until tender but still firm. Reserve.
3. Remove wings and neck from each pigeon and place in a heavy roasting pan. Truss the pigeons with kitchen string.
4. In a skillet, brown the pigeons on all sides. Season to taste with salt and pepper, arrange atop wings and necks in the roasting pan, and roast approximately 25 minutes, or until meat is medium rare. Remove the birds from the pan and keep warm. Discard wings, necks, and excess fat from the pan.
5. Add the shallots to the roasting pan and, over moderate heat, sauté until lightly browned. Deglaze the pan with ½ cup of the wine in which the pears were cooked. Add the stock and reduce until ½ cup remains. Strain into a small saucepan and whisk in the butter, one piece at a time. Correct seasonings and keep warm.
6. Cut each pear half lengthwise into three slices. Carve each pigeon into four pieces.

PRESENTATION: Nap each plate with sauce. Arrange six pear slices and one carved pigeon atop the sauce. Pass any remaining sauce in a sauceboat.

SUGGESTED WINE: A vintage Cabernet Sauvignon

TO SERVE 6

1 bottle (a fifth) dry red wine
½ cup sugar
1 teaspoon black peppercorns
6 Bosc pears, peeled, halved, and cored
6 young pigeons
Salt
Freshly ground pepper
4 medium shallots, minced
1 cup brown veal stock (page 66)
½ cup unsalted butter, cut into small pieces

Pigeon in Puff Pastry with Artichoke Mousse

Feuilletée de Pigeon à la Mousseline d'Artichauts

This dish is an excellent example of *nouvelle cuisine*; and it is sophisticated, yet an expression of the best California has to offer.

TO SERVE 6

1 pound puff pastry
  (page 200)
1 egg, lightly beaten, for
  egg wash
⅓ recipe mousseline
  d'artichauts (page 168)
1 carrot, peeled and cut
  into 1-inch pieces
1 leek, white part only
1 stalk celery, peeled and
  cut into 1-inch pieces
4 large mushrooms
½ pound unsalted butter
6 whole pigeon breasts
Salt
Freshly ground pepper
1 sprig fresh thyme or a
  pinch of dried thyme
2 shallots, minced
1 cup red wine
1 cup chicken stock
  (page 65)

1. Preheat oven to 425°.
2. Roll pastry ¼ inch thick and cut into six 2-by-3-inch rectangles. Brush with egg wash and bake for 20 to 25 minutes, or until golden brown. Reserve.
3. Prepare the *mousseline d'artichauts*. Reserve.
4. Cut the carrot, leek, celery, and mushrooms into julienne. Sauté in 2 tablespoons butter until *al dente*.
5. Season pigeon breasts with salt, pepper, and thyme and roast for 15 minutes.
6. Remove pigeon breasts from roasting pan and add shallots. Deglaze the pan with the wine and add the chicken stock. Reduce the sauce until slightly thickened. Add the remaining butter, one piece at a time, until sauce thickens. Strain and keep warm.
7. Slice pigeon breasts into *aiguillettes*.

PRESENTATION: Assemble each *feuilletée* on a warm plate as follows: julienne of vegetables, bottom half of *feuilletée* spread with 1 tablespoon *mousseline d'artichauts*, *aiguillettes* of pigeon, and top half of *feuillettée*. Spoon the sauce around the *feuilletée*.

SUGGESTED WINE: An elegant Bordeaux or a Cabernet Sauvignon from California

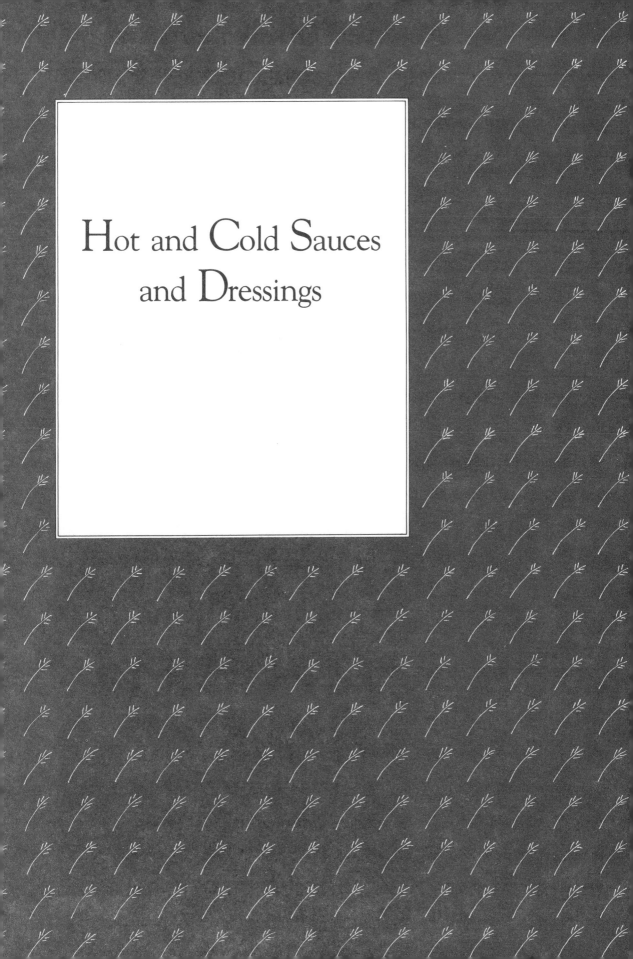

Hot and Cold Sauces and Dressings

Mustard Vinaigrette

Fresh Tomato Vinaigrette

Mayonnaise

Sauce Béarnaise

Sauce Hollandaise

White Butter Sauce

Red Butter Sauce

Dijon Mustard Sauce

Meaux Mustard Sauce

Sauce Béchamel

Sauce Mornay

Asparagus Sauce

Tomato Sauce

Creative sauces are still seen as the trademark of an inspired cook. In the professional kitchen, the *saucier* holds the most esteemed position after that of the head chef.

A good sauce is the balance of appropriate ingredients and specifically selected herbs, carefully combined and used in a discriminating manner. A dressing should, as the word implies, dress, not disguise, a salad. Certain spices, such as bay leaves and rosemary, impart an extremely strong, distinct flavor to food and should be used sparingly.

In this chapter I have included a number of basic recipes. Once you have mastered three or four, you will be able to create your own distinctive sauces and dressings with the addition of your favorite herb or spice. A sauce recipe is often the most well-kept secret of the protective chef. When your friends begin to covet your growing repertoire, be generous.

Mustard Vinaigrette
Vinaigrette à la Moutarde

This is an all-purpose vinaigrette that can be used on most salads. It can be refrigerated for up to a week.

1. With a wire whisk, combine all the ingredients except the oil.
2. Slowly, in a steady stream, add the oil, continuing to whisk all the while.

NOTE: Olive and walnut oils have very distinctive flavors; some people like them, others don't. By using a neutral oil you will please everybody.

TO MAKE 2½ CUPS

2 teaspoons Dijon
  mustard
2 teaspoons minced fresh
  tarragon
2 tablespoons sherry
  wine vinegar or good
  wine vinegar
2 egg yolks
¼ teaspoon salt
A large pinch of freshly
  ground pepper
2 cups salad oil, such as
  almond or safflower

Fresh Tomato Vinaigrette
Vinaigrette à la Tomate Fraîche

A light sauce for cold fish, vegetables, or chicken terrines.

1. In a small saucepan, combine the shallot, vinegar, tarragon, tomato paste, and water. Over medium heat, reduce until only ⅓ cup remains. Purée in a food processor until smooth.
2. Add the tomato and continue to process until smooth.
3. Add olive oil, tomato juice, and almond or safflower oil, and process briefly to blend. Season with salt and pepper to taste.
4. Chill until ready to use.

TO MAKE 4 CUPS

1 shallot, chopped
6 to 8 tablespoons sherry
  wine vinegar
Leaves from 2 sprigs
  fresh tarragon
1 tablespoon tomato
  paste
⅓ cup water
1 large ripe tomato,
  peeled, seeded, and
  diced
½ cup olive oil
2 cups tomato juice
½ cup almond or
  safflower oil
1 teaspoon salt
½ teaspoon freshly
  ground pepper

Mayonnaise

A very basic and useful sauce on which you can build many interesting variations, some of which are listed below.

TO MAKE 2½ CUPS

2 egg yolks
¼ teaspoon salt
Freshly ground pepper to taste
1 tablespoon Dijon mustard
2 cups mild-flavored oil, such as safflower or almond
1 tablespoon lemon juice or wine vinegar

1. Combine egg yolks, salt, pepper, and mustard in a mixing bowl. Whisk together.
2. Slowly add the oil, whisking all the while. Continue adding oil at a faster speed as the volume increases.
3. After whisking in all the oil, add the lemon juice. Taste, and correct seasonings.

Variations

Mayonnaise Légère

TO MAKE 1⅓ CUPS

⅓ cup whipped cream
1 cup mayonnaise

1. Fold the whipped cream into the mayonnaise. Chill and use as needed, mostly with fish terrines or cold fish.

Mayonnaise Cresson

TO MAKE 1⅓ CUPS

1 tablespoon minced watercress
1 or 2 teaspoons watercress juice
1 cup mayonnaise
⅓ cup whipped cream

1. Stir the watercress and the watercress juice into the mayonnaise.
2. Fold in the whipped cream. Chill and use as needed, mostly with cold fish or fish pâtés.

NOTE: To make watercress juice, purée watercress in a food processor. Transfer to a kitchen towel or double thickness of cheesecloth and squeeze to extract the juice.

Sauce Moutarde

1. Stir the mustard into the mayonnaise.
2. Fold in the whipped cream. Chill and use as needed, usually with cold fish, or deep-fried fish, or vegetables.

TO MAKE 1⅓ CUPS

1 tablespoon Dijon
  mustard
1 cup mayonnaise
⅓ cup whipped cream

Sauce Tartare

1. Combine the hard-boiled egg, capers, *cornichon*, anchovies, chives, and parsley with the mayonnaise.
2. Fold in the whipped cream. Chill and use as needed with cold or warm meat and fish dishes.

TO MAKE 2 CUPS

1 hard-boiled egg,
  minced
1 tablespoon capers,
  minced
1 cornichon, minced
1 or 2 anchovies, minced
1 teaspoon minced
  chives
2 teaspoons minced
  parsley
1 cup mayonnaise
½ cup whipped cream

Sauce Béarnaise

This sauce is an emulsion of egg yolks and butter. For the less experienced cook, it is best to whisk the sauce over hot water until it coats the back of a spoon.

TO MAKE 1½ TO 2 CUPS

2 medium shallots, minced
¼ teaspoon freshly ground pepper
½ cup dry white wine
½ cup white wine vinegar
3 egg yolks
4 tablespoons water
½ teaspoon salt
½ pound unsalted butter, clarified
1 tablespoon minced fresh tarragon

1. In a small saucepan, combine the shallots, pepper, white wine, and vinegar. Reduce over medium heat until 1 tablespoon liquid remains.
2. In a heat-resistant mixing bowl, combine the egg yolks, water, salt, and shallot mixture. Whip over hot, but not boiling, water until thick and creamy.
3. Slowly whisk in the butter, a few drops at a time, until the sauce begins to emulsify. In a slow stream, whisk in the remaining butter until it is completely incorporated.
4. Whisk in the tarragon. Correct seasoning to taste.
5. Keep warm until needed. *Sauce béarnaise* is served mostly with grilled red meat or fish.

Variation

TO MAKE 1½ TO 2 CUPS

1 tablespoon peeled, seeded, and finely chopped fresh tomato or 1 teaspoon tomato paste
1 recipe sauce béarnaise

Sauce Choron

1. Whisk the chopped tomato or tomato paste into the *sauce béarnaise.* Correct seasoning to taste.
2. Keep warm until needed. Serve with fish *en croûte* or grilled or roasted red meat.

Sauce Hollandaise

This sauce, most often served with poached fish, or vegetables such as asparagus and broccoli, may be made lighter by the addition of one part whipped cream to three parts sauce.

1. In a heat-resistant mixing bowl, combine the egg yolks, water, lemon juice, white pepper, and salt. Whip over hot, not boiling, water until thick and creamy.
2. Slowly whisk in the butter, a few drops at a time, until the mixture begins to emulsify. In a slow stream, whisk in the remaining butter until it is completely incorporated. Correct seasoning to taste.
3. Keep warm until needed.

TO MAKE 1½ TO 2 CUPS

3 egg yolks
4 tablespoons water
1 or 2 teaspoons lemon juice
A pinch of freshly ground white pepper
½ teaspoon salt
½ pound unsalted butter, clarified

Sauce Moscovite

1. Fold the caviar into the *sauce hollandaise* just before serving with delicately poached fish.

Variations

TO MAKE 1 CUP

1 tablespoon caviar
1 cup sauce hollandaise

Sauce Mousseline

1. Fold whipped cream into the *sauce hollandaise*.
2. Keep warm until needed.

TO MAKE 1¼ CUPS

¼ cup whipped cream
1 cup sauce hollandaise

White Butter Sauce
Beurre Blanc

This is a most versatile sauce that will enhance many shellfish, vegetable, or chicken dishes. Prepare only as much as needed, since *beurre blanc* separates when reheated.

TO MAKE APPROXIMATELY
1⅔ CUPS

1 cup dry white wine
2 shallots, chopped
1 tablespoon chopped
  fresh tarragon
½ cup whipping cream
¾ pound unsalted
  butter, cut into small
  pieces
Juice of half a lemon
½ teaspoon salt
¼ teaspoon freshly
  ground white pepper

1. In a medium saucepan, combine the wine, shallots, and tarragon. Over moderately high heat, reduce the liquid until approximately ⅓ cup remains.
2. Add cream and continue to reduce until ½ cup remains.
3. Lower heat and slowly whisk butter into the mixture, one piece at a time. Be careful to not let mixture boil or get too cold (temperature must not change).
4. Add the lemon juice, salt, and pepper. Taste and adjust seasonings.
5. Strain and serve.

Red Butter Sauce
Beurre Rouge

I recommend a heavy red wine to give this sauce its characteristic color and taste.

TO MAKE APPROXIMATELY
1⅔ CUPS

1 cup Petit Sirah
2 shallots, minced
A pinch of thyme
1 bay leaf
1 branch fresh tarragon
¼ cup whipping cream
¾ pound unsalted
  butter, cut into small
  pieces
Salt and freshly ground
  pepper to taste
Juice of half a lemon

1. In a medium saucepan, combine the wine, shallots, thyme, bay leaf, and tarragon. Reduce over moderately high heat until approximately ⅓ cup remains.
2. Add the cream and continue to reduce until approximately ½ cup remains.
3. Lower heat and slowly whisk the butter into the mixture, one piece at a time. Be careful to not let mixture boil or get too cold (temperature must not change).
4. Add lemon juice, salt, and pepper. Correct seasoning to taste.
5. Strain and serve.

Dijon Mustard Sauce

Sauce Moutarde Dijon

A derivation of *beurre blanc*, this sauce is used primarily for shellfish, but may also be served with fish or chicken.

1. In a saucepan, reduce the wine, shallots, and tarragon until 2 tablespoons of liquid remain.
2. Add the cream and reduce again until only 2 tablespoons remain.
3. Slowly whisk in the pieces of butter, keeping the sauce from boiling or getting cold. Strain.
4. Whisk in chives and mustard. Add salt, pepper, and lemon juice to taste.

TO MAKE 1¼ CUPS

1 cup dry white wine
3 shallots, chopped
1 tablespoon chopped
  fresh tarragon
¼ cup heavy cream
½ pound unsalted
  butter, cut into small
  pieces
2 tablespoons chopped
  chives
1½ tablespoons Dijon
  mustard
¾ teaspoon salt
A pinch of white pepper
Juice of half a lemon

Meaux Mustard Sauce

Sauce Moutarde de Meaux

This sauce goes well with chicken, beef, pork, or veal.

1. In a medium saucepan, combine the port and shallots and reduce until ¼ cup remains. Add the stock and continue to reduce until slightly thickened. Add the cream and reduce again until slightly thickened.
2. Whisk in the butter, one small piece at a time. Whisk in the mustard, adjusting amount to your own taste. Season with salt and pepper.

TO MAKE 1½ CUPS

1 cup port
1 tablespoon minced
  shallots
½ cup brown veal stock
  (page 66)
1 cup heavy cream
3 tablespoons unsalted
  butter, cut into small
  pieces
2 tablespoons Moutarde
  de Meaux
Salt and freshly ground
  pepper to taste

Sauce Béchamel

One of the basics of classical French cuisine, *sauce béchamel* is used infrequently today. However, I like it with certain egg dishes.

TO MAKE APPROXIMATELY
2 CUPS

¼ cup clarified unsalted butter
½ medium onion, minced
¼ cup all-purpose flour
2½ cups milk
A pinch of salt
A pinch of freshly ground white pepper
A pinch of freshly grated nutmeg
A sprig of fresh thyme

1. In a heavy saucepan, heat the butter. Add the onion and cook until translucent.
2. Add the flour to the butter-and-onion mixture and cook over low heat, stirring constantly, to form a *roux*. Set aside and reserve.
3. Bring the milk to a boil. Whisk into the *roux* and continue to whisk until smoothly blended. Add the seasonings and simmer gently for 30 minutes, stirring often until sauce is thick and smooth.
4. Strain the sauce and, if you are not using it right away, dot the top with butter to prevent a crust from forming.

Sauce Mornay

Derived from *sauce béchamel*, with an addition of cheese and egg yolks, *sauce Mornay* is used in "au gratin" dishes.

TO MAKE APPROXIMATELY
3 CUPS

2 cups sauce béchamel (above)
2 egg yolks, lightly beaten
½ cup grated Parmesan or Gruyère cheese
1 tablespoon unsalted butter
4 tablespoons whipped cream

1. In a heavy saucepan, heat the *sauce béchamel*. Add the egg yolks, stirring constantly. Just as the sauce is about to boil, remove the pan from the heat. (If the sauce boils it will curdle and lose its good flavor.)
2. Add the cheese and butter and stir until thoroughly combined.
3. When ready to use, fold in the whipped cream (this will give the dish you are making an even, golden brown glaze).

Asparagus Sauce
Sauce Asperge

An example of *cuisine minceur*, this sauce is very light and low in calories. It is delicious with steamed or broiled fish.

TO MAKE 1 CUP

1. In a large pot of boiling, salted water, cook the asparagus until tender, about 10 minutes. Remove them from the pot and place in ice water to stop the cooking process.
2. Stir the dry milk into the cold water until it is dissolved.
3. Cut off the tips of the asparagus and reserve them for garnish. Cut the remaining asparagus into 1-inch pieces and purée in a blender or food processor with milk and cream.
4. Transfer the mixture to a saucepan and reheat. Season to taste with salt, pepper, and lemon juice. Strain into a serving bowl.

12 large stalks asparagus
2 tablespoons nonfat dry milk
½ cup cold water
1 tablespoon heavy cream
½ teaspoon salt
¼ teaspoon freshly ground pepper
A few drops of lemon juice

Tomato Sauce
Sauce Tomate

A fundamental tomato sauce that combines well with any pasta.

TO MAKE 2 QUARTS

1. Chop the carrots, onion, and celery to make a *mirepoix*. In a large skillet, over medium heat, sauté the vegetables in the olive oil for about 10 minutes.
2. Add the tomato paste, tomatoes, basil, and bouquet garni. Lower the heat and simmer for 30 minutes, stirring occasionally.
3. Add the chicken stock and simmer for 1 hour longer.
4. Remove the bouquet garni and purée the sauce in the food processor. Strain it into a saucepan through a fine sieve.
5. Reduce until thickened. Whisk in cream and butter, and season with sugar, salt, and pepper. Taste and correct seasoning.

2 carrots, peeled
1 onion
1 stalk celery
3 tablespoons olive oil
3 tablespoons tomato paste
16 ripe tomatoes, peeled, seeded, and chopped
1 bunch fresh sweet basil
1 bouquet garni (page 5)
2 quarts chicken stock (page 65)
½ cup heavy cream
6 tablespoons unsalted butter, cut into small pieces
1 teaspoon sugar
1 teaspoon salt
Freshly ground pepper

Fish and Shellfish

Fillet of Sea Bass with Sorrel

Soft-Shell Crabs

Crayfish in Light Butter Sauce

Mousseline of Frogs' Legs with Watercress Sauce

Lobster with Herbs

John Dory with Red Wine

John Dory with Tomato Butter and Fresh Noodles

Steamed Pike with Chive Butter Sauce

Coulibiac of Pike with Crayfish

Salmon in Basil Sauce

Salmon or Bass in Puff Pastry

Provençal Salmon

Skate in Brown Butter

Red Snapper with Chives and Wild Mushrooms

Steamed Fillet of Red Snapper with Tarragon Butter

Red Snapper with Scallop Mousse

Fillet of Sole with Celery Cream Sauce

Fillet of Sole and Scallop Stew with Basil

Trout Fillets in Puff Pastry

Trout with Vegetables Cooked in Foil

Scallops in Cream Sauce

Scallops with Ginger

Shrimp with Pink Peppercorns

When fall arrives my thoughts drift back to brisk days in my little river in Austria. Standing knee-deep in icy waters where the river curved and I had built a dam of twigs and stone, I pursued, with bare hands and fevered enthusiasm, the red-spotted trout, the silvery whitefish, the elusive crayfish, and the sharp-toothed pike.

My personal sensibilities regarding fish preparation and presentation parallel the spirit and tradition of the Japanese, with their appreciation for seasonal fish cooked to the point of sheer perfection and their attention to composition, form, texture, and color, best exhibited in their love of sashimi (raw fish) meticulously selected, sliced, and served in the most artful manner. Besides my contemporary cooked fish recipes, I have included a few "sashimi-style" suggestions, such as my raw tuna with avocado. It is a combination of the very best of East-West philosophy with a distinctly California flair.

Because the United States has so many lakes and rivers and is bordered by two oceans, the supply of fish and shellfish is plentiful all year round. Since it is best to use the freshest fish available (fresh in terms of season as well as freshly caught), I often utilize fish procured on the West Coast, such as salmon, red snapper, crayfish, and sole. There are many suitable substitutions, and I have made mention of them with each recipe. Whatever fish may appeal to you, and wherever you live, there are wonderful regional possibilities: the Middle West has marvelous trout, whitefish, and pike; the South boasts frogs' legs and shrimp; and the East, blessed with its cold Atlantic water, has an enormous selection, including clams, soft-shell crab, lobster, scallops, and sea bass.

The preparation of fish is as versatile as your imagination will allow. It can be lightly grilled or broiled, gently steamed, served with a subtle sauce, or it can have a unique, elaborate preparation with a stuffing of fragilely seasoned mousse enveloped in a flaky puff-pastry crust. These recipes all require attention to exact cooking time, the second fundamental, after freshness, of preparing marvelous fish.

Fillet of Sea Bass with Sorrel

Filet de Bar à l'Oseille

In this recipe, the acidity of the sorrel sauce contrasts with the sweetness of the fish. You may substitute sole or salmon for the bass.

1. Preheat oven to 500°.
2. Cut the fillets into twelve strips weighing 4 ounces each. (Equal size portions ensure equal amount of doneness when cooked.) Season with salt and pepper.
3. Thoroughly wash sorrel and remove stems. Slice into julienne and reserve.
4. Butter a large oven-proof saucepan and sprinkle with the minced shallots. Arrange the fillets atop the shallots.
5. Pour in the vermouth and fish stock and add half the sorrel. Cover with buttered foil, buttered side down, touching the fish.
6. Over high heat, bring the liquid to a boil. Transfer the pan to the oven and bake the fish approximately 5 minutes, or until the fish feels springy to the touch. Transfer fish to a warm plate and cover with the foil. Reserve the cooking liquid.
7. In a separate pan, heat ½ tablespoon butter. Sauté the remaining half of the sorrel until wilted. Strain the reserved cooking liquid over the sorrel, add the cream, and reduce until thickened. Whisk in the remaining 7½ tablespoons butter, one piece at a time. Season with salt and pepper to taste.

PRESENTATION: Place two strips of bass on each plate and nap with sorrel sauce. Garnish with *fleurons*.

SUGGESTED WINE: A white Riesling from the Napa Valley

TO SERVE 6

3 pounds sea bass fillets
Salt
Freshly ground white pepper
1 pound sorrel
3 shallots, minced
½ cup dry white vermouth
½ cup fish stock (page 65)
¼ pound unsalted butter, cut into small pieces
1 cup heavy cream
6 fleurons (page 6)

Soft-Shell Crabs

Soft-shell crabs are harvested when their new shells are forming, after shedding their hard outer shells. They are in season during June and July, and most are found off the Maryland coast. Select small, live crabs.

TO SERVE 6

12 live soft-shell crabs
2 eggs, beaten
½ cup all-purpose flour
2 cups fresh bread crumbs
2 to 4 tablespoons unsalted butter
1 recipe beurre blanc (page 106)
3 tablespoons capers
1 tablespoon minced fresh herbs
Juice of 1 or 2 lemons

1. Rinse the crabs carefully under cold running water.
2. Dip the crabs first in beaten eggs, then in flour, and last in bread crumbs, shaking off any excess bread crumbs.
3. Heat a large skillet and add 2 tablespoons butter. Over moderate heat, sauté the crabs, shell side down, for 5 to 7 minutes. They should be golden brown and crisp. Turn the crabs and cook 6 to 7 minutes longer.
4. Meanwhile, prepare the *beurre blanc*. After it has been strained, add the capers, minced herbs, and lemon juice. Correct seasoning to taste.

PRESENTATION: Spoon the sauce into each of six plates. Place two soft-shell crabs on each plate.

SUGGESTED WINE: A Sauvignon blanc

Crayfish in Light Butter Sauce
Écrevisses à la Nage

Crayfish are in season from May to October and should be live when purchased. If the crayfish are overcooked, there will be no meat left. Lobster or shrimp may be substituted.

1. Separate crayfish tails from heads, reserving six whole crayfish for garniture.
2. Bring the court bouillon to a boil and add the crayfish tails. Cook for 2 minutes, or until tails turn red. Remove from liquid and reserve. Cook the whole crayfish for 3 to 4 minutes, or until bright red. Reserve.
3. Peel the onions and carrots. Cut them into very thin slices. Cook separately in 1 cup court bouillon until just tender. Reserve.
4. *To make the* nage: Reduce 1 cup court bouillon until only ½ cup remains. Whisk in the butter, one piece at a time. Add salt, pepper, and lemon juice to taste.

PRESENTATION: Peel crayfish tails and place nine tails in each of six warm soup plates. Arrange a few slices of the carrots and onions on each plate. Pour *nage* over all. Sprinkle with minced tarragon and garnish each plate with a whole crayfish.

SUGGESTED WINE: A Chardonnay

TO SERVE 6

5 dozen live crayfish
1 recipe court bouillon (page 66)
3 small white onions or 3 large boiling onions
2 medium carrots
1 pound unsalted butter, cut into small pieces
1 teaspoon salt
½ teaspoon freshly ground white pepper
Juice of half a lemon
1 tablespoon minced fresh tarragon

Mousseline of Frogs' Legs with Watercress Sauce
Mousse de Cuisses de Grenouille au Beurre de Cresson

This is an unusual way to prepare frogs' legs. It is better with fresh frogs' legs but the frozen ones can be used. Do not boil the watercress sauce or the lovely green color will turn grey. Since trout is also a freshwater fish, it can be substituted for the whitefish.

TO SERVE 6

12 pairs frogs' legs
1 pound unsalted butter
1 cup dry white wine
2 cups heavy cream
Salt and freshly ground
  pepper
4 shallots, chopped fine
1 pound whitefish
2 eggs
1½ bunches watercress
Juice of half a lemon

1. Sauté the frogs' legs in 2 tablespoons butter. Deglaze the pan with white wine; add ½ cup cream and season with salt and pepper. Cook until frogs' legs are tender, 5 to 6 minutes.
2. Bone the frogs' legs. (It is easy to remove the meat from the bones with your fingers.) Return the meat to the pan, and refrigerate.
3. Over low heat, sauté the shallots in 2 tablespoons butter until translucent. Set aside to cool.
4. Preheat oven to 400°.
5. In a food processor, purée the fish. Add salt, pepper, half the sautéed shallots, 12 tablespoons butter, and the eggs and process until blended. Transfer to a bowl and place over ice. Lightly whip 1 cup cream and fold it into the fish mixture. Correct seasoning to taste.
6. Butter six ½-cup molds. Half-fill with mousseline, add 1 tablespoon frogs' legs, and cover with the remaining mousseline. Set molds in a *bain-marie* and bake for 25 minutes.
7. *To make the sauce:* In a food processor, purée 1 bunch of watercress with the remaining ½ pound butter. In a medium saucepan, reduce the white wine and remaining sautéed shallots. Add the remaining ½ cup cream and reduce until sauce thickens. Add the watercress butter, bit by bit. Season with salt, pepper, and lemon juice to taste. Strain.

PRESENTATION: Unmold each mousseline onto a warm plate, nap with sauce, and decorate with the remaining frogs' legs and watercress.

SUGGESTED WINE: A Johannisberg Riesling

Lobster with Herbs

Homard aux Herbes

To preserve the sweetness of the lobster, it must be undercooked. Because of the richness of the two sauces, small lobsters should be served. Spiny lobsters, or *langoustes*, may be substituted.

1. Preheat oven to 500°.
2. Prepare the *sauce béarnaise*, adding the tomatoes and basil. Reserve and keep warm.
3. Prepare the *beurre blanc*, replacing the cream in the recipe with 2 tablespoons water and adding the *herbes de Provence*. Reserve and keep warm.
4. Cut each lobster in half lengthwise and remove the intestinal sac, leaving the coral inside. Cut off the claws and cook them in the court bouillon for approximately 5 minutes. Remove from the liquid and reserve.
5. Season the lobsters with salt and pepper and arrange in a roasting pan. Dot each lobster tail with ½ tablespoon butter. Bake for 8 to 10 minutes, until tender. Do not overcook. Turn the oven temperature up to broil after removing the lobsters.
6. Remove the lobster meat from the tails and cut into bite-size pieces. Return to their shells.
7. Remove lobster meat from the claws and arrange in the top cavity of the lobster. Nap with *sauce béarnaise* and set under the broiler to glaze, approximately 30 seconds.

PRESENTATION: Place lobsters on heated plates. Pour *beurre blanc* over the meat in the tail and serve immediately.

SUGGESTED WINE: A Chardonnay

TO SERVE 4

½ recipe sauce béarnaise (page 104)
2 very ripe medium tomatoes, peeled, seeded, diced, and drained
1 tablespoon minced fresh basil
½ recipe beurre blanc (page 106), without cream
1 teaspoon dried herbes de Provence, chopped very finely
4 live lobsters, 1½ pounds each
1 quart court bouillon (page 66)
Salt
Freshly ground pepper
2 tablespoons unsalted butter

John Dory with Red Wine

Saint-Pierre au Vin Rouge

The myth that fish must be prepared with and accompanied by white wine is a general rule that can be bent. Red wine can be used just as readily. John Dory is imported from New Zealand and France; red snapper and sea bass are suitable substitutes.

TO SERVE 6

3 John Dory, 2 to 2½
  pounds each
3 shallots, sliced
1 bunch parsley
1 stalk celery, sliced
3 medium leeks (white
  part only): 1 sliced, 2
  cut into julienne
½ teaspoon black
  peppercorns
2 cups dry red wine
6 ounces unsalted butter
2 cups heavy cream
12 large white
  mushrooms
Lemon juice
Salt
Freshly ground pepper

1. Fillet the fish. Skin the fillets and reserve them in the refrigerator.
2. Prepare a fish stock using the fish bones, shallots, parsley stems, celery, sliced leek, peppercorns, wine, and water to cover. Bring to a boil and simmer for 20 minutes. Strain and set aside.
3. Mince the parsley leaves and reserve.
4. *To make the leek ragout:* Sauté the julienne of leeks in 1 tablespoon butter until they are wilted. Add 1 cup cream and reduce over medium heat until the ragout has thickened. Reserve and keep warm.
5. Cut the mushrooms into julienne. Sprinkle with a little lemon juice and sauté them lightly in 1 tablespoon butter. Reserve and keep warm.
6. Reduce the fish stock to 1 cup. Add the remaining 1 cup cream and continue to reduce the sauce until it is thick enough to coat the back of a spoon. Whisk in 8 tablespoons of the remaining butter, one small piece at a time. Season to taste with salt, pepper, and lemon juice. Strain and keep warm.
7. Heat a heavy sauté pan and melt the remaining 2 tablespoons butter. Season the fish with salt and pepper. Sauté the fish fillets slowly over low heat until they feel springy to the touch.

PRESENTATION: Place a spoonful of the leek ragout in the center of each warm dinner plate. Cover the ragout with a fish fillet. Nap each fillet with sauce, top with julienne of mushrooms, and sprinkle lightly with minced parsley.

SUGGESTED WINE: A light St. Emilion or a Château Vignelaure

John Dory with Tomato Butter and Fresh Noodles

Saint-Pierre aux Nouilles Fraîches et Beurre de Tomate

In this recipe, worthy substitutes for the John Dory are lemon or grey sole or halibut.

1. Chop the tomatoes in a food processor. Pass the chopped tomatoes through a fine strainer and transfer the juice to a saucepan. Reduce until it begins to thicken. Set aside and reserve.

2. Butter a heavy flame-proof casserole. Arrange fish in one layer in the casserole and sprinkle with shallots. Season with salt and pepper, pour in the wine, cover, and bring to a boil. Simmer for 3 to 5 minutes, or until the fillets are springy to the touch. Transfer the fish to a hot plate and keep covered to prevent drying. (The fish will continue to cook after you remove it from the pan, so be sure to take it out when it is "medium rare.")

3. Add the tomato juice to the casserole and reduce until it begins to thicken slightly. Add ¾ cup cream and continue to reduce until sauce thickens. Whisk in the butter, one small piece at a time. Correct seasoning and add a dash of cayenne pepper.

4. In a separate saucepan, bring the remaining ¼ cup cream to a boil. Add cooked noodles and heat through.

PRESENTATION: Place noodles on heated dinner plates and top with fish. Strain sauce over fish and sprinkle with chopped tomatoes and parsley.

SUGGESTED WINE: A white wine from the Champagne region

SERVES 6

6 medium tomatoes
6 John Dory fillets, 6 ounces each
2 shallots, minced
Salt and freshly ground pepper
1 cup dry white wine
1 cup cream
½ pound unsalted butter, cut into small pieces
A pinch of cayenne pepper
Fresh pasta (page 208) cut into noodles and cooked
2 medium tomatoes, peeled, seeded, and chopped
1 tablespoon chopped parsley

Steamed Pike with Chive Butter Sauce
Brochet à la Vapeur au Beurre de Ciboulette

Pike is a freshwater fish commonly found in the Great Lakes. Steaming preserves its natural flavor.

TO SERVE 6

3 pounds pike fillets, cut into six serving pieces
Salt and freshly ground pepper
3 branches fresh thyme
2 medium carrots, cut into julienne
2 medium leeks, cut into julienne
3 small stalks celery, cut into julienne
1 pound unsalted butter
1½ cups dry white wine
1 bunch fresh tarragon
6 shallots, minced
1 cup heavy cream
Juice of 1 lemon
2 bunches chives, minced

1. Season fillets with salt, pepper, and a few thyme leaves. Refrigerate until needed.
2. In a medium sauté pan, sauté the julienne of carrots, leeks, and celery in 1 tablespoon butter until just tender. Set aside.
3. Fill the bottom of a steamer with water and ½ cup of the wine. Add ½ bunch tarragon, 2 shallots, and the remaining thyme; bring to a boil. Arrange fish fillets on the steamer rack, cover, and steam for 5 minutes. Arrange the julienne of vegetables on the fish and continue to steam for 5 minutes more, or until done.
4. Remove fish from the steamer and arrange on heated plates. Keep warm.
5. *To make the chive butter sauce:* In a saucepan, place 4 shallots, remaining tarragon, 1 cup wine, and a few leaves of thyme. Reduce until only ¼ cup of the liquid remains. Add the cream and reduce until mixture thickens slightly. Slowly whisk in the remaining butter, one small piece at a time. Add lemon juice, salt, and pepper to taste. Strain the sauce into a small saucepan and stir in the minced chives.

PRESENTATION: Nap the fillets with chive butter sauce and serve immediately.

SUGGESTED WINE: A white Graves or Sauvignon blanc

Coulibiac of Pike with Crayfish
Pain de Brochet aux Écrevisses

When crayfish is out of season small bay shrimp may be used. The *coulibiac* can be served cold the next day with *mayonnaise légère.*

1. Prepare the brioche dough a day in advance (through step 5).
2. Slice 1 pound of pike into small pieces. In a food processor, purée the pike with salt, pepper, cayenne pepper, and 1 egg. Transfer to a chilled bowl.
3. Whip 1¼ cups cream to a soft chantilly. Over ice, fold cream into pike mixture. Test mousse for taste and consistency in simmering water (see page 20) and correct seasoning. Refrigerate until needed.
4. Marinate the remaining 1 pound pike fillets in a mixture of ½ cup wine, 1 shallot, and minced tarragon.
5. Bring court bouillon to a boil. Add crayfish and return to a boil. Remove the crayfish and, when cool, shell twelve of them and reserve the other twelve whole.
6. Preheat oven to 400°.
7. Divide the brioche dough in half and roll out one piece ⅜ inch thick on a baking sheet. Spread half the fish mousse down the center. Arrange half the pike fillets over the mousse, top with the asparagus, and spread the remaining mousse over the asparagus. Finally, arrange the remaining fillets over the mousse.
8. Lightly beat the remaining egg for an egg wash and brush all around the edges of the dough. Roll out the remaining piece of brioche, large enough to cover the fish. Press edges together and trim. Brush with egg wash. Decorate with strips of dough and poke a vent in the top. Bake for 40 minutes.
9. While the fish is baking, reduce 1 cup wine, 1 minced shallot, tarragon stems, and ¼ cup cream until one third of the liquid remains or until bubbles are thick.
10. Using the food processor, purée the basil leaves. Add the butter and process until well blended.
11. Slowly add the basil butter to the reduced wine. Strain and correct seasonings, adding a bit of lemon juice if desired. Add shelled crayfish to the sauce just before serving.

TO SERVE 6 OR 8

1 recipe brioche dough (page 206)
2 pounds boneless pike fillets
1 teaspoon salt
½ teaspoon freshly ground pepper
¼ teaspoon cayenne pepper
2 eggs
1½ cups heavy cream
1½ cups white wine
2 shallots, minced
1 tablespoon minced fresh tarragon
6 tarragon stems
1 recipe court bouillon (page 66)
24 live crayfish
8 to 12 stalks asparagus, cooked until al dente
1 bunch basil leaves
½ pound unsalted butter, cut into small pieces
Lemon juice

PRESENTATION: Using an electric knife (or a very sharp chef's knife), slice the *coulibiac* into six or eight slices. Nap each plate with the sauce and arrange the whole crayfish decoratively on the plate. Center a slice of *coulibiac* in the plate.

SUGGESTED WINE: A Meursault or full-bodied Chardonnay

Salmon in Basil Sauce

Escalope de Saumon au Basilic

The sauce must go on room-temperature oven-proof plates so that it does not separate. Since the salmon is so easy to overcook, watch it carefully during the cooking process.

TO SERVE 6

3 medium shallots, peeled
2 medium mushrooms
2 bunches basil
10 tablespoons unsalted butter, cut into 10 pieces
2 cups dry white wine
2 cups fish stock (page 65)
2 cups heavy cream
6 ounces salmon escalopes per person (3 escalopes per plate)

1. Preheat oven to 450°.
2. Slice the shallots, mushrooms, and 1 bunch of the basil.
3. In a saucepan, melt 2 tablespoons butter. Add the shallots and mushrooms and sweat over low heat for 10 minutes.
4. Add the wine and sliced basil. Over moderate heat, reduce by half. Add the stock and again reduce the liquid by half.
5. Pour in the cream and continue to reduce the sauce, over medium heat, until it has thickened. (It will coat a spoon rather heavily.) Strain sauce into a clean saucepan.
6. In a blender or food processor, purée the remaining basil (save a few nice leaves for garnish) with ½ cup of the sauce. Whisk the purée into the remaining sauce and, over low heat, finish by whisking in the remaining 8 tablespoons butter, one piece at a time. Taste and add salt if necessary. Strain and reserve.
7. Nap the bottom of each plate with sauce. Place the salmon escalopes on top of the sauce and cook in the oven or under the broiler for 1 minute, or until slightly underdone. Serve immediately.

PRESENTATION: Garnish each plate with fresh basil leaves or salmon eggs.

SUGGESTED WINE: A Chardonnay or Fumé blanc

Salmon or Bass in Puff Pastry

Saumon ou Bar en Croûte

This is perfect for a special dinner party. The preparation can be done in advance and the presentation is spectacular.

1. Bone and skin the salmon. Season with salt, pepper, and 1 tablespoon tarragon. Reserve in the refrigerator.
2. *To make the fish mousse:* Purée the scallops in a food processor. Add one egg, mix well, and, with the motor running, add 8 ounces butter, cut into pieces. Set aside and chill. Lightly whip 1 cup cream (it should just begin to foam and thicken a little). Add the cream to the scallop purée. Season to taste with salt and pepper. Refrigerate immediately.
3. Divide the pastry dough in half and roll out each piece approximately ⅓ inch thick and larger than the fish. Line a 12-by-16-inch baking sheet with pastry. Cut the fish in half lengthwise and place the bottom half on top of the pastry. Spread the chilled mousse over the fish and cover with the top half of the fish.
4. Lightly beat the remaining egg for egg wash. Brush the pastry around the edge of the fish and cover with the second sheet of pastry. Press the layers of pastry around the fish to seal. Trim the pastry following the outlines of the fish, and use the leftover dough to decorate the fish with scales, an eye, and gills. Chill in the refrigerator for at least 30 minutes.
5. Preheat oven to 375°.
6. When ready, bake the fish for 30 to 45 minutes, or until the pastry is golden brown and the center of the mousse is hot (when you insert a skewer in the center for 1 minute, it should be hot when touched to the lip). While the fish cooks proceed with the sauces.
7. *To make the sauces:* Pour white and red wine into two separate saucepans. Divide shallots and add half to each pan. Add 1 tablespoon tarragon to the white wine and the thyme to the red wine. Reduce each until only 1 tablespoon remains.
8. Add ¼ cup cream to each pan. Bring both pans to a boil and reduce slightly. Whisk 8 ounces of butter into each sauce, one small piece at a time. Season each sauce with salt, pepper, and lemon juice. Keep warm.

TO SERVE 6

1 salmon or sea bass, approximately 4 pounds
Salt
Freshly ground pepper
2 tablespoons chopped fresh tarragon
1 pound fresh sea scallops or pike
2 eggs
1½ pounds unsalted butter
1½ cups heavy cream
2 pounds puff pastry (page 200)
1 cup dry white wine
1 cup red wine (such as Petit Sirah)
4 medium shallots, chopped
½ teaspoon thyme
Juice of 1 lemon

PRESENTATION: Present the fish whole on a serving platter. Using an electric knife (or very sharp chef's knife), slice it into six portions. Nap the bottom of each plate with the two sauces and place a slice of fish in pastry on top.

SUGGESTED WINE: A Meursault or a Chardonnay

Provençal Salmon
Saumon au Pistou

Ripe tomatoes and a very good olive oil are essential for a successful sauce.

TO SERVE 6 OR 8

Sauce Pistou:

1 cup olive oil
2 tablespoons sherry wine vinegar
1 bunch basil leaves, chopped
3 shallots, minced
4 ripe tomatoes, peeled, seeded, and chopped fine
Grated rind of half a lemon
Salt, freshly ground pepper, and cayenne pepper to taste
1 tablespoon minced fresh chives
1 tablespoon minced fresh tarragon

Salmon:

2 carrots, peeled
1 leek, white part only
2 stalks celery, with strings removed
2 quarts court bouillon (page 66)
2 pounds Chinook or King salmon fillets

1. Combine all ingredients for the *sauce pistou* and let marinate overnight, unrefrigerated.
2. Cut carrots, leek, and celery into julienne. Cook them in 1 cup strained court bouillon until tender but still crisp. Drain and reserve.
3. Wrap each salmon fillet in aluminum foil and poach in court bouillon for approximately 5 minutes. To check the degree of doneness, remove one package from the liquid and unwrap. The center should still be slightly pink.

PRESENTATION: Divide julienne of vegetables among serving plates. Arrange salmon fillets in the center of the julienne and top each fillet with a tablespoon of the *sauce pistou.* Serve remaining sauce separately.

SUGGESTED WINE: A white Châteauneuf-du-Pape or a Château St. Jean Chardonnay

Skate in Brown Butter

Raie au Beurre Noir

This is a French bistro dish, little known in America. Skate is delicate and easy to digest. Only the "wings" are consumed.

1. Skin the skate wings (place in boiling water for 3 minutes, remove, and use a small knife to scrape off the skin), or have your fishmonger skin them at the market.
2. Prepare a court bouillon with the milk, thyme, bay leaf, celery, salt, peppercorns, and enough water to cover the fish.
3. When court bouillon comes to a boil, add skate wings and simmer until fish begins to separate from middle bone, 5 to 8 minutes. Immediately remove fish from liquid. Place on a hot platter and bone, using a large metal spatula.
4. Melt the butter until it is light brown. Add the capers and deglaze the pan with vinegar.

PRESENTATION: Pour the butter over the fish and sprinkle with fresh herbs. Or you may serve the fish with a *beurre blanc* seasoned with mustard or fresh ginger.

SUGGESTED WINE: A Pouilly Fumé

TO SERVE 6

3 pounds skate wings (or stingray)
2 cups milk
A pinch of thyme
1 bay leaf
1 stalk celery, sliced
1 teaspoon salt
6 peppercorns
Water
6 ounces unsalted butter
4 tablespoons capers
3 tablespoons sherry wine vinegar
Chopped fresh herbs

Red Snapper with Chives and Wild Mushrooms
Filet de Rouget à la Ciboulette et Champignons Sauvages

Red snapper from Florida is one of my favorite fish. If it is not available, use sea bass, halibut, John Dory, or pike.

TO SERVE 6

8 ounces puff pastry (page 200)
2 bunches chives, minced
14 ounces unsalted butter, at room temperature
Juice of 1 lemon
1 medium tomato, peeled and seeded
2½ pounds red snapper fillets
Salt
Freshly ground pepper
3 medium shallots, minced
1 cup dry white wine
½ cup fish stock (page 65)
6 tablespoons heavy cream
1 pound Japanese tree mushrooms, cleaned, or any kind of fresh mushrooms available

1. Preheat oven to 450°.
2. Roll out the puff pastry to a rectangle, ¼ inch thick, approximately 12 by 18 inches. Cut out six diamond-shaped shells, each 3 inches wide, and arrange on a baking sheet. Chill at least 10 minutes.
3. Bake the pastry for 15 minutes, reduce heat to 325°, and continue baking until shells are golden brown, approximately 10 minutes longer. Reserve.
4. Reserve 1 tablespoon of the chives for garnish and place the remainder in a food processor with 12 ounces of butter, cut up, and the lemon juice. Process until smooth and creamy. Set aside and reserve.
5. Cut tomato into ¼-inch dice and reserve for garnish.
6. Cut the fish into 18 diamond shapes, each approximately 3 inches wide, and season with salt and pepper. Butter a large, heavy sauté pan and sprinkle with half the shallots. Arrange the fish fillets on top of the shallots, pour in the white wine and fish stock, and cover with buttered foil, buttered side down. Bring to a boil and transfer to the oven. Bake 5 to 7 minutes, until "medium rare." Remove fish to a warm platter and cover with the foil. (Remember, the fish will continue to cook slightly.)
7. Reduce the cooking liquid until 1 cup remains, add the cream, and continue to reduce until sauce thickens. Whisk in the chive butter, a small amount at a time. Taste and correct seasoning. Strain and keep warm.
8. Melt the remaining 4 tablespoons butter in a skillet. Over high heat, sauté the mushrooms and remaining half of the shallots until mushrooms are golden brown. (You may have to use more or less butter, depending on the type of mushroom.)
9. Slice off the top third of each pastry shell to form a lid. Gently remove moist dough inside shell and fill with sautéed mushrooms. Keep warm in the turned-off oven.

PRESENTATION: Warm six large dinner plates and nap each with sauce. Place the filled pastry shell at the base of the plate and arrange three fillets above the shell. Lightly nap each fillet with sauce and garnish with diced tomatoes and reserved chives.

SUGGESTED WINE: A Chardonnay or Pouilly-Fuissé

Steamed Fillet of Red Snapper with Tarragon Butter
Filet de Rouget à la Vapeur au Beurre Estragon

Steaming is one of the oldest methods of cooking. Almost forgotten, it has lately been revived because people have become very health-conscious.

TO SERVE 6

1. Season the red snapper fillets with 1 teaspoon salt, ¼ teaspoon pepper, and 1 tablespoon minced tarragon.
2. Wrap each of the fillets in four or five spinach leaves.
3. In the bottom of a steamer combine the water, wine, shallots, celery, tarragon branches, and the 1 tablespoon butter. Bring to a boil.
4. Place the spinach-wrapped fillets on a buttered steamer rack and steam for 10 to 12 minutes. The fish should be slightly undercooked. Remove the fish to a warm plate and cover loosely with foil.
5. *To make the sauce:* Take approximately one fourth of the liquid from the bottom of the steamer and reduce until ½ cup remains. Add the cream and reduce until ¾ cup remains.
6. Slowly whisk in the remaining 1 pound of butter over a very low heat, one small piece at a time. Do not let the sauce boil or get cold.
7. Strain the sauce and stir in the remaining 1 tablespoon minced tarragon. Taste carefully and correct the seasoning with the lemon juice and remaining salt and pepper, or to taste.

6 red snapper fillets, 8 ounces each
1½ teaspoons salt
¾ teaspoon freshly ground pepper
2 tablespoons minced fresh tarragon leaves, plus 3 branches fresh tarragon
24 to 30 large spinach leaves, cleaned, with stems removed
2 cups water
2 cups dry white wine
2 medium shallots, chopped
1 stalk celery, sliced
1 pound unsalted butter, cut into small pieces, plus 1 tablespoon
½ cup heavy cream
Juice of half a lemon

PRESENTATION: Serve the fish on hot plates. Cover with sauce and garnish with fresh tarragon leaves.

SUGGESTED WINE: A Chénin blanc

Red Snapper with Scallop Mousse
Rouget à la Mousseline de Coquilles Saint-Jacques

Because of the presentation, this is a perfect entrée for three or four people.

TO SERVE 4

1 whole 3-pound red
   snapper
1 pound fresh sea
   scallops (with small
   side muscles removed
   as necessary)
2 cups heavy cream
1 egg
Salt
Cayenne pepper
Freshly ground pepper
1 bunch fresh tarragon
4 medium shallots,
   minced
2 cups dry white wine
½ pound unsalted
   butter, cut into small
   pieces
6 whole mushrooms,
   medium-size
Juice of 1 lemon
4 slices truffle
4 fleurons (page 6)

1. Preheat the oven to 375°. Remove the bones from the snapper, leaving the fish whole. Set aside.
2. In a food processor, purée the scallops. Add 1 cup cream, the egg, 1 teaspoon salt, ½ teaspoon cayenne pepper, and the leaves from half the bunch of tarragon, and process until blended.
3. Season the inside of the fish with salt, pepper, and a few tarragon leaves. Stuff with the scallop mousse.
4. Sprinkle the shallots in a roasting pan; add the wine and 1 tablespoon butter. On the stove top, bring the mixture to a boil, place the stuffed fish in the pan, and cover with buttered aluminum foil, buttered side down.
5. Over high heat, bring the liquid back to a simmer. Place the pan in the oven and bake about 30 minutes, until the fish is just barely done.
6. Transfer the fish to a buttered warm platter and raise oven temperature to 450°.
7. Over high heat, reduce the liquid in the roasting pan by half. Add the remaining 1 cup cream and continue to reduce until the sauce is slightly thickened. Whisk in 7 ounces butter, one piece at a time. Strain, taste, and adjust seasonings.
8. Remove the stems from the mushrooms, reserving them for another use. Cook the mushroom caps in 1 table-spoon butter and lemon juice for 3 to 4 minutes.
9. Heat the *fleurons* for 1 or 2 minutes in the oven.

PRESENTATION: Nap the fish, already on a warm serving platter, with sauce. Garnish with truffle slices and mush-room caps. Decorate the platter with *fleurons*.

SUGGESTED WINE: A Chardonnay

Fillet of Sole with Celery Cream Sauce

Filet de Sole à la Crème de Céleri

An intelligent way to prepare fish without too many calories, using a vegetable purée as a sauce.

1. Peel the carrots, turnip, and asparagus; place the peelings in the bottom of a steamer. Cut the carrots, turnip, asparagus, and mushrooms into 1-by-¼-inch pieces. Cook each vegetable separately in boiling, salted water with a small amount of lemon juice until tender but still crisp. Drain and keep warm.
2. Peel the celery roots and cut them into quarters. In lightly salted boiling water, cook until very tender. In a blender or food processor, process the celery roots with enough of the reconstituted milk to make a very smooth, thick purée. Set aside and keep warm.
3. Add to the bottom of the steamer the wine, water, fish bones, peppercorns, parsley, bay leaf, and *herbes de Provence.* Bring to a boil.
4. Cut the fish fillets into thick, finger-size strips (approximately 1 by 3 inches). Brush the steamer rack with oil and arrange the fish in a single layer. Cover and steam for 5 to 7 minutes, or until slightly underdone. Remove from the steamer and keep warm.
5. Strain the liquid from the steamer into a saucepan, and, over high heat, reduce until only 1 cup remains. Thicken the sauce with the celery-root purée. Taste and correct seasonings with salt, pepper, and lemon juice.

PRESENTATION: Place the strips of fish in a deep oval dish. Cover with the cooked vegetables and nap with the sauce. Since this is a "diet" dish, serve it with a large glass of mineral or spring water instead of wine.

TO SERVE 6

2 medium carrots
1 medium turnip
1 pound asparagus
1 pound mushrooms
Salt
1 lemon
4 small celery roots (celeriac)
4 to 6 tablespoons nonfat dry milk, dissolved in ¼ cup water
2 cups Chardonnay or white Burgundy
2 cups water
Bones from fish fillets
¼ teaspoon peppercorns
4 sprigs parsley
1 bay leaf
A pinch of herbes de Provence
2 pounds fillet of sole, pike, or turbot
Almond or safflower oil

Fillet of Sole and Scallop Stew with Basil

Filet de Sole et Coquilles Saint-Jacques à la Nage au Pistou

Fresh scallops and small pieces of sole are cooked in their own juices with a light flavor of Provence.

TO SERVE 6

2 large whole sole
1 stalk celery, chopped
1 medium leek, cleaned
  and chopped
1 small onion, chopped
2 cups dry white wine
A pinch of thyme
3 tomatoes, peeled and
  seeded
Salt and freshly ground
  pepper
1 cucumber
24 asparagus tips,
  blanched
24 green beans, blanched
1 shallot, minced
12 tablespoons unsalted
  butter
12 large sea scallops (or
  24 bay scallops)
1 bunch fresh basil
1 lemon

1. Remove the fillets from the sole. Cut fillets into finger-size strips and reserve. Place fish bones and trimmings in a stockpot with celery, leek, and onion. Add 1½ cups wine, the thyme, and enough water to cover. Bring to a boil and simmer 20 minutes. Strain the *fumet* into a clean saucepan and reduce to 3 cups (approximately) while continuing with the preparation of the stew.

2. Dice the tomatoes and cook them in 1 tablespoon butter with the minced shallot, over moderate heat, until the moisture has evaporated and the sauce is thick. Season to taste with salt and pepper.

3. Turn the cucumber into oval shapes (see page 14). Sauté the asparagus tips, green beans, and cucumber in 2 tablespoons butter for 1 minute. Add remaining ½ cup wine and bring to a boil. Cook vegetables until they are *al dente.*

4. In a saucepan or sauté pan combine vegetables and their liquid, reduced *fumet,* scallops, and sole. Simmer for 2 or 3 minutes; the fish should be just tender, not dry or flaky.

5. Reserve six nice basil leaves. Cut remaining basil into *chiffonade.* Add the *chiffonade,* tomato sauce, and remaining butter to the stew. Stir to blend and season with salt, pepper, and lemon juice to taste.

PRESENTATION: Divide the stew among six heated soup plates. Garnish with one basil leaf per plate.

SUGGESTED WINE: A Blanc de Blancs

NOTE: This dish is lovely when eaten cold. Just omit the butter enrichment in step 5.

Trout Fillets in Puff Pastry

Filets de Truite en Chemise

Trout can be purchased all year round. By stuffing the trout and wrapping it in puff pastry, you have a very elegant presentation.

1. *To make the fish mousse:* Purée the scallops in a food processor. Add the egg and process until very smooth. Season with 1 teaspoon salt, ¼ teaspoon white pepper, cayenne pepper, and chopped tarragon.
2. With the motor running, pour the cream through the feed tube. Process until blended. Test for texture and seasoning by poaching in simmering water (see page 20).
3. Season trout fillets with remaining ½ teaspoon salt and ¾ teaspoon white pepper. Lay six trout fillets, skin side (the side where the skin was) down, on a flat surface. Fill a pastry bag with the fish mousse and pipe the mousse onto each fillet. Top with the remaining six fillets, skin side up, and chill.
4. Divide the pastry into six equal portions. Roll out each piece large enough to enclose a trout. Enclose and mold pastry around each trout, removing excess pastry. Brush with egg wash and decorate as desired. Refrigerate until ready to bake.
5. Preheat oven to 375°.
6. Arrange trout on a baking sheet and bake 20 to 25 minutes, or until pastry is golden brown.

PRESENTATION: Place the trout on a heated platter and garnish with flowers, if desired. To serve, slice into portions and nap with *beurre blanc*.

SUGGESTED WINE: A white Hermitage

TO SERVE 12

½ pound sea scallops (with small side muscles removed as necessary)
1 egg
1½ teaspoons salt
1 teaspoon freshly ground white pepper
A pinch of cayenne pepper
½ cup heavy cream
Chopped fresh tarragon to taste (optional)
6 trout, 10 ounces each, boned, skinned, and filleted
2 pounds puff pastry (page 200)
1 lightly beaten egg, for egg wash
3 cups beurre blanc (page 106)

Trout with Vegetables Cooked in Foil
Truite en Papillote

This recipe is for the weight-conscious. It is low in calories but still has good flavor.

6 trout, 8 to 10 ounces
  each
1 tablespoon minced
  fresh dill, tarragon, or
  chervil
Salt
Freshly ground pepper
1 carrot, cut into thin
  julienne
1 small leek, cut into
  thin julienne
1 small turnip, cut into
  thin julienne
1 teaspoon unsalted
  butter
2 tablespoons water
2 lemons, thinly sliced
1 recipe asparagus sauce
  (page 109)

1. Bone and skin the trout. Season it inside and out with fresh herbs, salt, and pepper.
2. Sauté the vegetables in the butter until they are tender but still crisp. Add the water and remove the pan from the heat.
3. Cut six pieces of aluminum foil, each large enough to enclose one trout.
4. Preheat oven to 450°.
5. Arrange three or four lemon slices on each piece of foil. Lay the trout on the lemon slices. Place some of the julienne of vegetables on the bottom half of each trout and top with the other half of the trout. Close the foil so it is airtight.
6. Place the *papillotes* on a baking sheet and bake them for 12 to 15 minutes, or until they look like balloons.

PRESENTATION: Serve each *papillote* on a dinner plate. Let the guests open their own packages so they can savor the aroma. Serve the sauce separately.

SUGGESTED WINE: A Vouvray or Fumé blanc

Scallops in Cream Sauce

Coquilles Saint-Jacques à la Crème

I prefer the sweet little bay scallops for this dish. However, if they are not available, you may substitute sea scallops cut in half horizontally so that the slices will be more uniform. It is very important to undercook scallops; if too well done, they become tough and chewy. The tenderness of the scallops and the crispness of the julienne of vegetables impart a touch of *nouvelle cuisine.*

1. Cut carrots, turnip, leek, and celery root into julienne.
2. In a skillet, heat the 1 tablespoon butter and slowly sauté vegetables until tender but still crisp. Salt to taste. Reserve.
3. If scallops are large, slice in half horizontally, retaining disklike shape. If small, leave whole.
4. In a saucepan combine vermouth, shallots, and a dash of salt and pepper. Add scallops and bring to a boil. Boil no more than 2 minutes, less if scallops are small. Remove scallops and reserve.
5. Cook liquid until reduced by half. Add ½ cup cream and continue cooking until mixture thickens.
6. Whisk ½ pound butter into sauce, 2 tablespoons at a time. Add lemon juice to taste. Do not let the sauce boil or get cold.
7. Lightly whip remaining ½ cup cream and add to the sauce, a few spoonfuls at a time.
8. Arrange cooked scallops in six or eight gratin dishes and garnish with vegetables. Place in a preheated 400° oven and heat to serving temperature.
9. Pour the sauce over each serving and glaze under a hot broiler (about 2 minutes). Watch carefully to avoid burning.

PRESENTATION: Place the individual gratin dishes on plates and serve.

SUGGESTED WINE: A Sancerre or Chénin blanc

TO SERVE 6 OR 8 AS AN ENTRÉE, 12 OR 14 AS AN APPETIZER

2 medium carrots, peeled
1 turnip, peeled
1 small leek, white part only
1 small celery root (celeriac), peeled
Salt and freshly ground pepper
½ pound unsalted butter, plus 1 tablespoon
2 pounds bay scallops
1 cup dry white vermouth
3 shallots, minced
1 cup whipping cream
Lemon juice to taste

Scallops with Ginger

Coquilles Saint-Jacques au Gingembre

An impressive presentation, this dish is a combination of *nouvelle* and Oriental cuisines.

TO SERVE 2

6 ounces puff pastry
(page 200)
1 egg, lightly beaten, for
egg wash
½ cup Sauternes
1 shallot, minced
½ tablespoon minced
fresh ginger
10 ounces bay scallops
(or sea scallops, cut in
half horizontally), with
small side muscles
removed as necessary
3 tablespoons heavy
cream
6 ounces unsalted butter
Salt
Freshly ground pepper
Lemon juice
2 scallions or 1 small
leek, cut into ¼-inch
slices

1. Preheat oven to 450°.
2. Roll out the puff pastry to a 10-inch circle (or square, if you prefer), ¼ inch thick. Place on a baking sheet and cut out an 8-inch circle from the center, removing the excess pastry. Brush with egg wash. Cut a concentric circle 1 inch in from the edge and halfway through the pastry. Chill for 10 minutes.
3. Bake 15 minutes, reduce heat to 350°, and continue to bake 15 to 20 minutes longer, or until the pastry is golden brown. Do not turn off the oven after removing pastry.
4. Carefully cut off the cover formed by the concentric circle and gently remove the moist dough inside the shell.
5. In a saucepan, combine the wine, shallot, and ginger and bring to a boil. Add the scallops and cream and cook, over moderate heat, for 1 or 2 minutes. Remove the scallops.
6. Over high heat, reduce the cooking liquid, adding any juices that have drained from the scallops. Slowly, one small piece at a time, whisk in all but 1 teaspoon of the butter. Season to taste with salt, pepper, and lemon juice. Set aside.
7. In a small sauté pan, melt the remaining 1 teaspoon butter. Over high heat, wilt the scallions for 30 seconds. Set aside.
8. Return the scallops to the sauce and heat through. Reheat the pastry shell in the hot oven (returned to 450°) for 2 minutes.

PRESENTATION: Place the pastry shell on a warm platter and fill with the scallops and sauce. Garnish with the sautéed scallions and decoratively top with the pastry lid.

SUGGESTED WINE: The same one used in the recipe

Shrimp with Pink Peppercorns

Crevettes au Poivre Rose

For best results, sauté the shrimp very quickly, as the Chinese do, so the shrimp stay plump and juicy.

1. Peel the shrimp, leaving the tails intact. Season with salt and black pepper.
2. Heat a large sauté pan until it is very hot. Add the olive oil, and, over high heat, sauté the shrimp, 2 minutes on each side. Remove the shrimp from the pan and keep warm.
3. Add the shallot to the pan and deglaze with vermouth. Add the fish stock and pink peppercorns and reduce until sauce has thickened slightly. Whisk in 4 tablespoons butter, a small piece at a time. Set aside and keep warm.
4. Heat a sauté pan, add the remaining 2 tablespoons butter, and cook until it begins to turn light brown (*noisette*). Add the cleaned spinach, salt lightly, and sauté, covered, over medium heat until spinach is wilted (approximately 1 minute). Remove from the heat.

PRESENTATION: Arrange a few wilted leaves of spinach on a plate. Place four shrimp on each plate and nap lightly with the sauce.

SUGGESTED WINE: A Chardonnay

TO SERVE 6

24 plump fresh shrimp, medium-size
Salt
Coarsely ground black pepper
1 tablespoon olive oil
1 shallot, minced
3 tablespoons dry white vermouth
1 cup fish stock (page 65)
1 tablespoon pink peppercorns
6 tablespoons unsalted butter
½ pound spinach, cleaned, with stems removed

Meats

Lamb Chops with Cream of Shallots

Noisettes of Lamb with Zucchini and Eggplant

Veal Stew

Veal Medallions with Port Wine Sauce

Veal Medallions in Meaux Mustard Sauce

Veal Medallions with Onion Marmalade

Stuffed Veal Loin with Orange Sauce

Fillet of Beef in Puff Pastry with Sauce Béarnaise

New York Steak with Four Peppers and Port Wine

Ground Steak with Roquefort Cheese and Green
Peppercorn Sauce

Chopped Steak with Béarnaise and Cabernet Sauces

Roast Pork Normandy

Medallions of Pork

Pork Chops with Cabbage and Sherry Vinegar Sauce

Calf's Liver with Ginger and Pink Peppercorns

Calf's Tongue Braised in Red Wine and Onions

Calf's Tongue with Vinegar and Capers

Veal Kidneys with Leeks and Vinegar Sauce

Sweetbread Tourte

Sweetbreads in Sorrel Sauce

Meat, often maligned in this era of health and weight consciousness, supplies myriad nutrients in relatively small volume. The French eat the most meat among Europeans; thus the wealth of classic French meat recipes is not surprising. America, too, is a nation of meat eaters, perhaps because our meat is among the best in the world.

America produces delicious grain-fed lamb, particularly in Pennsylvania, New Jersey, and northern California. After eating a lamb dish at Ma Maison, Roger Vergé, chef and owner of the renowned three-star restaurant Moulin de Mougins, observed that our lamb was comparable to any found in France. Perhaps the reason many Americans are not fond of lamb is because they don't have a chance to taste it; some restaurants and butchers present mutton instead. You must find a high-quality meat market to procure good lamb; buy it during the months of April through July, when the animal is more likely to be young.

Veal's neutral character presents a perfect backdrop for an undeterminable variety of sauces, and yet it is nearly as flavorful when prepared simply as *veal paillard* (grilled with the juice of a lemon). It is understandable that the greatest sauce lovers, the Italians, are the greatest veal eaters as well. Italians eat four times as much veal as Americans; but considering our constantly improving breed of veal, which I contend is already the best in the world, our appreciation is likely to increase.

Pork is the leading meat of the world because it is economical. There is virtually no waste, since almost all of the animal can be eaten. It is also the easiest of meats to preserve. The poet Monselet declared: "The pig is nothing but an immense dish which walks while waiting to be served."

I have also included recipes for the variety meats (sweetbreads, kidneys, liver, tongue, and brains), which are unfairly underrated in America. In France, the kidney is a delicacy.

When grilling or sautéing meat, I first heat my pan to a high temperature and then add the meat; this sears in the juices and preserves the flavor. I select the most tender parts (racks, fillets, or loins) for quick sautéing or grilling. Less tender sections, such as legs, shoulders, or neck, are generally roasted, braised, or boiled in order to tenderize the meat. Marinating also helps to give meat a more delicate texture and heightened flavor; it also reduces cooking time.

A word of caution: Cook meat carefully, and don't over-cook it; at today's prices, you can't afford to let any flavor escape!

Lamb Chops with Cream of Shallots
Côtes d'Agneau Échalotes

Quickly searing the lamb chops on both sides keeps the meat juicy. The vinegar sauce and the fresh chopped shallots give it a piquant flavor.

1. Season lamb chops with salt and pepper.
2. Heat a heavy sauté pan, add the oil, and cook lamb chops until they are medium rare, approximately 3 or 4 minutes on each side. Transfer to a warm platter and pour off any accumulated fat.
3. In the same pan, sauté three fourths of the shallots for 2 minutes, reserving the remaining shallots. Deglaze the pan with the vinegar, pour in the white wine, and reduce the liquid until only 2 tablespoons remain.
4. Add the stock and thyme and reduce by half. Add the heavy cream and cook over moderate heat until lightly thickened (approximately half the original volume).
5. Whisk in the butter, a small amount at a time. Taste and correct seasonings. Strain the sauce.

PRESENTATION: Place two lamb chops on each heated serving plate. Nap with sauce and garnish each lamb chop with some of the reserved shallots. Serve with *pommes Lyonnaise* (page 176).

SUGGESTED WINE: A Cabernet Sauvignon

TO SERVE 6

12 lamb chops, approximately 1½ inches thick
Salt
Freshly ground pepper
1 tablespoon mild-flavored oil, such as almond or safflower
10 shallots, minced
½ cup good red wine vinegar
½ cup dry white wine
1 cup brown veal stock (page 66)
2 sprigs fresh thyme
1 cup heavy cream
6 tablespoons unsalted butter, cut into small pieces

Noisettes of Lamb with Zucchini and Eggplant

Noisettes d'Agneau avec Courgettes et Aubergines

Only lamb of excellent quality can be used for *noisettes*. Cook lamb medium rare to ensure tender meat.

TO SERVE 6

2 tablespoons olive oil or unsalted butter
½ pound eggplant, cut into ½-inch cubes
½ pound zucchini, cut into ½-inch cubes
Salt and freshly ground pepper
2 cloves garlic, chopped
2 sprigs fresh thyme
½ pound fresh tomatoes, peeled, seeded, and cut into ½-inch cubes
1 tablespoon vegetable oil
12 noisettes of lamb, 3 to 4 ounces each (from saddle or rack)
1 cup dry white wine
1 cup brown veal stock (page 66)
1 tablespoon chopped fresh tarragon
4 tablespoons unsalted butter
Tarragon leaves for garnish

1. Heat the olive oil in a large heavy saucepan. Add the eggplant and zucchini cubes and season with salt, pepper, garlic, and thyme. Sauté the vegetables until *al dente.*
2. Drain the tomatoes, add to the vegetables, and stir thoroughly. Set aside and reserve in a warm spot.
3. Heat a medium sauté pan and add the vegetable oil. Season the *noisettes* with salt and pepper and cook to desired degree of doneness (3 or 4 minutes on each side for medium rare). Transfer to a warm plate and reserve.
4. Pour out grease from the pan, deglaze with white wine, and reduce slightly. Add the veal stock and chopped tarragon and continue to reduce until slightly thickened. Whisk in the butter, one piece at a time. Correct seasoning to taste and keep warm.

PRESENTATION: In the center of each hot serving plate, arrange some of the vegetable mixture. Top with two *noisettes* and nap with sauce. Decorate with tarragon leaves.

SUGGESTED WINE: A Pinot Noir

Veal Stew

Blanquette de Veau

An old country French recipe that will satisfy gourmets. Cooking slowly over low heat ensures tender and juicy meat. The ideal accompaniment is rice, so that every last drop of the sauce can be enjoyed.

1. Cut the veal into 2-inch cubes.
2. In a wide, heavy saucepan, heat the oil. Brown veal cubes on all sides, removing from pan as browned. Pour out any oil that remains after all the meat is browned.
3. In the same saucepan, melt the butter. Sauté the onion until translucent. Return the meat to the pan and sprinkle with flour. Continue to stir until the flour is absorbed.
4. Deglaze with white wine and bring to a boil. Add stock, thyme, bay leaf, celery leaves, salt, and pepper. Cover and let simmer for 35 to 45 minutes, or until the veal is tender. If it is cooking too rapidly, remove the cover.
5. While the veal is cooking, separately blanch the carrots, celery, and broccoli in boiling, salted water until *al dente*. Reserve until needed.
6. Transfer cooked veal to a clean saucepan, reserving the liquid. Add cream to the liquid and reduce until thickened. Strain over meat, bring to a boil, and add the vegetables.
7. Add lemon juice and correct seasonings.

PRESENTATION: Serve the stew with rice pilaf.

SUGGESTED WINE: A light red wine

TO SERVE 6

3 pounds veal shoulder and neck
2 tablespoons mild-flavored oil, such as almond or safflower
1 tablespoon unsalted butter
1 large onion, chopped fine
3 tablespoons all-purpose flour
2 cups dry white wine
3 cups chicken stock (page 65) or brown veal stock (page 66)
A pinch of thyme
1 bay leaf
Leaves from 2 celery stalks, chopped fine
1 teaspoon salt
Freshly ground pepper to taste
6 large carrots, peeled and cut into bâtonnettes
1 stalk celery, cut into bâtonnettes
1 medium head broccoli, cut into florets
1 cup heavy cream
Juice of half a medium lemon

Veal Medallions with Port Wine Sauce

Médaillons de Veau avec Sauce Porto

Using a good port will give your sauce a better flavor.

TO SERVE 6

3 pounds veal loin,
  boned and cut into 12
  equal medallions
Salt and freshly ground
  pepper
1 tablespoon mild-
  flavored oil, such as
  almond or safflower
1 cup port
½ cup brown veal stock
  (page 66) or chicken
  stock (page 65)
½ cup heavy cream
5 tablespoons unsalted
  butter
Lemon juice
3 pounds spinach,
  cleaned, with stems
  removed

1. Season the veal medallions with salt and pepper.
2. Heat oil in a skillet. When oil is hot, sauté veal medallions in two batches, 3 minutes on each side. Transfer to a warm platter and keep warm.
3. Deglaze skillet with port. Over high heat, reduce until ½ cup remains. Add the stock and cream; then continue to reduce, over medium heat, until slightly thickened. Off the heat, slowly whisk in 4 tablespoons butter, one small piece at a time. Adjust seasonings and add drops of lemon juice to taste.
4. Sauté spinach in 1 tablespoon butter or 3 to 4 tablespoons water until just wilted. Season to taste with salt and pepper. Drain and keep warm.

PRESENTATION: Place two veal medallions on a bed of spinach on each heated serving plate. Nap each medallion with a spoonful of sauce.

SUGGESTED WINE: A fruity white wine or a light red one

Veal Medallions in Meaux Mustard Sauce

Médaillons de Veau à la Moutarde de Meaux

The sauce for this dish can also be served with chicken, lamb, or beef. The Meaux mustard adds just the right piquant touch.

TO SERVE 6

6 veal medallions, 6
  ounces each
1 ounce clarified
  unsalted butter
3 shallots, minced

1. Over moderate heat, sauté the veal in clarified butter, for 2 or 3 minutes on each side, until golden brown. Pour out the grease.
2. Add shallots to pan and deglaze with port. Let it reduce by half.

3. Add heavy cream and reduce to thicken lightly. Remove from heat, add mustard, and then whisk in butter, one small piece at a time.

PRESENTATION: Pour sauce on each serving plate and top with the veal medallions.

SUGGESTED WINE: A Merlot

½ cup port
1 cup heavy cream
3 tablespoons Moutarde de Meaux
2 ounces unsalted butter, cut into small pieces

Veal Medallions with Onion Marmalade
Médaillons de Veau aux Oignons

Cooking the onions until all the liquid evaporates, then binding with cream, brings out the very special flavor of this marmalade sauce.

1. Season the onions with ½ teaspoon salt and pepper to taste. Into a medium saucepan, put 1½ cups stock, the vinegar, and the onions. Cover the pan, and cook over moderate heat, until liquid has evaporated, about 15 minutes.
2. In a small saucepan, reduce the cream until 3 tablespoons remain. Add the cream to the onions and bring to a boil. Remove the onions from the heat and reserve in a warm spot.
3. Season the veal with the remaining ½ teaspoon salt and pepper to taste. Dust lightly with the flour. Heat a heavy skillet and add ½ teaspoon each of butter and oil. Sauté the medallions until golden brown on both sides but still pink inside (3 or 4 minutes on each side). Transfer to a platter and keep warm.
4. Pour grease from the skillet and deglaze with port. Add the remaining ½ cup stock and reduce until 3 tablespoons remain. Slowly whisk in the remaining 1½ tablespoons butter.

TO SERVE 4

2 large or 3 medium onions, cut into eighths
1 teaspoon salt
Freshly ground pepper
2 cups chicken stock (page 65)
1 tablespoon good red or sherry wine vinegar
1 cup heavy cream
1½ pounds veal loin, cut into 8 medallions, 3 ounces each
1 tablespoon all-purpose flour
2 tablespoons unsalted butter
1 tablespoon mild-flavored oil, such as almond or safflower
½ cup port

PRESENTATION: Arrange onions on each serving plate, top with two veal medallions, and lightly nap with sauce.

SUGGESTED WINE: A Chardonnay

Stuffed Veal Loin with Orange Sauce

Rognonnade de Veau à l'Orange

White Eastern veal is preferable to Western veal. Timing is very important: To test for doneness, poke a large-tined fork or a skewer into the center of the roast for 1 minute; if it comes out feeling hot when you touch it, the roast is ready.

TO SERVE 6

1 veal loin with flank, about 6 pounds
2 veal kidneys
1 tablespoon mild-flavored oil, such as almond or safflower
Salt
Freshly ground pepper
6 oranges
2 lemons
2 tablespoons sugar
1 cup port
2 cups brown veal stock (page 66)
¼ pound unsalted butter, cut into small pieces

1. Preheat oven to 400°.
2. Bone the loin, removing all the fat and sinew, and reserve them. Season the inside of the loin with salt and pepper. Remove fat and skin from the kidneys and slice each kidney in half lengthwise.
3. In a heavy sauté pan, heat the oil and sauté the kidneys for 1 minute on each side. Set aside and cool. Arrange in the center of the veal loin and roll the loin over the kidneys. Tie the roast with string at regular intervals. Season with salt and pepper.
4. Place fat and trimmings in the bottom of a roasting pan and set the loin on top. Roast for 1½ hours. The roast should still be pink inside, not well done. Transfer it to a warm platter.
5. While the meat is roasting, peel the skins of the oranges and the lemons and cut into julienne. Place in a small saucepan with the sugar and enough water to cover. Boil until the sugar begins to caramelize. Pour the julienne into a strainer and rinse briefly under water. Set aside.
6. Squeeze the juice from the oranges. Remove fat and trimmings from the roasting pan and pour off any fat that has accumulated. Deglaze with the port and add the veal stock and orange juice. Simmer 15 minutes, strain, and reduce until only 1 cup remains. Whisk in the butter, one piece at a time, to slightly thicken the sauce. Reserve and keep warm.

PRESENTATION: Place a slice of the roast on a warm plate. Nap with sauce and sprinkle with the julienne of orange and lemon peels.

SUGGESTED WINE: A light St. Emilion or a fruity Chardonnay

Fillet of Beef in Puff Pastry with Sauce Béarnaise

Filet en Croûte avec Sauce Béarnaise

A classic, elegant entrée for a formal dinner party. Because most of the preparation can be done early in the day, you will be able to spend more time with your guests and less in the kitchen.

1. Over high heat, sauté *tournedos* in 3 tablespoons butter for 30 seconds on each side. Set aside to cool completely.
2. In a hot skillet, with the remaining 3 tablespoons butter, cook shallots and mushrooms until all liquid evaporates. Add cream, salt, and pepper. Reduce over moderate heat to a thick purée. Cool.
3. Preheat oven to 450°.
4. Divide pastry into six portions. On a lightly floured board, roll out each portion to a rectangle approximately 6 by 12 inches and ¼ inch thick. Place each *tournedo* on one side of a pastry rectangle, leaving enough room to fold over.
5. Top each *tournedo* with mushroom purée. Brush edges of the pastry with egg wash and then fold it over and shape it to the contours of the meat. Cut away excess pastry and decorate as desired. The recipe can be prepared ahead to this point.
6. Glaze the tops of the pastry with egg wash.
7. Bake the *tournedos* 15 to 20 minutes, or until the pastry is golden brown.

PRESENTATION: Arrange the *tournedos* on a heated platter and garnish with watercress. Serve with the *sauce béarnaise.*

SUGGESTED WINE: A Gevrey-Chambertin

TO SERVE 6

6 tournedos, 6 ounces each
6 tablespoons unsalted butter
2 shallots, minced
1 pound mushrooms, chopped fine
4 tablespoons heavy cream
Salt and freshly ground pepper to taste
2 pounds puff pastry (page 200)
1 egg, lightly beaten, for egg wash
1 recipe sauce béarnaise (page 104)

New York Steak with Four Peppers and Port Wine

Entrecôte au Quatre Poivres

The flavor of the green and pink peppercorns and the sharpness of the black and white peppers blend to give this steak its distinctive taste.

TO SERVE 6

2 tablespoons whole
white peppercorns
2 tablespoons whole
black peppercorns
6 entrecôtes, 8 ounces
each
Salt
2 tablespoons mild-
flavored oil, such as
almond or safflower
1 cup port or dry sherry
1 cup heavy cream
½ cup brown veal stock
(page 66)
3 tablespoons unsalted
butter, cut into small
pieces
2 tablespoons pink
peppercorns, soaked
overnight in port
2 tablespoons green
peppercorns

1. With the back of a heavy saucepan, crush the white and black peppercorns.
2. Remove all fat from the *entrecôtes*. Season with salt and crushed peppercorns.
3. Heat a large heavy saucepan. Pour in oil and, over high heat, cook the *entrecôtes* 4 minutes on each side (for medium rare). Transfer meat to a warm platter and reserve.
4. Pour out grease from pan, deglaze with port, and reduce. Add cream and veal stock and continue to reduce until sauce is thick enough to coat the back of a spoon.
5. Whisk in butter, one small piece at a time. Season to taste with salt.

PRESENTATION: Place one *entrecôte* on each warmed serving plate. Ladle sauce over steaks and divide peppercorns equally over each portion.

SUGGESTED WINE: A heavy red wine such as a Côte de Beaune

Ground Steak with Roquefort Cheese and Green Peppercorn Sauce

Biftek Haché au Roquefort avec Poivre Vert

The combination of Roquefort cheese, green peppercorns, and port wine transforms the common hamburger into an elegant dish.

1. In a bowl, combine meat, eggs, shallots, and salt and pepper to taste. Mix well. Divide into twelve rounds.
2. Stuff each round with Roquefort cheese, taking care to cover cheese completely. Flatten slightly.
3. Heat a heavy sauté pan. Add the oil and sauté the meat, turning once until cheese melts and *haché* is rare.
4. Transfer meat to a heated platter. Pour off fat from sauté pan. Deglaze with the port. Add peppercorns and cream. Reduce until sauce begins to thicken. Whisk in the butter, one small piece at a time.

VARIATION: Do not stuff meat rounds with cheese. Deglaze the sauté pan with port, add cream, and reduce. Thicken the sauce with the Roquefort cheese.

PRESENTATION: Place two *hachés* on each dinner plate. Serve with *pommes Lyonnaise.*

SUGGESTED WINE: A Côte Rôtie or a Châteauneuf-du-Pape

TO SERVE 6

3 pounds coarsely chopped beef (fillet tips or ends of New York steak)
2 eggs
2 shallots, minced
Salt and freshly ground pepper
¾ cup Roquefort cheese, crumbled
3 tablespoons mild-flavored oil, such as almond or safflower
1 cup port
3 to 4 tablespoons green peppercorns
1 cup heavy cream
½ cup unsalted butter, cut into small pieces
1 recipe pommes Lyonnaise (page 176)

Chopped Steak with Béarnaise and Cabernet Sauces

Biftek Haché Béarnaise et Cabernet

Again, the ordinary hamburger becomes an elegant offering. The meat should be coarsely ground or chopped with a knife for the maximum flavor.

TO SERVE 6

2½ pounds coarsely
  ground beef (lean
  trimmings of tenderloin
  or New York strip loin)
2 shallots, minced
½ teaspoon chopped
  fresh thyme
Salt and freshly ground
  pepper to taste
1 egg
1 tablespoon mild-
  flavored oil, such as
  almond or safflower
½ tablespoon unsalted
  butter

Sauce Cabernet:

3 shallots, minced
3 tablespoons unsalted
  butter
2 cups dry red wine
A pinch of thyme
½ bay leaf
Freshly ground pepper
1 cup brown veal stock
  (page 66)

1 recipe sauce béarnaise
  (page 104)

1. *To prepare* biftek haché: Combine ground meat, shallots, thyme, salt, pepper, and egg. Mix well. Shape into six patties, ¾ inch thick. Refrigerate until needed.
2. *To prepare* sauce Cabernet: Reserve 1 tablespoon of the minced shallots and sauté the remaining shallots in 1 tablespoon butter until they just begin to brown.
3. Deglaze the pan with red wine and add thyme, bay leaf, and pepper to taste. Reduce until 1 cup remains. Add brown stock and, over moderate heat, continue to reduce until the sauce becomes syrupy. Strain into a small saucepan. Whisk in the remaining 2 tablespoons butter and add the reserved 1 tablespoon shallots. Correct seasoning and keep warm.
4. Prepare *sauce béarnaise.* Reserve and keep warm.
5. In a heavy sauté pan, heat 1 tablespoon oil and ½ tablespoon butter until it begins to color. Cook the patties to desired degree of doneness. Transfer to a warm platter.

PRESENTATION: Place a *biftek haché* on each heated plate and cover half the steak with *sauce béarnaise* and half with *sauce Cabernet.* Serve immediately, with *pommes Lyonnaise.*

SUGGESTED WINE: A Zinfandel or Petit Sirah

Roast Pork Normandy

Rôti de Porc Normande

Pork should stay slightly pink when cooked so that it will be tender and retain its juices.

1. Preheat oven to 450°.
2. Season the roast with salt and pepper. Roast in a heavy pan on top of the trimmings, or on a rack, for 40 minutes. Pork should be slightly pink inside.
3. Transfer to a warm platter and discard the trimmings and excess fat. Deglaze the pan with Calvados. Add the veal stock and heavy cream and boil for approximately 15 minutes, or until sauce is slightly thickened. Strain and keep warm.
4. Heat a heavy sauté pan and add 1 tablespoon butter. Sauté the apples until tender and golden brown.
5. Heat a separate sauté pan, add the remaining 1 tablespoon butter, and sauté the mushrooms for 3 or 4 minutes.
6. Combine the mushrooms with the strained sauce. Correct seasoning to taste.

PRESENTATION: Nap the heated plates with the sauce. Place 2 slices of meat on each plate. Garnish with apple slices.

SUGGESTED WINE: A Zinfandel

TO SERVE 4

2 pounds pork loin, with ribs attached
Salt
Freshly ground pepper
4 tablespoons Calvados
1 cup brown veal stock (page 66)
1 cup heavy cream
2 tablespoons unsalted butter
2 apples, Golden or Red Delicious, peeled, cored, and cut into 8 segments
½ pound mushrooms, sliced

Medallions of Pork

Noisettes de Porc Sonoma Valley

The light acidity of the grapes combined with the richness of the pork and the fruity essence of the wine produces an enchanting balance of aroma and taste. In particular, the acidic grapes tend to reduce the slightly fatty quality of most pork.

TO SERVE 4

½ pound seedless grapes, peeled
1½ cups Johannisberg Riesling
8 pork medallions, each ½ inch thick
Salt
Freshly ground pepper
Flour
5 tablespoons unsalted butter
1½ cups brown veal stock (page 66)

1. Marinate the grapes in the wine overnight.
2. Drain the grapes and reserve ½ cup of the marinade.
3. Season the medallions with salt and pepper. Dust very lightly with flour.
4. Heat a heavy sauté pan and add 2 tablespoons butter. Sauté the medallions, 3 or 4 minutes on each side, until golden brown and still slightly pink inside. Transfer to a heated platter and pour off the excess fat.
5. Deglaze the pan with the reserved ½ cup wine and reduce by one third. Add the stock and continue to reduce until the sauce is slightly thickened. Season to taste with salt and pepper. Whisk in 2 tablespoons butter.
6. In a separate saucepan, melt the remaining 1 tablespoon butter and gently heat the grapes. Drain off any accumulated liquid and add the grapes to the hot sauce.

PRESENTATION: Place two medallions on each heated plate. Spoon the sauce and grapes over the medallions. Serve with *pommes Lyonnaise* (page 176).

SUGGESTED WINE: A Johannisberg Riesling

Pork Chops with Cabbage and Sherry Vinegar Sauce

Côtes de Porc au Vinaigre Xérès avec Salade de Chou Tiède

This is a specialty of my native Austria that I have refined to please the American palate.

1. Season both sides of pork chops with salt and pepper.
2. Heat a heavy sauté pan and add 1 tablespoon butter and the oil. Over medium heat, sauté the chops for 5 minutes on each side, or until slightly pink on the inside.
3. Remove chops to a heated platter and pour off the excess fat. Deglaze the pan with 3 tablespoons of the vinegar and the sherry. Add the veal stock and, over moderate heat, reduce until slightly thickened. Reserve.
4. Sauté the bacon until crisp. Spoon off all but 2 tablespoons of the bacon fat and deglaze the pan with the remaining 4 tablespoons of sherry wine vinegar. Add the cabbage and stir, over high heat, until heated through. Season to taste with salt and pepper.
5. Heat the sauce and whisk in the Dijon mustard and remaining 1 tablespoon butter.

PRESENTATION: Divide the cabbage on heated plates. Place a pork chop on each bed of cabbage and nap each chop with the sauce. Garnish with chopped tomatoes and sprinkle with chives.

SUGGESTED WINE: A Merlot

TO SERVE 2

2 center-cut pork chops, 1 inch thick
Salt
Freshly ground pepper
2 tablespoons unsalted butter
1 tablespoon mild-flavored oil, such as almond or safflower
7 tablespoons sherry wine vinegar
3 tablespoons sherry
1 cup brown veal stock (page 66)
4 slices bacon, cut into ¼-inch slices
6 ounces cabbage, cut into julienne
1 teaspoon Dijon mustard
2 tablespoons peeled, seeded, and chopped tomatoes
1 teaspoon minced chives

Calf's Liver with Ginger and Pink Peppercorns
Foie de Veau au Gingembre et Poivre Rose

The sauce, flavored with ginger and pink peppercorns, converts liver from the ordinary to the exceptional. The liver should be pale pink in color for the best flavor.

TO SERVE 6

3 pounds calf's liver
Salt and freshly ground
  pepper
2 tablespoons all-purpose
  flour
2 tablespoons mild-
  flavored oil, such as
  almond or safflower
½ cup port
2 tablespoons pink
  peppercorns
1 tablespoon minced
  fresh ginger
1 cup brown veal stock
  (page 66)
½ cup heavy cream
3 tablespoons unsalted
  butter, cut into small
  pieces

1. Trim off any excess fat and membrane from the liver. Cut it into ¼- to ⅓-inch-thick slices. Season both sides of each slice with salt and pepper to taste and dust lightly with flour.
2. Heat a heavy sauté pan. Add the oil and, over high heat, sauté the liver quickly, until golden brown on the outside but still pink on the inside, approximately 1 minute on each side. Set aside and reserve on a heated platter.
3. Deglaze the pan with port. Add the peppercorns, ginger, and veal stock and reduce by half. Pour in the cream and continue to reduce until slightly thickened. Reduce heat and whisk in the butter, one small piece at a time.

PRESENTATION: Place the sautéed liver on warm plates, nap with sauce, and serve immediately.

SUGGESTED WINE: A Cabernet Sauvignon

Calf's Tongue Braised in Red Wine and Onions

Langue de Veau à la Fondue d'Oignons

This is an inexpensive and low-calorie dish that is satisfying to those who are watching their weight.

TO SERVE 6

1. In a large saucepan, cook the tongues in boiling, salted water for 45 minutes. Refresh under cold running water and peel if possible. If the tongues do not peel easily, continue with recipe and peel just before slicing.
2. Preheat oven to 400°.
3. In a saucepan, reduce the wine until only 1 cup remains. Add the stock and heat through.
4. Place tongues in an oven-proof casserole. Top with onions, vinegar, tomatoes, celery, bay leaf, thyme, garlic, and tarragon sprig. Add wine, stock, and salt and pepper. Cover and cook in the oven for approximately 1 hour, or until tender. As the liquid reduces, add a bit more stock or water, if necessary, to prevent burning.
5. Remove the tongues from the casserole and keep warm. Transfer the vegetables to a food processor or blender and purée. Reheat. Season with salt and pepper to taste.

PRESENTATION: Slice tongues and cover each serving with the vegetable sauce. Sprinkle with minced tarragon.

SUGGESTED WINE: A light St. Emilion

2 calf's tongues, approximately 2 pounds
2 cups red wine (such as a Petit Sirah)
2 cups chicken stock (page 65)
2 pounds onions, thinly sliced
1 tablespoon good red or sherry wine vinegar
3 medium tomatoes, peeled, seeded, and diced
1 stalk celery, sliced
1 small bay leaf
A pinch of thyme
2 cloves garlic, unpeeled
1 sprig fresh tarragon
Salt
Freshly ground pepper
1 tablespoon minced fresh tarragon

Calf's Tongue with Vinegar and Capers
Langue de Veau au Vinaigre et Câpres

Tongue has always been considered a delicacy in Europe and it is becoming widely popular in the United States. Calf's and lamb's tongues are the best.

TO SERVE 6

2 calf's tongues, approximately 1 pound each

Stock:

1 medium onion, quartered
2 stalks celery, sliced
2 medium carrots, sliced
1 bay leaf
A pinch of dried thyme
Salt
½ teaspoon whole black peppercorns
2 cups dry white wine

Tomato Sauce:

1 cup dry white wine
3 tablespoons wine vinegar
4 ripe tomatoes, peeled, seeded, and diced
1 tablespoon minced shallots
½ tablespoon chopped fresh tarragon
½ cup unsalted butter, cut into small pieces
2 tablespoons capers
Chopped fresh chervil or chives (for garnish)

1. Blanch tongues for 30 minutes in boiling, salted water to cover.
2. *To make the stock:* Combine vegetables, seasonings, and wine and cook tongues in mixture until tender, approximately 1½ hours.
3. *To make the sauce:* Reduce the white wine, vinegar, tomatoes, shallots, and tarragon until tomatoes give up most of their liquid. Transfer to a blender or food processor and purée. Return sauce to a saucepan.
4. Whisk the butter into the sauce, one small piece at a time. Strain, if desired. Add 2 tablespoons capers and correct seasonings to taste. Keep warm.
5. Remove the tongues from the stock, carefully peel them, and slice into ⅜-inch-thick pieces.

NOTE: If you wish to serve the tongue cold, substitute ½ cup olive oil for the butter in the sauce.

PRESENTATION: Nap each plate with sauce, arrange slices of tongue on the sauce, and sprinkle with fresh herbs.

SUGGESTED WINE: A Chénin blanc

Veal Kidneys with Leeks and Vinegar Sauce
Rognons de Veau avec Poireaux et Sauce Vinaigre

The kidneys *must* be fresh. Cook over high heat to seal the meat and help retain the flavor. The leeks and vinegar sauce are the perfect complement.

1. Cut leeks into julienne.
2. Heat a heavy saucepan and melt 1 tablespoon butter. Add the leeks and sauté slowly until they are cooked through and appear glossy.
3. Add the cream and reduce until it becomes a thick compote.
4. Remove the fat and nerves from the kidneys and slice across the width into ¼-inch-thick pieces. Season to taste with salt and pepper.
5. Heat a sauté pan. Heat walnut oil and 2 tablespoons butter until very hot. Sauté the kidneys for 30 seconds on each side; they must stay pink.
6. Pour out fat from pan, deglaze with vinegar, and reduce until only 1 tablespoon remains. Add veal stock and reduce again until it thickens. Remove from heat, whisk in remaining butter, and keep warm.

PRESENTATION: Arrange a small mound of leek compote in the middle of a hot plate. Arrange kidney slices around the leeks. Reheat, under a broiler, if necessary. Strain the sauce over the kidneys. Sprinkle leeks with minced chives.

SUGGESTED WINE: A Zinfandel such as Château Montelena

TO SERVE 6

2 medium-size leeks, white part only
6 ounces unsalted butter
¾ cup cream
3 or 4 veal kidneys (only fresh ones with a nice pale color and white fat)
Salt and freshly ground pepper
2 tablespoons walnut oil
4 tablespoons sherry or honey vinegar
1 cup brown veal stock (page 66)
1 teaspoon minced chives

Sweetbread Tourte
Feuilletée de Ris de Veau

This is my own favorite recipe for sweetbreads. The combination of the creamy sauce, the sweetbreads, and the puff pastry is heaven.

TO SERVE 6 OR 8

2 pounds calves'
  sweetbreads
Salt and freshly ground
  pepper
Juice of half a lemon
3 tablespoons unsalted
  butter
1 large carrot, cut into
  mirepoix
1 stalk celery, cut into
  mirepoix
1 medium onion, cut
  into mirepoix
A pinch of thyme
½ cup port
1 cup chicken stock
  (page 65) or brown
  veal stock (page 66)
½ pound mushrooms,
  cut into ¼-inch dice
1 large shallot, minced
2 cups heavy cream
6 thin slices cooked
  ham, cut into brunoise
2 cooked chicken
  breasts, cut into
  brunoise
½ cup Greek or Niçoise
  olives, pitted
½ pound puff pastry
  (page 200)
1 egg, lightly beaten, for
  egg wash

1. Soak the sweetbreads in cold water overnight. Drain.
2. Preheat oven to 400°.
3. Place the sweetbreads in a saucepan and cover with cold water. Add 1 tablespoon salt, freshly ground pepper, and the lemon juice, and bring to a boil. Remove from the heat and immediately place under cold running water until cool. Remove the nerves, tubes, and extra fat.
4. Heat a heavy, oven-proof sauté pan and add 2 tablespoons butter. Sauté the *mirepoix* of carrots, celery, and onion until barely tender. Stir in the thyme and deglaze the pan with the port. Add the stock and sweetbreads and transfer to the oven for 20 minutes.
5. In a sauté pan, heat the remaining 1 tablespoon butter and, over moderate heat, sauté the mushrooms and shallot for 3 to 4 minutes.
6. Remove the sweetbreads from the pan and reserve. Strain the pan liquid into a saucepan and reduce to a glaze. Add the cream and reduce the sauce until it coats the back of a spoon. Stir in the ham, chicken, mushrooms, and olives. Boil lightly for 5 minutes.
7. Break the sweetbreads into small pieces and add to the ham-and-chicken mixture. Remove from the heat and season to taste with salt, pepper, and lemon juice. Cool slightly.
8. Roll out two thirds of the puff pastry large enough to line a 10-by-1¼-inch flan ring. Place the flan ring on a heavy baking sheet. Mold pastry into the ring and chill.
9. Increase the oven temperature to 450°.
10. Spoon in the cooled filling and brush the edge of the pastry with egg wash.
11. Roll out the remaining pastry large enough to cover the top. Press the edges together and trim. Brush with egg wash.

12. Bake the tourte for 20 minutes, reduce the heat to 350°, and cook 25 minutes longer, or until the crust is golden brown and the tourte is cooked through.

PRESENTATION: Place the *feuilletée* of sweetbreads on a serving platter and remove the flan ring. Present as is.

SUGGESTED WINE: A Sauvignon blanc

Sweetbreads in Sorrel Sauce
Ris de Veau à la Sauce Oseille

Sorrel is available all year round. For the home gardener, it is very easy to grow.

1. Soak the sweetbreads overnight in cold water.
2. Drain the sweetbreads, place them in a saucepan, and cover with cold water. Add 1 tablespoon salt and bring to a boil.
3. As soon as the water boils, remove the sweetbreads and cool them under cold running water. Remove the nerves and excess fat.
4. Cut the sorrel into julienne.
5. Slice the sweetbreads into scallops ½ inch thick. Season with salt and pepper and dust very lightly with flour.
6. In a heavy sauté pan, heat 2 tablespoons butter. Sauté the sweetbreads 3 to 4 minutes on each side, until cooked. Sweetbreads should not be overcooked. Transfer to a warm platter and keep warm.
7. In the same sauté pan, over medium heat, melt 1 tablespoon butter. Stir in the sorrel and cook until wilted.
8. Deglaze the pan with vermouth and reduce until only 1 tablespoon remains. Add the veal stock and heavy cream and reduce until the sauce coats the back of a spoon. Season to taste with salt and pepper. Whisk in 2 tablespoons butter and keep warm.
9. Heat another sauté pan and melt the remaining 1 tablespoon butter. Over medium heat, sauté the spinach until wilted.

TO SERVE 4

1¼ to 1½ pounds
  calves' sweetbreads
Salt
1 bunch sorrel
Freshly ground pepper
All-purpose flour
6 tablespoons unsalted
  butter
½ cup dry white
  vermouth
1 cup brown veal stock
  (page 66)
1 cup heavy cream
1 pound spinach,
  cleaned, with stems
  removed

PRESENTATION: On a heated serving platter, make a bed of spinach. Arrange the sweetbreads on the spinach and nap with half the sauce. Serve the remaining sauce in a separate bowl.

SUGGESTED WINE: A light red wine or a fruity white one

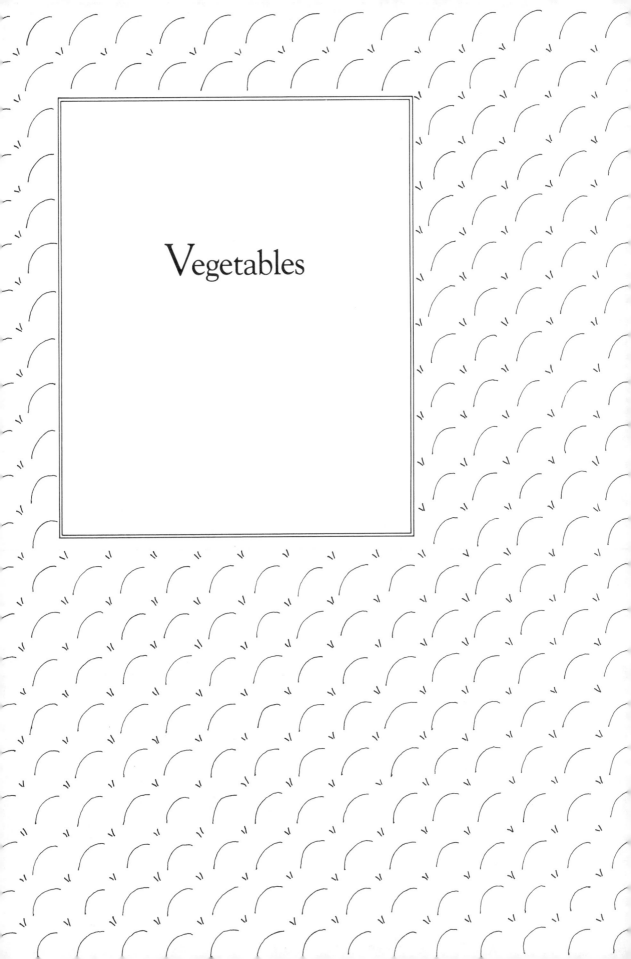

Vegetables

Purée of Artichokes

Artichoke Mousse

Green Beans in Fresh Butter

Carrot Loaf

Carrot Purée

Eggplant Gratin

Cucumbers with Dill

Celery Root Purée

Braised Endives

Leek Timbales

Macaroni with Basil

Mushrooms with *Fines Herbes*

Duxelles

Crisp Potato Flowers

Gratinéed Potatoes

Potato Purée with Truffles

Lyonnaise Potatoes

Spinach Flan with Fresh Tomato

Spinach Tart

Turnips with Parsley

Zucchini with Basil and Tomatoes

Zucchini Casserole

Some children grow up surrounded by cars and city lights, and others, as I did, grow up alongside cornstalks and neat rows of bountiful and assorted vegetables in the farmer's field.

As a child, I never had the advantages of visiting art museums or exploring libraries. But the changing of the seasons, the planting and harvesting of the fields, and mostly the countless hours of reflection I spent among the glorious scents and colors of the vegetable fields allowed me to develop my deep respect and understanding of the beauty of simplicity — in taste and aroma, form and color.

My fond memories of those fields, and some early lessons in my grandmother's kitchen, translate directly into my simple preparation and presentation of salads and vegetables. I would often eat many of the vegetables raw, having discovered that the young, small selections were most tender and sweet. Today, I still favor vegetables that retain their just-picked aroma and texture and I find this is best achieved by using only the freshest vegetables and cooking them very delicately.

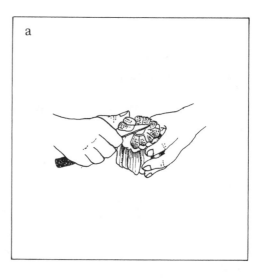

a

Purée of Artichokes

Purée d'Artichauts

This is for the weight-conscious household. It is excellent with roast meat, and I use it often as a garniture for fish.

1. Cut off the stem of each artichoke, and trim the green leaves around the bottom (a). Slice off the bottom (b), exposing the choke (c). Rub the artichoke bottoms with the cut lemon.
2. Boil artichoke bottoms in heavily salted water until they are very tender. This should take 30 to 40 minutes. Drain and cool slightly. Remove the fiber from the center of the artichoke bottoms, using a small knife or spoon.
3. Cut the artichoke bottoms into quarters; place them in a blender or food processor and purée. Rub the purée through a fine sieve or *tamis*.
4. Dilute dry milk in the water and stir into the purée. The mixture should be very smooth and stiff enough to mound or to pipe through a pastry tube.
5. Heat through and season with salt, pepper, and lemon juice.

TO SERVE 6

10 large artichokes
1 lemon, halved
3 tablespoons nonfat dry milk
½ cup water
1 teaspoon salt
½ teaspoon freshly ground pepper
Juice of 1 lemon

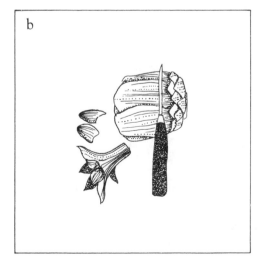

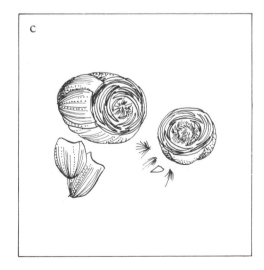

Artichoke Mousse

Mousseline d'Artichauts

This is my favorite accompaniment to lamb and a good garniture for fish. The artichokes *must* be fresh, not frozen or canned.

TO SERVE 6 OR 8

12 large artichokes
Juice of 2 lemons
1 teaspoon salt
3 tablespoons unsalted
  butter
3 tablespoons heavy
  cream
Freshly ground pepper

1. To prepare artichokes for cooking, break off stems. Cut artichokes down to bottom and trim away leaves, exposing the artichoke heart.
2. Rub entire surface of each artichoke with lemon to prevent browning.
3. Bring a large pot of water to a boil. Add salt and lemon juice, and place artichokes in pot. Cover and cook until tender, about 40 or 50 minutes.
4. Drain and remove fiber from center of artichokes. Cool.
5. Purée the artichokes in a food processor.
6. Pass through a fine sieve or *tamis* and transfer to a heavy saucepan. Stir in butter and cream and heat through. Correct seasonings with salt and freshly ground pepper. Serve immediately.

NOTE: To reheat, add 1 tablespoon butter and 1 tablespoon cream.

Green Beans in Fresh Butter

Haricots Verts au Beurre Frais

Green beans are available a good part of the year; they taste best when prepared in this simple way.

TO SERVE 4

1 pound green beans
Salt
3 tablespoons unsalted
  butter
Freshly ground pepper

1. Cut the string beans in approximately 2-inch lengths, diagonally, for attractive shapes.
2. Bring a large pan of heavily salted water to a boil. Add the beans and boil for 3 or 4 minutes, or until barely tender.
3. Drain and refresh in ice water. Drain and dry well.
4. When ready to serve, heat the butter in a sauté pan until it is foamy. Add the beans and toss in the butter for 1 or 2 minutes, until heated through. Season with salt and pepper to taste.

Carrot Loaf

Gâteau de Carotte

A perfect dinner-party vegetable. The loaf can be prepared in advance and baked when needed.

1. Sauté the carrots slowly in 2 ounces butter until tender. Chop coarsely and reserve in a large mixing bowl.
2. Over high heat, sauté the mushrooms in 1 ounce butter for 2 minutes. Chop coarsely and add them to the carrots.
3. Sauté spinach in 1 ounce butter. Chop coarsely and reserve separately. When the spinach is cool, add 1 egg and mix thoroughly.
4. Beat together the remaining eggs and the cheese. Combine this mixture thoroughly with the carrots and mushrooms. Add salt and pepper. Taste and correct seasonings if necessary.
5. Line an 8½-by-4½-by-2½-inch loaf pan with aluminum foil. Butter the foil with the remaining ounce of butter. Fill the pan with half the carrot mixture, cover with the spinach, and top with the remaining carrot mixture.
6. Place in a *bain-marie,* and bake at 400° for 1 hour and 15 minutes, or until a knife plunged into the center comes out clean.

PRESENTATION: Invert onto a warm serving platter and remove the foil. Slice and serve immediately.

TO SERVE 8

2 pounds carrots, peeled and cut into ¼-inch slices
5 ounces unsalted butter
¼ pound mushrooms, sliced
½ pound spinach, cleaned, with stems removed
5 eggs
4 ounces grated Swiss cheese
1 teaspoon salt
1 teaspoon freshly ground pepper

Carrot Purée
Mousseline de Carotte

It is very easy to obtain a wonderful mousseline of carrots. The trick is cooking the carrots slowly in butter instead of with water. Serve it as an accompaniment to a main course such as veal or chicken.

TO SERVE 4

1 pound carrots, peeled and cut in ¼-inch slices
4 tablespoons unsalted butter
Salt
Freshly ground white pepper
¼ cup heavy cream
3 tablespoons sour cream

1. In a large sauté pan, melt the butter. Add the carrots and sauté over a low flame for 20 to 25 minutes, until tender. Season to taste with salt and pepper.
2. Transfer carrots to a food processor and process until smooth. Add the heavy cream and sour cream and continue to process until well combined. (If the mousseline is too stiff, add more sour cream, a teaspoonful at a time).
3. Correct seasoning to taste.

Eggplant Gratin
Aubergines au Gratin

It is better to use small eggplants for this recipe, since they are usually firmer than the larger ones. You can prepare this ahead of time and gratinée when needed.

TO SERVE 4 OR 6

1 pound eggplant, cut in ½-inch slices
Salt
1 to 1¼ cups peeled, seeded, and chopped tomatoes
Freshly ground pepper
½ cup grated Swiss cheese

1. Salt both sides of each eggplant slice and let drain for 1 hour. Pat the slices dry.
2. Preheat oven to 350°.
3. Butter a shallow round or oval oven-proof dish. Overlap the eggplant slices to cover the bottom of the dish in a single layer. Season with pepper.
4. Spread a thin layer of chopped tomatoes over the eggplant and sprinkle with cheese.
5. Bake for 25 to 30 minutes, until the eggplant is tender when pierced with the tip of a sharp knife.

PRESENTATION: Serve as is.

Cucumbers with Dill

Concombres à l'Aneth

For this recipe young cucumbers are best because they contain fewer or undeveloped seeds.

1. Cut off the tips of the cucumbers and slice into 2-inch pieces. Quarter each piece vertically and cut into olive-shaped pieces. (Skin will automatically be removed as the pieces are shaped.)
2. Bring a pot of salted water to a boil and blanch cucumbers for 10 seconds. Refresh under cold water.
3. In a large skillet, melt the butter and add the chopped dill. Slowly sauté the cucumbers until tender but still crisp. Do not allow the butter to color.
4. Serve as an accompaniment to fish.

TO SERVE 6

2 Japanese or regular cucumbers, 8 ounces each
2 tablespoons unsalted butter
1 tablespoon chopped fresh dill

Celery Root Purée

Purée de Céleri-Rave

Celery roots are more tender in fall and winter. They contain a lot of salt, so salt them lightly at the beginning and add salt at the end if needed. This purée goes well with fish or game.

1. Cut the celery root into 1-inch cubes and place in a large saucepan.
2. Cut the potato into 1-inch cubes. Add to the celery root and cover with water. Add the salt and bring to a boil.
3. Cook at a slow boil for approximately 20 minutes, or until vegetables are tender. Drain and transfer to a food processor.
4. Process until puréed. Add the cream and butter and continue to process until thoroughly combined.
5. Correct seasoning with salt and pepper to taste. Add a pinch of cinnamon, if desired.

TO SERVE 6

1 large or 2 small celery root (celeriac), about 1 pound, peeled
1 large potato, approximately 8 ounces, peeled
1 teaspoon salt
2 tablespoons heavy cream
3 tablespoons unsalted butter
Freshly ground white pepper
A pinch of cinnamon (optional)

Braised Endives

Endives Meunière

Endives are in season during the winter months. The best ones traditionally have come from Belgium and now are grown in New Zealand. When choosing endives, look for nice white ones with leaves that are close together.

TO SERVE 6

12 medium Belgian
  endives
Salt
Freshly ground white
  pepper
2 teaspoons sugar
Juice of 1 lemon
3 tablespoons unsalted
  butter
1 tablespoon minced
  parsley

1. Preheat oven to 500°.
2. Make a small incision in the stem end of each endive (this helps them cook evenly). In a large, shallow oven-proof sauté pan, arrange the endives in a single layer. Pour in enough water to halfway cover the endives. Season with salt, pepper, sugar, and lemon juice. Add 1½ tablespoons butter.
3. Cover the pan with parchment paper and weight down with a heavy plate.
4. On the stove top, bring the contents to a boil. Transfer pan to the oven and braise for 35 to 40 minutes, until tender. (Do not allow the liquid to evaporate, or the endives will be very bitter.) Let the endives cool, then drain off the liquid.
5. In a sauté pan, heat the remaining 1½ tablespoons butter until foamy. Add endives and sauté on all sides until golden brown.

NOTE: If not serving the endives the same day, store them in their liquid after completing step 4. Proceed with step 5 just before serving.

PRESENTATION: Place on a heated platter and dust with minced parsley.

Leek Timbales

Timbales de Poireaux

Leeks are one of the finest vegetables. The many different preparations (as a vegetable, in soups, in salads) make the leek one of the most used onion varieties.

1. Preheat oven to 350°. Butter four ½-cup soufflé dishes or timbale molds.
2. Wash the leeks. Slice them thinly, crosswise. Melt butter in a sauté pan and sauté the leeks until translucent but not brown. Cool and transfer to a 4-cup measure.
3. Lightly whisk the eggs. Stir into the leeks with enough cream to make 2 cups. Mix well. Season with salt and pepper to taste.
4. Spoon into prepared molds. Place molds in a *bain-marie* and cover with buttered foil, buttered side down. Bake 25 to 30 minutes, or until set.

PRESENTATION: Unmold on individual plates as an appetizer or serve with the main course as a garniture.

TO SERVE 4

2 medium leeks, white part only
2 tablespoons unsalted butter
3 eggs
Heavy cream
Salt
Freshly ground white pepper

Macaroni with Basil

Macaroni au Gratin

This dish may be served as an appetizer or as an accompaniment to certain veal dishes.

1. In a large saucepan reduce the cream until 2 cups remain. Add the julienne of basil and continue to reduce until the cream coats the back of the spoon.
2. Pour the macaroni into a large pot of boiling, salted water. Add the oil and cook for 10 minutes, or until *al dente*. Drain.
3. Preheat the broiler.
4. Add the drained macaroni to the basil cream and stir thoroughly. Turn into a shallow buttered oven-proof serving dish.
5. Combine the cheeses and sprinkle over the macaroni. Place under the broiler for a few minutes until the cheese melts and the top is lightly browned.

TO SERVE 4 OR 5

1 quart heavy cream
1 bunch fresh basil, cut in julienne
8 ounces macaroni
1 tablespoon mild-flavored oil, such as almond or safflower
Salt
Freshly ground white pepper
¼ cup grated Parmesan cheese
¼ cup grated Swiss cheese

Mushrooms with *Fines Herbes*
Champignons aux Fines Herbes

A very simple way to prepare mushrooms, fast and liked by everyone. Serve with fish or meat.

TO SERVE 6

1½ to 2 pounds mushrooms (such as cèpes, chanterelles, champignons de Paris, or oyster mushrooms)
Juice of half a lemon
3 tablespoons unsalted butter
3 shallots, minced
1 tablespoon minced fresh tarragon, chervil, or flat-leaf parsley
Salt
Freshly ground pepper
1 tablespoon fresh fines herbes

1. Cut the mushrooms into halves or quarters. If they are small, leave whole.
2. Place in a bowl and sprinkle with lemon juice. In a large sauté pan, heat 2 tablespoons butter. Add the shallots and tarragon and sauté over moderate heat for 1 minute.
3. Add the mushrooms and sauté until tender. Strain off any excess liquid, return mushrooms to the pan with the remaining 1 tablespoon butter, and over high heat cook until golden brown.
4. Season with salt and pepper.

PRESENTATION: Place in a warm serving dish, sprinkle with *fines herbes* and serve.

Duxelles

This is a basic recipe. *Duxelles* can be used as a stuffing, as a filling for omelettes, or as the base for mushroom soup.

TO MAKE APPROXIMATELY 1 CUP

3 tablespoons unsalted butter
1 pound mushrooms, minced
2 medium shallots, minced
3 to 4 tablespoons heavy cream
Salt
Freshly ground pepper

1. Melt the butter in a hot sauté pan. Add the mushrooms and shallots, and sauté over moderate heat until all the liquid evaporates. Stir occasionally so that the mixture cooks evenly.
2. Stir in enough cream to bind the mushroom mixture.
3. Season to taste with salt and pepper. Use as directed.

Crisp Potato Flowers
Galettes de Pommes de Terre

This makes an ideal accompaniment to duck.

1. Preheat oven to 450°.
2. Thinly slice the potato. Place the slices in a bowl and toss with salt, pepper, and duck fat so that they are well coated.
3. Arrange the potato slices in a flowerlike fashion in individual baking pans.
4. Bake 20 to 25 minutes, or until potatoes are brown and crisp.

PRESENTATION: Turn out on a plate to accompany almost any entrée.

SPECIAL EQUIPMENT: 2 nonstick baking pans, 4 inches in diameter and ½ inch deep

TO SERVE 2

1 medium baking potato, peeled
Salt
Freshly ground pepper
1 to 2 tablespoons melted duck fat or unsalted butter

Gratinéed Potatoes
Gratin Dauphinois

This hearty but elegant dish is the ideal accompaniment for roast lamb or any grilled meat.

1. Preheat oven to 325°.
2. Slice the potatoes ⅛ inch thick. In a large bowl, combine the potatoes, cream, minced garlic, salt, and pepper. Place in a casserole and cook in a *bain-marie* for 1 to 1½ hours or until the potatoes are just tender. Remove from oven.
3. Raise the oven temperature to 450°.
4. Rub a large gratin dish with the remaining clove of garlic and spread with 4 tablespoons of the *crème fraîche*. Pour in half the potatoes. Spread with remaining *crème*

TO SERVE 6

12 medium potatoes, peeled
3 cups heavy cream
3 cloves garlic (2 of them minced)
1 teaspoon salt
½ teaspoon freshly ground pepper
6 tablespoons crème fraîche
6 tablespoons grated Swiss cheese

fraîche and sprinkle with the grated cheese. Set gratin dish in a *bain-marie* and place in the hot oven until the potatoes are brown (about 15 minutes).

PRESENTATION: Serve from the gratin dish.

Potato Purée with Truffles

Mousseline de Pommes de Terre aux Truffes

An old favorite of the Périgord region. It is simple to prepare and certainly expensive, but worth it.

TO SERVE 6

2½ pounds Idaho
 potatoes, peeled
Salted water
1 whole truffle
¾ cup cream
2 to 3 tablespoons truffle
 juice
4 ounces butter
Salt and freshly ground
 white pepper to taste

1. Cut potatoes into large pieces of equal size. Cover with salted water. Bring to a boil and cook until tender. Drain thoroughly.
2. Cut truffle into very fine julienne.
3. In a small saucepan, heat the cream.
4. Purée the potatoes. (Either force them through a sieve or place them in a food processor and turn it on for a few seconds.) Add butter, hot cream, and truffle juice.
5. Stir in the julienne of truffles. Correct seasonings with salt and pepper.

Lyonnaise Potatoes

Pommes Lyonnaise

TO SERVE 6

1 medium onion, thinly
 sliced
4 tablespoons clarified
 unsalted butter
3 large Idaho or baking
 potatoes, peeled
1½ teaspoons salt
1 teaspoon freshly
 ground pepper

You must do this in a nonstick pan; otherwise the potatoes will not unmold properly.

1. Preheat oven to 400°.
2. Sauté sliced onions in 1 tablespoon butter until lightly golden brown. Reserve.
3. Cut the potatoes into ⅛-inch slices. (Do not soak in water when sliced.) Immediately mix with the remaining 3 tablespoons butter, salt, and pepper.

4. In a 10-inch nonstick baking pan, arrange half the potatoes in one layer. Cover with the sautéed onions and top with the remaining potatoes.
5. Bake approximately 30 minutes, until the potatoes are golden brown and crispy. If the underside of the potatoes is not browned when the potatoes are tender, finish over high heat on the stove top.

NOTE: Potatoes may be baked in individual 4-inch pans for 12 to 15 minutes.

PRESENTATION: Invert potatoes on a platter and serve immediately.

SPECIAL EQUIPMENT:
One 10-inch nonstick pan or six 4-inch nonstick pans

Spinach Flan with Fresh Tomato
Darioles d'Épinard à la Tomate Fraîche

This can be served as an appetizer or as an accompaniment to fish or meat. A knife carefully slipped around the sides of the timbales will aid in the unmolding of the *darioles*.

TO SERVE 4

1. Preheat oven to 400°.
2. Sauté the spinach and garlic in 3 tablespoons butter for 5 minutes. Transfer the mixture to a chopping board and chop coarsely. Set aside to cool.
3. In a bowl, combine milk, cream, eggs, salt, pepper, and nutmeg. Add the sautéed spinach and mix well.
4. Butter the *dariole* molds. Fill them with the spinach mixture and cover the molds with buttered foil, butter side down.
5. Place the molds in a *bain-marie* and bake for 20 minutes, or until they are firm to the touch.
6. Blanch, peel, seed, and roughly chop the tomatoes.
7. Over high heat, sauté the minced shallot in the remaining 1 tablespoon butter for 1 minute. Add tomatoes and reduce until the liquid is evaporated. Season to taste with salt and pepper. Reserve until ready to serve.

¾ pound spinach, cleaned, with stems removed
1 clove garlic, minced
4 tablespoons unsalted butter
½ cup milk
½ cup heavy cream
3 eggs
1 teaspoon salt
Freshly ground pepper
A pinch of nutmeg
6 medium tomatoes
1 shallot, minced

PRESENTATION: Unmold the *darioles* onto heated plates and serve the chopped tomatoes on the side.

Luncheon Variation: Serve the *darioles* topped with a poached egg and surrounded by chopped tomatoes.

SPECIAL EQUIPMENT: Four ½-cup *dariole* molds

Spinach Tart
Tarte d'Épinard

Reserved scraps of puff pastry can be used for this tart. To keep the pastry crisp, be sure the spinach is well drained before placing it on the circles of pastry. Other vegetables may be substituted for the spinach. The amounts are up to you.

TO SERVE ANY NUMBER

Puff pastry (page 200)
Spinach
Unsalted butter
Garlic clove
Salt
Freshly ground pepper
Peeled, seeded, and
  chopped fresh tomatoes

1. Preheat oven to 350°.
2. Roll out pastry very thin and cut it into 4- or 5-inch circles. Prick all over with the tines of a fork. Bake until the pastry is golden brown.
3. Sauté fresh spinach in butter together with the garlic clove, until wilted. Season with salt and pepper to taste, remove garlic, and divide among the pastry circles.

PRESENTATION: Garnish with chopped tomatoes and serve as an appetizer or luncheon entrée. It is very good when served with *beurre blanc* (page 106).

Turnips with Parsley

Navets Sautés au Persil

Young turnips must be used for this recipe. Older ones can be woody. Serve this dish with a main course of lamb or duck.

1. Cut the turnips into quarters or turn them into oval shapes (see page 14).
2. Blanch the turnips in boiling, salted water for 10 minutes.
3. In a sauté pan, melt 2 tablespoons butter. Add the turnips and, over a low flame, sauté for 8 to 10 minutes, or until just tender when pierced with the tip of a sharp knife.
4. When tender, stir in the parsley, the remaining tablespoon of butter, and pepper to taste.

TO SERVE 4

4 turnips, about 4
  ounces each, peeled
Salt
3 tablespoons unsalted
  butter
2 tablespoons minced
  parsley
Freshly ground pepper

Zucchini with Basil and Tomatoes

Courgettes avec Basilic et Tomates

The zucchini should be small and firm, the tomatoes ripe and juicy; and only fresh basil will give you the special flavor.

1. Cut the zucchini into ¼-inch slices or ¼-inch cubes.
2. Heat the olive oil in a large sauté pan. Add the zucchini, garlic, basil, and tomatoes. Over high heat, cook until the zucchini is tender.
3. Season with salt and pepper to taste. Serve hot or cold.
4. If using the onion, sauté briefly in the hot olive oil before adding the remaining ingredients.

PRESENTATION: Serve in a heated serving bowl or arrange attractively on each plate as an accompaniment to an entrée.

TO SERVE 6

12 to 15 baby zucchini,
  approximately 1 pound
2 tablespoons olive oil
2 cloves garlic, minced
3 branches basil leaves,
  removed from stems
  and cut into fine
  julienne
3 ripe medium tomatoes,
  peeled, seeded, diced,
  and drained
Salt
Freshly ground pepper
½ medium onion,
  minced (optional)

Zucchini Casserole
Tian de Courgettes

Use small, firm zucchini and very ripe tomatoes for the best flavor. This can be made ahead of time and baked at the last minute.

TO SERVE 6

2 medium onions
4 tablespoons olive oil
¾ pound zucchini
2 pounds tomatoes
3 cloves garlic, halved
Salt
Freshly ground pepper
Fresh or dried thyme

1. Preheat oven to 400°.
2. Peel the onions and cut into fine slices. Cook slowly in olive oil until translucent. Do not allow to color.
3. Cut zucchini into ¼-inch slices. Reserve.
4. Peel and seed tomatoes and cut into ¼-inch slices. Reserve.
5. Rub the inside of a large gratin dish with garlic. Arrange a layer of onions on the bottom of the dish. Season with salt and pepper. Over the onions, arrange tomatoes and zucchini in alternating rows. Season with salt and pepper. Sprinkle with thyme and drizzle with olive oil.
6. Bake for approximately 30 minutes, or until zucchini is tender. Press vegetables flat with a wide spatula or the back of a spoon two or three times during the baking period.

PRESENTATION: Serve directly from the gratin dish.

VARIATIONS:
1. When the vegetables are cooked, sprinkle with grated Swiss cheese and place under the broiler to melt.
2. To serve as a lunch or a light supper entrée, cook the vegetables for 20 minutes, using individual gratin dishes. Make a well in the center and break one or two eggs into the well. Return to the oven and bake until the eggs are cooked.

Salads

Pigeon Salad with Walnuts

Duck Salad

Summer Salad with Fresh Tuna

Spinach Salad

Warm Lobster Salad

Fisherman's Salad

Salad with Scallops and Watercress

Ma Maison's Chicken Salad

Asparagus Vinaigrette

Baumanière Salad

Spring Salad

Green Beans and Mushrooms with Walnut Dressing

A good salad can consist of a few sweet inner leaves of a young butter lettuce sprinkled with a feathery light vinegar-mustard dressing or the successful combination of a variety of vegetables and assorted condiments and herbs. Regardless of content, the most important "ingredient" is freshness and quality. No amount of dressing or quantity of herbs will disguise the disappointing texture and flavor of wilted, overly mature vegetables. Select your vegetables carefully.

American cuisine has traditionally made use of many salad dressings, most of which lack a delicacy of taste and consistency that I find essential if a salad, particularly a green or simple mixed one, is to maintain a light, refreshing quality. For me, the sharpness and tartness of vinegar and mustard mingled with the body and fragrance of a fine oil, fresh herbs, a dash of freshly ground pepper, and a touch of salt is the ideal enhancement for any garden green or raw vegetable.

Since so many people have become more health-conscious, salads play an important role in meal planning. A salad served in small portions makes a perfect appetizer — light and stimulating for the palate; a larger portion becomes a satisfying yet refreshing main course on a warm day. A simple salad served with a slice of cheese is a classic and natural way to complete a meal.

I have not included many recipes for simple green salads because you can find them in other cookbooks. Instead, I offer some of my favorite creations that are now classics at Ma Maison. Many embody warm and cold ingredients of different textures, which, when combined, create a surprising taste. What is most delightful and notable about these selections is the blending of carefully prepared and seasoned duck, pigeon, or fish with greens and other vegetables to create attractive, delicious salads without sacrificing the fresh, light quality essential to the ideal salad.

Pigeon Salad with Walnuts

Petite Salade de Pigeon aux Noix

If pigeons are not available, pheasants or Cornish hens may be substituted. My recipe calls for walnuts, but for a more delicate taste, try pine nuts.

1. Preheat oven to 450°.
2. Separate the pigeon breasts from the legs. (Reserve the legs for another dish.) Season the breasts with salt and pepper. Heat an oven-proof sauté pan and brown the breasts in oil. Then bake for 15 minutes; the meat should still be pink. Remove from the oven and keep warm.
3. Deglaze the pan with vinegar, add the chicken stock, and reduce by half. Whisk in 2 tablespoons of the butter, a small amount at a time, and keep warm.
4. Sauté the shallot and mushrooms in the remaining 1 tablespoon butter. Set aside and keep warm.
5. In a salad bowl, toss the salad greens, nuts, and vinaigrette. Slice the pigeon breast into thin slices.

PRESENTATION: Place the tossed salad on cold salad plates, arrange the mushrooms on top, and cover with sliced pigeon breasts. Nap the breasts with the vinegar sauce.

SUGGESTED WINE: A lightly chilled Cabernet from northern California

TO SERVE 6

6 pigeons, 8 ounces each
Salt
Freshly ground pepper
1 teaspoon mild-flavored oil, such as almond or safflower
6 tablespoons good red or sherry wine vinegar
6 tablespoons chicken stock (page 65)
3 tablespoons unsalted butter
1 medium shallot, minced
½ pound wild mushrooms, such as chanterelles, mousserons, or Japanese tree mushrooms (cultivated white mushrooms may be substituted)
1 head curly endive
4 heads limestone or Boston lettuce
4 tablespoons walnuts
4 tablespoons mustard vinaigrette (page 101)

Duck Salad
Salade de Canard

One of my favorite creations and a popular choice of Ma Maison regulars, this salad combines the flavors of French, American, and Japanese cuisines.

TO SERVE 2

1 whole duck with legs removed
2 tablespoons red wine vinegar
½ cup duck stock (page 67)
¼ pound Japanese tree mushrooms
2 tablespoons butter
1 tablespoon minced shallots
1 tablespoon minced fresh tarragon
4 French bread slices, ½ inch thick
1 clove garlic, peeled
1 head curly endive, washed
¼ cup mustard vinaigrette (page 101)
3 medium tomatoes, peeled, seeded, and diced into ¼-inch pieces

1. Preheat the oven to 550°.
2. Prick the duck with a fork. Place, breast side up, in a roasting pan and roast for 20 minutes. (It is important to roast the duck breast side up; you will find that the meat will retain more of its natural juices and remain tender and moist.) The breast should be crispy on the outside and pink on the inside. Remove and keep warm.
3. Pour off the grease and deglaze the pan with the vinegar. Add the duck stock, bring it to a boil, and reduce the liquid by two thirds. Keep this sauce warm.
4. Sauté the mushrooms in 1 tablespoon butter together with the shallots and tarragon.
5. Sauté the bread slices in the remaining 1 tablespoon butter. Remove the bread slices and rub them with the garlic.

PRESENTATION: Toss the curly endive with the vinaigrette and place it in the center of a platter. Surround with tomatoes, bread slices, and sautéed mushrooms. Slice the warm duck breast against the grain and arrange the slices over the endive. Pour the deglazed sauce over the slices.

SUGGESTED WINE: A hearty Zinfandel or a Merlot

Summer Salad with Fresh Tuna

Salade d'Été au Thon Cru

This is a California version of the French *salade Niçoise*. The tuna must be absolutely fresh; salmon or bass may be substituted.

1. *To make the marinade*: In a salad bowl, combine lime juice, anchovies, tarragon, shallots, olive oil, salt, and pepper. Mix well.
2. Cut tuna into ¼-inch-thick strips. Marinate for 1 hour.
3. Break up two heads of lettuce, and combine with cucumber, avocado, eggs, celery heart, and tomatoes. Mix well with vinaigrette.

PRESENTATION: Arrange remaining head of lettuce leaves on a platter. Form a dome with the vegetables and top with tuna.

TO SERVE 6

Juice of 2 limes
6 anchovy fillets, chopped
1 tablespoon chopped fresh tarragon
3 shallots, chopped
3 tablespoons olive oil
Salt and freshly ground pepper
1 pound fresh tuna
3 heads butter lettuce
1 cucumber, peeled, seeded, and chopped
1 avocado, peeled and sliced
2 hard-boiled eggs, chopped
1 celery heart, chopped
6 tomatoes, peeled, seeded, and sliced
½ cup mustard vinaigrette (page 101)

Spinach Salad

Salade d'Épinards

Created in America and often imitated in France, spinach salad can be prepared all year round.

1. Cook bacon until crisp. Drain it on a paper towel.
2. Place spinach in a large salad bowl. Add mushrooms, eggs, bacon, and cheese. Dress with mustard vinaigrette and toss.

PRESENTATION: Arrange on individual plates and serve.

TO SERVE 6

½ pound bacon, cut into ½-inch slices
2 pounds spinach, washed, dried, and stems removed
¾ pound mushrooms, sliced
3 hard-boiled eggs, chopped
3 cups Swiss cheese, shredded
½ cup mustard vinaigrette (page 101)

Warm Lobster Salad

Salade d'Homard Tiède

This is an expensive but worthwhile salad that can be served as a luncheon entrée or first course at dinner. Using the lobster while it is still warm gives maximum flavor. A truffle butter would be a wonderful substitution for the simple *beurre blanc*.

TO SERVE 6

6 heads limestone lettuce (or substitute butter lettuce)
1 ripe avocado, sliced
2 medium tomatoes, peeled, seeded, and coarsely chopped
1 pound green beans, cooked until tender but still crisp
6 firm white mushrooms, sliced
2 gallons court bouillon (page 66)
6 live lobsters, 1 pound each
2 tablespoons dry vermouth
6 tablespoons heavy cream
½ pound unsalted butter, cut into small pieces
Salt
Freshly ground pepper
Lemon juice
2 tablespoons caviar

1. Prepare all the vegetables. In the center of each of six soup plates, arrange a mound of lettuce. On the rim of each plate, arrange avocado slices, tomatoes, green beans, and mushrooms so they surround the lettuce mound.
2. Bring the court bouillon to a boil and cook the lobsters for 5 minutes (or until done).
3. While the lobsters are cooking, reduce the vermouth and cream until it coats the back of the spoon. Whisk in the butter, one small piece at a time. Season to taste with salt, pepper, and lemon juice. Keep warm.

PRESENTATION: For each soup plate slice one lobster tail and place on top of the lettuce mound. Place the claw meat decoratively in one corner and cover the lobster with warm sauce. With a teaspoon, place an equal amount of caviar on each plate. Serve immediately.

SUGGESTED WINE: A Johannisberg Riesling

Fisherman's Salad

Salade des Pêcheurs

I like to cook the shellfish shortly before serving, so that it does not need refrigeration; it loses its flavor if chilled.

TO SERVE 6

1. *To make the vinaigrette:* Combine vinegar, mustard, lemon juice, and tarragon. Whisk in oil. Season with salt and pepper to taste.
2. Cut carrots, leek, and turnip into fine julienne. Sauté in the butter until they are *al dente*. Cool and marinate in the vinaigrette.
3. Bring the court bouillon to a boil. Plunge lobster into the liquid and cook for 5 minutes. Remove from court bouillon and cool.
4. Bring the court bouillon back to a boil. Add the shrimp and cook just until the liquid returns to a boil. Remove the shrimp and set aside to cool.
5. In a small saucepan, bring ¼ cup court bouillon to a boil. Add the scallops and cook for about 2 minutes. Do not overcook. Remove from liquid and cool.
6. Remove shells from lobster and shrimp. Slice all the seafood into serving-size pieces.
7. Carefully wash and dry the lettuce or watercress. Remove the vegetables from vinaigrette and reserve. Toss greens with remaining vinaigrette.

PRESENTATION: Arrange dressed greens on six chilled plates. Sprinkle with vegetable julienne. Top with sliced seafood. (Garnish with thin slices of truffle if you're feeling extravagant.)

SUGGESTED WINE: A Sauvignon blanc

3 tablespoons good red or sherry wine vinegar
2 tablespoons Dijon mustard
Juice of half a lemon
2 sprigs fresh tarragon leaves, minced
1 cup almond oil (or any oil with a very mild or neutral flavor)
Salt and freshly ground pepper
1 or 2 medium carrots
1 leek
1 or 2 medium turnips
1 ounce unsalted butter
1 recipe court bouillon (page 66)
1 live lobster, 1½ pounds
1 pound fresh shrimp (16 per pound)
12 large scallops (with small side muscles removed as necessary)
2 heads butter lettuce or 3 bunches watercress

Salad with Scallops and Watercress
Salade de Coquilles Saint-Jacques au Cresson

Undercooked scallops are tender and sweet; when over-cooked, they become tough and rubbery. Bay scallops can be used instead of sea scallops in this recipe.

TO SERVE 6

Salad:

15 sea scallops, medium-size (with small side muscles removed as necessary)
Juice of half a lemon
Salt and freshly ground pepper
18 peeled asparagus spears
6 ripe medium-size tomatoes
3 bunches watercress
1 or 2 hard-boiled eggs
1 bunch chives, chopped

Vinaigrette:

1 tablespoon good red or sherry wine vinegar
1 tablespoon lemon juice
1 tablespoon Dijon mustard
1 tablespoon chopped chives
Salt and freshly ground pepper
6 to 8 tablespoons almond oil (or any oil with a very mild or neutral flavor)

To prepare the salad:
1. Cut each scallop into two or three slices. Poach lightly, for approximately 1 minute, in lemon juice, water to cover, salt, and pepper. Drain and refrigerate.
2. Cook asparagus in boiling, salted water until tender but still crisp. Refresh in cold water. Cut each spear in half. Refrigerate.
3. Plunge tomatoes into boiling water for 30 seconds. Remove and refresh immediately in cold water. Remove skin. Refrigerate.
4. Wash watercress two or three times until absolutely clean.
5. Chop eggs coarsely.

To make the vinaigrette:
1. Using a wire whisk, combine vinegar, lemon juice, and mustard.
2. Whisk in chives and season lightly with salt and pepper.
3. Slowly add almond oil, whisking all the while. Correct seasonings.

PRESENTATION: To assemble salad, arrange bouquets of watercress on six individual plates. Sprinkle a spoonful of dressing over the watercress. Slice the tomatoes and arrange decoratively around the watercress. Arrange asparagus between scallops to form a dome. Sprinkle with chives and chopped eggs. Nap with additional dressing. Serve very cold.

SUGGESTED WINE: A crisp white wine such as an Entre-deux-Mers

Ma Maison's Chicken Salad

Salade de Poulet "Ma Maison"

The chicken should be torn apart and mixed with all the seasonings when still warm. It does not have to be refrigerated and should be served at room temperature.

1. Remove the skin from the chicken. Peel meat from the bones and shred. Do not cut with a knife.
2. Peel and core the apple. Cut into ½-inch cubes.
3. Cut the celery stalk into ¼-inch cubes.
4. Mix chicken, apple, celery, capers, and mustard. Add enough mayonnaise to coat lightly.
5. Taste and correct seasoning with salt, pepper, and lemon juice. Add more mustard if desired. Serve without refrigeration.

PRESENTATION: Season lettuce with mustard vinaigrette and place it in the center of a serving platter. Top with chicken salad and garnish with tomatoes, green beans, and slices of hard-boiled egg.

SUGGESTED WINE: A Pinot Chardonnay

TO SERVE 4

1 3-pound chicken, boiled
1 medium-size Golden Delicious apple
1 stalk celery
1 tablespoon capers
2 tablespoons Moutarde de Meaux
½ cup mayonnaise (page 102), approximately
Salt
Freshly ground pepper
Lemon juice
¼ cup mustard vinaigrette (page 101)

Garnish (optional):
Slices of hard-boiled egg
Cooked green beans
Tomato slices
2 heads Boston lettuce, washed and broken up

Asparagus Vinaigrette

Asperges Vinaigrette

It is very important to cook asparagus in boiling salted water until *al dente* only; it should still be crisp. To achieve a good color, refresh very quickly in a bowl of cold water and ice cubes. Never refrigerate asparagus or it will lose all its taste. For the best flavor, serve it lukewarm.

1. Peel the asparagus.
2. In a large pot, bring heavily salted water to a boil. Place asparagus in the water and cook until tender but still firm (about 5 minutes from the time the water returns to a boil).

TO SERVE ANY NUMBER

4 to 6 asparagus spears per person
2 tablespoons vinaigrette per person

3. Remove the asparagus from the pot and refresh in ice water to stop the cooking process.

PRESENTATION: Arrange asparagus on individual plates and spoon over the dressing. When the asparagus is served warm, the vinaigrette can be replaced by a *sauce mousseline* (page 105) or a *beurre blanc* (page 106). Wine and asparagus do not go well together.

Baumanière Salad
Salade Baumanière

This is served in the spring and summer at L'Oustau de Baumanière, where I spent a good part of my apprenticeship.

TO SERVE 6

6 medium tomatoes
12 medium asparagus
  spears or green beans
6 medium Belgian
  endives
1 medium avocado
2 or 3 artichoke
  bottoms, cooked
6 tablespoons heavy
  cream
Salt
Freshly ground pepper
Juice of 1 lemon
2 tablespoons minced
  chives
1 cup mustard
  vinaigrette (page 101)
3 heads limestone lettuce
  (or substitute Boston or
  butter lettuce)
1 tablespoon pine nuts
  or diced walnuts
6 thin slices prosciutto,
  cut into julienne

1. Peel, seed, and dice the tomatoes. Place them in a strainer to drain.
2. Peel and cook the asparagus (or green beans) in salted boiling water for 4 to 5 minutes, or until tender but still crisp. Refresh in cold water, pat dry, and reserve.
3. Cut the endives into ½-inch slices. Reserve 24 nice leaves.
4. Cut the asparagus, avocado, and artichoke bottoms into ⅜-inch cubes.
5. Whip the cream until stiff and season it with salt, pepper, lemon juice, and 1 tablespoon chives. Reserve in the refrigerator.
6. Prepare the vinaigrette. Mix the artichokes, asparagus, lettuce, pine nuts, and sliced endive with enough of the dressing to coat the salad lightly.

PRESENTATION: On a large round platter arrange the reserved endive leaves to form a star. Spoon the salad on top of the center of the star. Decorate with the diced tomatoes and prosciutto. Garnish with the seasoned whipped cream and sprinkle with remaining chives.

Spring Salad
Salade de Printemps

The combination of the cold greens and the warm dressing gives this salad its interesting flavor.

1. Wash all the salad greens and dry thoroughly. Combine them, reserving a few limestone leaves for garniture. Tear any oversized or long leaves into bite-size pieces.
2. *To make the hollandaise*: Combine egg yolks, water, lemon juice, salt, and pepper in a bowl set over simmering water. Using a whisk, whip until mixture is thick. Allow to cool slightly and whisk in the soft butter, one small piece at a time.
3. Meanwhile, in a 6-quart stockpot, bring salted water to a boil. Add asparagus and cook until *al dente*, 4 to 6 minutes, and remove from the water right away. Set aside and keep warm.
4. Toss the salad greens with the avocado, mushrooms, and vinaigrette.

PRESENTATION: Place the tossed salad on individual salad plates. Top with the hot asparagus, cover with *hollandaise*, and sprinkle with chopped herbs.

TO SERVE 6

6 heads limestone lettuce (or substitute Boston or butter lettuce)
6 bunches arugula (roquette) or watercress
1 head curly endive
3 egg yolks
2 tablespoons water
Lemon juice
Salt
Freshly ground pepper
3 tablespoons unsalted butter, at room temperature
36 asparagus spears, peeled
2 avocados, peeled and sliced
½ pound white, firm mushrooms, sliced
1 recipe mustard vinaigrette (page 101)
1 teaspoon minced fresh herbs (tarragon, chives, and parsley)

Green Beans and Mushrooms with Walnut Dressing

Salade d'Haricots Verts et Champignons au Noix

Small green beans and large, white, firm mushrooms are necessary for this salad's taste and appearance.

TO SERVE 6

1 pound small green
  beans
1 pound large white
  mushrooms
Juice of 1 lemon
2 tablespoons walnuts
1 tablespoon Dijon
  mustard
2 tablespoons sherry
  wine vinegar
Salt and freshly ground
  pepper to taste
½ cup light oil, such as
  almond oil
1 tablespoon minced
  fresh tarragon or chives

1. Remove the ends and strings of the green beans. Cook in boiling, salted water until *al dente*. Refresh in ice water.
2. Slice the mushrooms into strips the size of the beans. Sprinkle with lemon juice.
3. In a blender or food processor, purée the walnuts, mustard, vinegar, salt, and pepper. Add the oil and blend well.
4. Combine green beans and mushrooms. Add dressing to taste, and refrigerate any unused dressing.

PRESENTATION: Arrange the salad on a serving platter. Sprinkle with minced tarragon or chives.

Doughs

Sugarless Pastry Dough

Sweet Pastry Dough

Puff Pastry

Cream Puff Paste

Crêpe Batter

Croissants

Brioche

Walnut Bread

Pasta

Technically, a dough is a simple flour-water mixture. It becomes refined with the addition of butter, eggs, cream, sugar, and other ingredients. Some cooks might include margarine with this list; in my opinion margarine can never replace butter in any dough.

Dough containing large amounts of butter, such as puff pastry, should always be prepared in the morning, when the kitchen is cool, since heat causes the butter to run out of the dough, making the combining of ingredients very difficult.

Some of these doughs will require a certain amount of savoir-faire and even more muscle power. A good food processor or electric mixer will prove most helpful.

By mastering these basic recipes and techniques, you will be able to prepare an astonishing number of dishes, from appetizers through desserts. From the simple pie dough used to mold a tart shell, you will soon advance to the more complex technique of the flaky croissant. Similarly, you may begin making desserts with unadorned sugar dough, but with patience and practice you can shortly discover the more imposing secrets of airy puff pastry.

Sugarless Pastry Dough
Pâte Brisée

Use this pastry for savory dishes such as quiche and *oeufs pochés au beurre rouge*.

1. In an electric mixer, using the paddle, cream the butter and salt. Add the eggs and milk and mix for a few seconds.
2. Add all the flour at one time and beat just until the pastry forms a ball.
3. Chill at least 1 hour before use.

NOTE: If you do not have an electric mixer or food processor, place the flour on a clean work surface, form a crater in the center, place all the remaining ingredients in the crater, and knead well together.

TO MAKE 2 POUNDS

12 ounces unsalted butter at room temperature
2 teaspoons salt
2 eggs
2 tablespoons milk
1 pound all-purpose flour (4 to 5 cups)

Sweet Pastry Dough
Pâte Sucrée

Pâte sucrée is used for most dessert shells as well as for small cookies.

1. In a food processor, combine the flour, butter, sugar, and vanilla. Process until mixture resembles coarse meal, approximately 15 seconds.
2. Combine the egg yolks and 1 tablespoon water and, with the motor running, add to the flour mixture and process until a ball forms on the blade, adding more water if necessary.
3. Seal in plastic wrap and refrigerate overnight.

TO MAKE 1 POUND

½ pound all-purpose flour
5 ounces cold unsalted butter, cut into 5 pieces
¼ cup sugar
2 to 3 drops vanilla extract
2 egg yolks
1 to 2 tablespoons water

Puff Pastry
Pâte Feuilletée

This is an extremely versatile pastry. I recommend preparing a large amount at one time and cutting it into desired quantities and shapes for freezing. (It freezes very successfully. Remove it from the freezer and place in the refrigerator the day before you plan to use it.)

TO MAKE APPROXIMATELY 2½ POUNDS

Détrempe:

½ pound pastry flour
½ pound all-purpose flour
3 ounces chilled unsalted butter, cut into six pieces
2 teaspoons salt
¾ to 1 cup ice water

Pastry butter for rolling:

1¼ pounds unsalted butter, chilled
¼ cup all-purpose flour

1. *To make the* détrempe: Combine the pastry flour, all-purpose flour, butter, and salt in a food processor or electric mixer. Process until the mixture resembles coarse meal. With machine running, add just enough water to make a stiff but pliable dough. Shape into a flattened ball (a) and wrap tightly in plastic wrap. Refrigerate for 30 minutes.
2. Remove the butter for rolling from the refrigerator, sprinkle with flour, and knead until soft but still cold. Shape into a rectangular block, approximately 6 by 9 inches (b).
3. Remove the *détrempe* from the refrigerator. Cut a deep cross in the dough (c). Spread out the sections of dough so that the center is the thickest part (d). Roll it in opposite directions to form a four-leaf clover, keeping the center thicker (e). Place the block of butter diagonally in the center of the cloverleaf (f) and bring the edges of the *détrempe* to the center, enclosing the butter completely (g). Wrap tightly in plastic wrap and chill for 1 hour.
4. *To make the "turns":* Place the chilled dough on a lightly floured surface. Pound lightly and evenly with your rolling pin to make the dough malleable. Roll out into a rectangle approximately 9 by 16 inches (h). With the 9-inch side in front of you, fold into thirds, starting with the bottom third (i) and folding over the top third (j). You have now completed the first turn.
5. Turn the dough so that the narrow end faces you (k), keeping the seam on your right (a quarter turn). Again, roll out the dough into a rectangle approximately 9 by 16 inches (l) and again fold (m) into thirds (n). You have now completed two turns. Wrap in plastic wrap and refrigerate for 30 minutes.

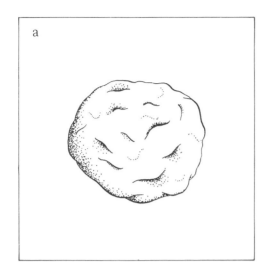

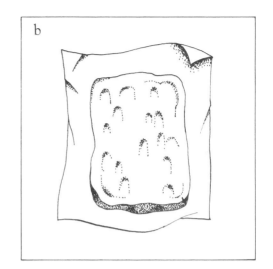

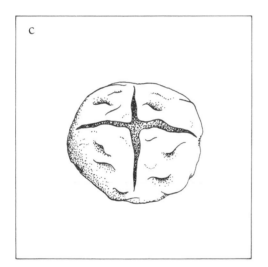

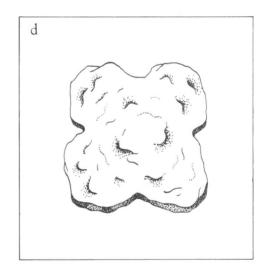

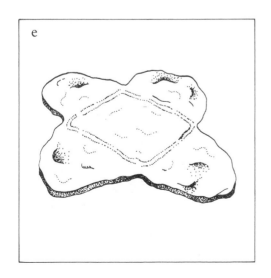

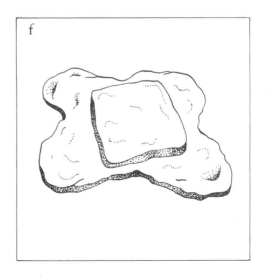

g

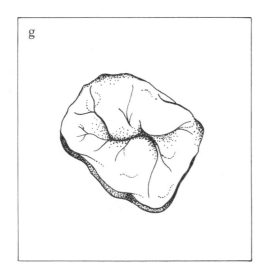

h

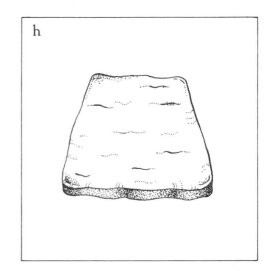

i

j

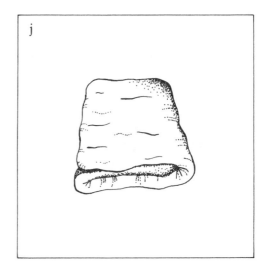

k

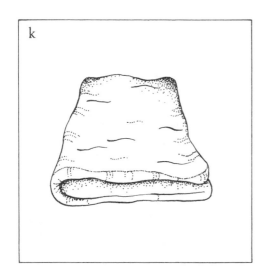

l

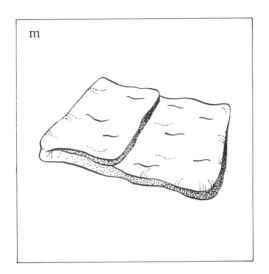

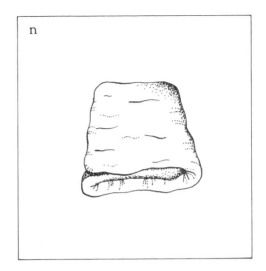

6. Pound the dough evenly and again roll out into a 9-by-16-inch rectangle. Complete two more turns as in steps 4 and 5 to make four turns. Wrap in plastic wrap and refrigerate for 50 to 60 minutes. Repeat procedure for two more turns to make a total of six turns. Refrigerate until needed.

7. Use as desired. The dough may be frozen successfully for up to six months if wrapped airtight.

Thoughts on making the pastry:

1. Do not overwork the *détrempe* or it will be impossible to roll out. If the *détrempe* is rubbery and not pliable, it is best to toss it out and begin again.

2. When making the butter-and-*détrempe* package, the two parts should be about the same temperature and consistency.

3. As you roll and turn the pastry, use as little flour as possible, brushing away excess flour with a large pastry brush.

4. The chilling times are approximate; the important thing to remember is that the pastry should be chilled all the way through and have sufficient time to rest between turns.

5. After the first two turns, it is possible to refrigerate the pastry overnight and then continue with the remaining turns.

Cream Puff Paste
Pâte à Chou

This is an all-purpose dough that can be used for pastries as well as savouries, depending upon the filling.

TO MAKE APPROXIMATELY 48 PUFFS

1 cup milk
4 ounces butter
½ tablespoon sugar
1 teaspoon salt
1 cup flour
5 eggs
1 egg, lightly beaten, for egg wash

1. Bring milk, butter, sugar, and salt to a boil. Add flour all at once and stir over low heat until mixture comes away from the sides of the pan. Continue stirring, over very low heat, until a film forms on bottom of the pan.
2. Using a large food processor or a wooden spoon, incorporate the eggs, one at a time, until mixture is smooth and shiny.
3. Preheat oven to 375°.
4. Fill a pastry bag and pipe out pastry into 1-inch mounds. Brush with egg wash and bake for 10 minutes. Reduce heat to 325° and bake 10 minutes longer. Do not peek while *choux* are baking or they will deflate, never to rise again.

Crêpe Batter
Appareil à Crêpe

Crêpes should be very thin. With the help of a nonstick pan and a little practice, you will be able to make perfect crêpes, suitable for either entrées or desserts.

TO MAKE EIGHTEEN OR TWENTY 7-INCH CRÊPES

¾ cup all-purpose flour
1 teaspoon sugar
A pinch of salt
3 eggs
1 tablespoon melted unsalted butter
1½ cups milk

1. In a bowl, combine flour, sugar, salt, eggs, and melted butter. Stir until smooth. Add milk and mix well. Strain.
2. Heat a 7-inch crêpe pan or nonstick omelette pan and melt 1 teaspoon butter over moderate heat.
3. Pour in 2 or 3 tablespoons of batter. Cook the crêpe until it is golden brown on the bottom; then flip it, using a spatula. Remove when golden brown on both sides. Continue until all the batter is used up.

NOTE: Crêpes can be wrapped airtight and stored in the refrigerator or freezer.

Croissants

Everybody thinks croissants were invented by the French, but it was in Budapest in 1686 that the first croissant was born. I recommend doubling this recipe, since croissants can be baked, immediately frozen, and reheated as needed. (Reheat in a 350° oven for 5 minutes, or until the crust is crisp. They will always taste fresh if this procedure is followed.)

1. Using the dough hook of an electric mixer, combine flour, sugar, and salt in the bowl.
2. Dissolve the yeast in 1 cup lukewarm milk. Add to the flour mixture, together with the remaining milk, and mix until dough forms a ball.
3. Remove dough hook. Cover bowl with plastic wrap and allow dough to rest for 1 or 1½ hours, until double in bulk. Punch down the dough and refrigerate it, covered, for 30 minutes.
4. Mold the butter into a block and proceed as for puff pastry (see page 200), giving the dough four turns. Refrigerate again for 30 minutes.
5. Preheat oven to 400°.
6. Roll out dough into two rectangles ⅙ inch thick. Cut into triangles and shape into crescents. Put them on a baking sheet and allow to rise for 20 minutes.
7. Brush each croissant with egg wash and bake for 15 minutes, or until golden brown.

TO MAKE 24 CROISSANTS

1 pound all-purpose flour
4 tablespoons sugar
1 teaspoon salt
½ ounce fresh yeast (or 1 tablespoon dry)
1¼ cups milk
12 ounces unsalted butter, at room temperature
1 egg, lightly beaten, for egg wash

Brioche

If brioche dough is allowed to rise in too warm a spot the yeast will be killed and an odor will develop. This recipe should give you perfect results; smaller proportions will not be as successful.

TO MAKE 2 LARGE BRIOCHES
OR 16 to 18 INDIVIDUAL ONES

1 pound 2 ounces all-
  purpose flour
2 tablespoons sugar
1 tablespoon salt
2 tablespoons dry yeast
½ cup milk
6 eggs
10 ounces unsalted
  butter, at room
  temperature
1 egg, lightly beaten, for
  egg wash

1. In the bowl of an electric mixer, using the paddle, combine the flour, sugar, salt, and yeast. Add enough of the milk to make a stiff dough that pulls away from the sides of the bowl.
2. Add the eggs, one at a time, beating thoroughly after each addition. Continue to beat until elastic.
3. If your machine has a dough hook, substitute it for the paddle and add the softened butter, a small amount at a time, until it is well incorporated and the dough pulls away from the sides of the bowl.
4. Transfer dough to another bowl, cover with a damp cloth, and allow to rise at room temperature for approximately 1 hour, until double its original size.
5. Punch down the dough, cover again with the damp cloth, and allow to rise overnight in the refrigerator. Be sure to cover the bowl with a plate weighted with a brick (or other heavy object) to prevent the dough from overrising and overfermenting.
6. Form the dough into two large brioches and place in lightly buttered 6-cup molds. Allow to rise until double in size.
7. Preheat oven to 350°.
8. When brioches have risen, and are ready to bake, brush with egg wash and bake for 20 minutes. Reduce heat to 350° and continue to bake for 30 minutes more, or until a skewer inserted in the center comes out clean. Baking time will be shorter for smaller brioches.

VARIATION: For head brioche use a 4-inch diameter by 2-inch-high ripple-edged tart mold. Fill with a brioche dough ball to a height of one third of the mold. Brush with egg wash, form a second ball one sixth of the size of the first one, and place it on top of the first dough ball.

Walnut Bread

Pain de Noix

This bread takes a very slow rise. Using plastic wrap will aid the process.

To make the sponge:
1. Dissolve the yeast in ¼ cup water.
2. Place the flour in a large mixing bowl and whisk in the remaining 1½ cups water. Whisk in the dissolved yeast.
3. Cover tightly with plastic wrap and let rise until double in bulk, approximately 2½ to 3 hours. Or let rise in the refrigerator overnight.

To make the bread dough:
1. Dissolve the yeast in ¼ cup water.
2. In a large bowl, thoroughly combine all the flours. Add 4 cups of the flour, the salt, the dissolved yeast, the honey, and the remaining 1½ cups water to the sponge. Mix with a wooden spoon, adding small amounts of additional flour until the dough is too stiff to beat.
3. Turn out onto a lightly floured surface and let the dough rest for 5 minutes. Sprinkle with ⅓ cup flour and knead until the flour is absorbed. The dough will be sticky.
4. Knead vigorously for several minutes, adding a little more flour if the dough is too sticky. Continue to knead until the dough is smooth and elastic. Let rest for 5 minutes. Knead again for 1 minute.
5. Place the dough in a large bowl, 6 to 8 quarts, and cover tightly with plastic wrap. Let rise at room temperature (75°) until tripled in bulk, about 3 hours.
6. Lightly flour the work surface and scatter ½ cup nuts on the flour. Turn out the dough on top of the nuts, sprinkle with the remaining ½ cup nuts, and knead until all the nuts are combined with the dough.
7. Butter two 8-cup loaf pans or molds. Divide the dough in half and shape loaves to fit each pan. Cover loosely with plastic wrap and let rise at room temperature until doubled in bulk.

TO MAKE TWO 1½-POUND LOAVES

Sponge:

¼ ounce fresh yeast or
  ½ tablespoon dry yeast
1¾ cups lukewarm
  water
2 cups unbleached all-
  purpose flour

Bread Dough:

½ ounce fresh yeast or 1
  tablespoon dry yeast
1¾ cups lukewarm
  water
2 cups rye flour
2 cups stone-ground
  whole-wheat flour
2 cups unbleached all-
  purpose flour
The sponge
1½ tablespoons salt
2 tablespoons honey
1 cup chopped walnuts

8. Preheat oven to 450°.
9. Using a razor blade or a very sharp knife, make a slash down the length of each loaf. Spray with water and place in the hot oven. Spray two more times at 3-minute intervals.
10. Bake 20 minutes, reduce heat to 350°, and bake 20 to 25 minutes longer. The bread will shrink slightly from the sides of the pan and sound hollow when tapped on the bottom of the loaf.
11. Turn off the oven. Remove the loaves from the pans and set on a rack in the oven with the door slightly ajar for 20 minutes, to dry out.

Pasta

This is a very basic recipe that can be used for fettuccine, lasagne, ravioli, or any other pasta you choose.

TO SERVE 6

3 to 3½ cups all-purpose flour
A pinch of salt
4 eggs
2 tablespoons water
2 tablespoons oil

1. In a food processor, using the steel blade, place the flour and salt. Add the eggs, water, and oil and process until dough begins to form a ball.
2. Remove from work bowl and wrap securely in plastic wrap. Use as needed. (If using the dough within 2 hours, let it rest unrefrigerated. For best results, pasta should be used within 24 hours.)
3. Divide into four pieces and knead through a pasta machine as per manufacturer's directions, keeping unused portions wrapped.
4. Cut as desired. Once you have cut the pasta to the desired form, it will stay the freshest if you freeze it.

SPECIAL EQUIPMENT: Pasta machine

Desserts

Ladyfingers

Matchsticks

Palmiers

Almond Tiles

Marjolaine

Wolfgang's Sachertorte

Chocolate Cake

Chocolate Mousse Cake: Variation on a Theme

For Chocolate Lovers Only

Apple Tart

Kiwi Fruit Tart

Raspberries in Puff Pastry

Pear Tart with Caramel Sauce

Saint-Honoré with Pears

Candied Grapefruit Peel

Chocolate Bread Pudding

Chocolate Mousse

Chocolate Meringue

Floating Island

Glacéed Pears with Champagne Sabayon

Crêpes with Cheese and Raisins

Pear Soufflé

Frozen Strawberry Mousse

Coffee-Caramel Mousse

Vanilla Ice Cream

Hazelnut Parfait

Honey Ice Cream

Frozen Grand Marnier Soufflé

Meringue with Ice Cream

Cantaloupe with Port Wine Sherbet and Raspberries

Melon Sherbet

Champagne Pineapple Sherbet

Raspberry Sherbet

Champagne Sherbet

Chocolate Chantilly

Almond Cream

Pastry Cream

Ganache

Praline

Sauce Caramel

A wonderful meal can be compared to fine theater: Both are well composed and performed with skill and feeling. Desserts are the dénouement of the meal. As appetizers present you with your first impression of a meal, desserts offer the final statement. Care should be taken to prepare a last, lingering echo that is stimulating and refreshing to the palate, appealing to the eye, and light on the stomach.

It is possible to create lovely-looking desserts that are also light and delicious. One of my favorites is a moderately simple yet artistic presentation of a hot fruit tart with a cool, refreshing sherbet of the same flavor. I enjoy the compatibility of the similar flavors, with the contrast of the hot and cold temperatures. I prefer the natural sweetness or tartness of fruit and use a minimum amount of sugar and only seasonal fresh fruit. Sherbets may be prepared a few days in advance of a dinner party and kept frozen, allowing you more time with your guests.

There is a distinct difference between desserts prepared in restaurants or the home and those offered in pastry shops. A restaurant or home dessert should be much lighter and served in smaller portions. I would never serve a heavy cake after a multicourse dinner. With this in mind, I have selected some of my favorite desserts, most of which can be prepared in advance and will complement any meal.

Many people enjoy coffee with dessert. If you prefer to drink wine, I suggest a Johannisberg Riesling, Trockenbeerenauslese, Sauternes, or demi-sec champagne.

Ladyfingers
Biscuits à la Cuiller

Ladyfingers are used for various pastry presentations. If baked in advance, they can be stored in airtight boxes.

TO MAKE 4 DOZEN
LADYFINGERS, 4 INCHES LONG

5 eggs, separated
1 whole egg
⅔ cup plus 2 tablespoons sugar
1 cup sifted flour
1 teaspoon vanilla extract or ½ teaspoon orange flower water (optional)
2 generous tablespoons powdered sugar

1. Preheat oven to 350°. Line two large (approximately 14 by 19 inches) baking sheets with parchment paper.
2. With an electric mixer, whip the egg yolks, the whole egg, and ⅔ cup sugar until the mixture is very light and very thick. This will take 3 to 5 minutes on high speed.
3. Sift the flour over the egg yolk mixture and fold it in quickly. Set the batter aside.
4. Whip the egg whites into soft peaks. Add the remaining 2 tablespoons sugar and whip until stiff and shiny, but not dry. Stir one fourth of the egg whites into the egg yolk mixture; then quickly but gently fold in the remaining egg whites.
5. Spoon the batter into a large pastry bag fitted with a plain ½-inch (number 6) tip. On the parchment paper, pipe out the ladyfingers 4 inches long, and sift powdered sugar over the tops.
6. Place the trays in the oven and bake for 15 to 18 minutes. The ladyfingers will be golden brown when done. After 10 minutes, reverse the baking sheets to ensure even baking.
7. Cool the ladyfingers on a rack. They can be kept for a week in an airtight container. They can also be frozen in an airtight container, as long as they are defrosted while in the container.

PRESENTATION: Use the ladyfingers as an accompaniment when serving ice cream or sherbet, or as part of an assortment of petits fours. When they are to be used in this manner it is advisable to use the optional flavoring in the recipe. Use the biscuits to line a mold and fill with a mousse, charlotte, or bavarian cream.

SPECIAL EQUIPMENT:
Pastry bag and number 6 tip

Matchsticks

Allumettes

It is important to freeze the pastry after applying the icing. The "matchsticks" can be sliced more easily and the icing will not drip down the sides. As a result, the puff pastry will rise evenly.

1. Roll out puff pastry ⅛ inch thick, to a rectangle approximately 12 by 14 inches. Place on a baking sheet and chill in the freezer for 30 minutes.
2. In a mixing bowl, combine the egg white and powdered sugar until smooth. Sift in the cornstarch and beat with a hand whisk until creamy and completely smooth.
3. Spread the sugar mixture in an even layer on the cold puff pastry. Allow the pastry to rest in the freezer for another 30 minutes, or until firm.
4. Preheat oven to 350°.
5. Using a chef's knife, cut the pastry into "matchsticks" approximately 3½ inches by ¾ inch. Bake for 22 to 25 minutes, or until the tops are delicately browned on the edges and the pastry is crisp.

NOTE: When measuring the powdered sugar, sift it into a measuring cup and sweep off the excess with a knife. Take care not to pack down the sugar.

PRESENTATION: Serve the *allumettes* as an accompaniment to sorbets, or as part of an assortment of petits fours.

TO MAKE 36 TO 40 COOKIES

1 pound puff pastry (page 200)
1 egg white
1 cup sifted powdered sugar
2 tablespoons cornstarch

Palmiers

These can accompany sorbets or can be included on a tray of petits fours served with coffee.

TO MAKE APPROXIMATELY 24 COOKIES

8 ounces puff pastry (page 200)
4 ounces crystallized sugar
1 egg, lightly beaten, for egg wash

1. Roll out the puff pastry over crystallized sugar to a rectangle approximately 6 inches wide and 20 inches long. Fold each end, meeting in the center. Brush with egg wash and fold again, with each end meeting in the center. Then fold in half. Freeze for 5 to 10 minutes to firm the pastry.
2. Preheat oven to 400°.
3. Remove pastry from the freezer and slice into ¼-inch slices. Lay slices, flat side down, on a baking sheet and bake for 10 minutes. Turn the cookies over and bake for an additional 10 minutes, or until lightly brown. To avoid sticking, remove cookies from the baking sheet as soon as they are done.

Almond Tiles

Tuiles aux Amandes

The classic way is to make *tuiles* look like roof tiles, but they can also be molded over a cup and used to hold mousses or sorbets.

TO MAKE APPROXIMATELY 6 DOZEN

1. Spread the almonds on a baking tray and toast for 3 to 4 minutes, until lightly browned.
2. Melt the butter and let it cool. In a bowl, combine the sugar, flour, almonds, and lemon rind.
3. In a separate bowl, using a whisk, combine the egg whites, butter, vanilla extract, and Grand Marnier until well blended. Add the flour mixture to the egg white mixture, being careful not to overmix. Allow the mixture to rest in the refrigerator overnight.
4. Preheat oven to 375°.
5. Lightly butter a baking sheet and spoon out the batter by teaspoonfuls two inches apart. Using a fork, spread until almost flat. (To mold shells over a cup, use 1 tablespoon of the batter.)
6. Bake until the edges turn golden brown, approximately 4 to 6 minutes. Immediately remove from the baking sheet and place in a *tuile* cup or drape over a rolling pin.

½ cup blanched, sliced almonds
3½ ounces unsalted butter
1 cup minus 2 tablespoons sugar
1 cup sifted all-purpose flour
Grated rind of half a lemon
6 egg whites
1 teaspoon vanilla extract
3 tablespoons Grand Marnier

PRESENTATION: Serve *tuiles* as an accompaniment to or shell for sorbets, or fill with chocolate mousse (page 231) and serve with *crème anglaise* (page 233).

SPECIAL EQUIPMENT: *Tuile* cups (optional)

Marjolaine

Though this recipe is lengthy, it is not difficult; and it is very well worth the effort. When making the butter cream, be sure the egg-syrup mixture is cool before the butter is added.

Meringue layers:

4 ounces hazelnuts
1¾ cups blanched, sliced almonds
1¾ cups sugar
2 tablespoons all-purpose flour
3 tablespoons melted butter
8 egg whites
A pinch of salt

Praline butter cream:

1 cup sugar
¾ cup water
¼ cup toasted hazelnuts
¼ cup toasted almonds
3 egg yolks
½ pound unsalted butter, softened
2 tablespoons each espresso coffee and hazelnut liqueur

Chocolate cream:

½ pound bittersweet chocolate
⅔ cup crème fraîche

Whipped cream filling:

1½ cups crème fraîche
or
¾ cup heavy cream, whipped
2 tablespoons sour cream
1 tablespoon sugar (optional)

To make the meringue layers:
1. Preheat oven to 400°.
2. Place hazelnuts and almonds on separate baking sheets. Roast almonds approximately 5 minutes and hazelnuts 10 to 12 minutes. Nuts should be golden brown. Transfer hazelnuts to a clean towel and rub with towel to remove as much of the peel as possible.
3. Reserve 2 tablespoons sugar and combine the remaining sugar with nuts and flour in a food processor. Process until mixture resembles coarse flour. Set aside to cool.
4. Line two 12-by-16-inch baking sheets with parchment paper. Brush generously with melted butter.
5. Whip egg whites and salt to soft peaks. Add reserved 2 tablespoons sugar and continue to beat to stiff peaks. Fold in cooled nut mixture. Pour meringue on the prepared baking sheets. Spread each evenly over entire sheet. The layers should be very thin, approximately ⅛ inch deep.
6. Bake for 10 to 12 minutes, until golden brown. Remove from oven and let cool.
7. When cool enough to handle, turn layers out on a smooth work surface and carefully remove the paper.

To prepare the praline butter cream:
1. In a small saucepan, cook ¾ cup sugar and ¼ cup water until the bubbles are clear and syrup is thick. Add the nuts and cook until syrup is a dark caramel color (the nuts will turn brown as well). Add the remaining ½ cup water and cook 1 to 2 minutes longer to liquefy the caramel.
2. In an electric mixer, beat the egg yolks with the remaining ¼ cup sugar until light and fluffy. Strain the hot caramel syrup into the egg yolks, reserving the nuts for another use. Continue to beat until mixture is cool.
3. Slowly add the butter, 1 tablespoon at a time. When incorporated, add the coffee and liqueur. Chill.

To prepare the chocolate cream (ganache):
1. Cut chocolate into small pieces. Combine with *crème fraîche* and cook over simmering water until chocolate is melted. Stir until smooth. Cool to spreading consistency.

To prepare the whipped cream filling:
1. Whip *crème fraîche* until stiff (or whip heavy cream and fold in sour cream. Add sugar, if desired).

To assemble:
1. Cut each meringue layer in half, lengthwise, making four 5-by-14-inch rectangles. Reserve the smoothest layer for the top. Place the first layer on a plate and spread with two thirds of the *ganache*. Top with the second layer and spread with whipped cream. Top with the third layer and spread with praline butter cream. Top with the fourth layer. Finish with a *ganache* glaze, which is made by melting the remaining *ganache* until it is the consistency of heavy cream. Pour it over the cake and smooth with a spatula to form an even glaze. Chill the *marjolaine*. Trim sides if necessary with a serrated knife.
2. When ready to serve, sprinkle with sifted powdered cocoa or powdered sugar.

PRESENTATION: *Marjolaine* can be served as above or it can be cut into bite-size portions and placed in petit four cups.

Wolfgang's Sachertorte

This is my version of the world-famous chocolate cake from the Hotel Sacher in Vienna.

TO SERVE 10

Cake:

1 pound bittersweet
  chocolate, cut into
  small pieces
2 ounces unsweetened
  chocolate, cut into
  small pieces
8 ounces unsalted butter
¾ cup plus 2
  tablespoons sugar
12 eggs, separated
1 teaspoon vanilla
  extract
½ teaspoon salt
8 ounces flour

Filling:

1 cup apricot preserves
1 tablespoon apricot
  brandy

Glaze:

8 to 10 ounces
  bittersweet chocolate
2 tablespoons butter

1. Preheat oven to 350°. Butter and flour a 9-inch spring-form pan.
2. Melt the chocolate over simmering water. Set aside to cool.
3. Cream the butter, ¾ cup sugar, egg yolks, and vanilla. Stir in the chocolate and set aside.
4. In an electric mixer, beat the egg whites and salt to stiff peaks. With the machine running, add the remaining 2 tablespoons sugar. Stir one third of the egg whites into the chocolate mixture to lighten it. Fold in the remaining egg whites, gently but thoroughly. Turn into the springform pan.
5. Bake approximately 1 hour. To check for doneness, insert a toothpick gently into the cake. It should come out dry. Remove the ring of the pan and cool the cake on a rack.
6. *To make the apricot filling:* Purée the apricot jam through a food mill fitted with the finest disk (or use a food processor). Stir in the apricot brandy. Set aside until ready to use.
7. Slice cake in half horizontally to make two layers. Spread the bottom layer with two thirds of the apricot filling and top with the second layer. Spread top and sides of the cake with a thin layer of filling. Chill.
8. *To make the glaze:* Melt chocolate and butter over simmering water. Remove from heat and cool until it reaches glazing consistency. Spread over cake and chill.
9. Remove sachertorte from refrigerator 1 hour before serving.

PRESENTATION: Serve a wedge of cake with *crème chantilly* (page 246).

SPECIAL EQUIPMENT:
9-inch springform pan
Food mill

Chocolate Cake

Gâteau au Chocolat

A chocolate cake that needs no garnish, just a sprinkling of powdered sugar.

TO MAKE ONE 10-INCH CAKE

1. Preheat oven to 325°. Butter and flour a 10-inch round cake pan.
2. Combine chocolate and butter and melt over simmering water.
3. Whisk together the egg yolks and all but 3 tablespoons of the sugar. Stir melted chocolate into egg yolks until thoroughly combined.
4. With an electric mixer, on medium speed, beat egg whites until soft peaks form. Gradually beat in the remaining sugar and continue to whip until egg whites are stiff but not dry.
5. Carefully fold chocolate mixture into egg whites. Pour into prepared pan.
6. Bake for 1 hour and 15 minutes. Turn out onto a rack immediately. As the cake cools, the center will sink and crack — do not worry.

8 ounces bittersweet chocolate, cut into small pieces
4 ounces unsalted butter, cut into small pieces
5 eggs, separated
A pinch of salt
⅔ cup sugar

PRESENTATION: Dust the cake with powdered sugar and serve with unsweetened whipped cream.

Chocolate Mousse Cake: Variation on a Theme

This is Chocolate Charlotte Ma Maison, created especially for chocolate lovers.

TO SERVE 10 OR 12

½ recipe sachertorte (page 220)
1 recipe chocolate mousse (page 231)
1 recipe ladyfingers (page 214)

1. Bake the sachertorte for 40 minutes; then cool.
2. With the sachertorte still in the pan, pour chocolate mousse over top. Refrigerate for several hours.
3. Place the cake on a serving plate and remove ring of springform. Smooth the sides with a spatula and surround with ladyfingers, with their flat sides pressed against the cake.

SPECIAL EQUIPMENT: 9-inch springform pan

For Chocolate Lovers Only

Chocolate . . . Chocolate . . . Chocolate. A small piece goes a very long way.

TO SERVE 10 TO 12

1. Place the chocolate cake on a plate.
2. Split and fill with *ganache* that has been softened until spreadable. The *ganache* layer should be approximately ¾ inch thick.
3. Cover with chocolate chantilly.
4. Top chantilly with chocolate mousse.
5. Smooth sides with spatula and spread a thin layer of *ganache* on sides.
6. Arrange raspberries on top of cake and dust lightly with powdered sugar. Decorate with chocolate leaves if you wish.

1 chocolate cake (page 221)
2 cups ganache (page 247)
1 cup chocolate chantilly (page 246)
½ recipe chocolate mousse (page 231)
Fresh raspberries (1½ to 2 pints)
Powdered sugar

NOTE: To make chocolate leaves, melt bittersweet chocolate and spread in a very thin layer (about ⅛ inch thick) on a sheet of waxed paper. Refrigerate until hard and then cut out leaf shapes with the tip of a sharp knife. Peel away paper.

Apple Tart
Tarte Tatin

There are many versions of *tarte tatin*. Cooking the apples and puff pastry separately and combining them at the last moment ensures the pastry will be light and stay crisp. Glazing with a hot iron pan produces the carmelized flavor.

TO SERVE 8

½ cup unsalted butter
12 large Golden Delicious apples, cored, quartered, and peeled
1 cup sugar
8 ounces puff pastry (page 200)
Sugar for glaze

1. Preheat oven to 450°.
2. Using half the butter, heavily coat the bottom and sides of a 10-by-3-inch round cake pan.
3. Arrange apples in the pan in a continuous circle (starting at the edge of the pan), piling one on top of the other — the first row of apples with rounded side down, the remaining rows with rounded side up. Sprinkle top with 1 cup sugar and dot with remaining butter.
4. Bake for 30 minutes. Reduce oven temperature to 350° and continue to bake 1 hour longer, or until apples are soft and brown on top. Remove from the oven and cool completely.
5. While apples are baking, prepare the crust. Roll out enough puff pastry to form a 12-inch square ⅛ inch thick and place it on a buttered cookie sheet. Cut out a circle a bit larger than the 10-inch apple-baking pan (a large plate can be used to form the circle). With tines of two forks, prick pastry over the entire surface to prevent curling during baking. Bake in a 350° oven until lightly browned, 25 to 35 minutes. Cool.
6. *To assemble:* Set pastry shell on a serving dish and place it upside down over the apples. Invert pan. Apples are now on top of shell. Heat the bottom of an old frying pan until very hot (about 15 minutes). Sprinkle sugar liberally over the surface of the apples and sear with the hot pan to glaze apples. Repeat this procedure three or four times, keeping the pan hot when not in use.

PRESENTATION: Cut into wedges and serve warm with whipped cream.

Kiwi Fruit Tart

Clafoutis aux Kiwis

Clafoutis are usually prepared with cherries. Kiwis are an exotic and wonderful replacement.

1. Preheat oven to 350°.
2. Roll out the dough to fit a 10-inch quiche pan 1½ inches deep. Crimp edges and remove excess dough. Line the pan with parchment paper or aluminum foil. Fill with aluminum beans (or use dried beans or rice), and bake for 15 to 20 minutes, until brown. Remove pan from oven and reduce temperature to 325°.
3. Combine eggs, cream, sugar, and *eau-de-vie* in a small bowl. Stir until blended. Strain.
4. Cut each kiwi into four slices and arrange in the pastry shell. Cover with the egg mixture and bake for 45 to 50 minutes.
5. Remove tart from oven. Dust top with powdered sugar and glaze under the broiler for about 1 minute. Cool on a rack and serve at room temperature.

TO SERVE 8

½ pound puff pastry (page 200) or pâte sucrée (page 199)
4 eggs
1 cup heavy cream
6 ounces sugar
4 teaspoons eau-de-vie de mirabelle or pear brandy
8 kiwis, peeled

Raspberries in Puff Pastry

Feuilletée aux Framboises

This is one of my favorite desserts. Once all the components are ready — and they can be prepared earlier in the day — it is a simple matter to put them together.

1. Preheat oven to 450°.
2. Roll out puff pastry to a rectangle slightly larger than 6 by 9 inches, ⅜ inch thick. Cut pastry into six 3-by-3-inch pieces. Place them on a baking sheet and brush with egg wash, being careful not to let it drip onto the baking sheet. Bake for 5 minutes; then lower the heat to 350°, and bake 20 minutes longer.
3. While the pastry is baking, whisk together in a mixing bowl the whipped cream, pastry cream, and Grand Marnier. Chill until needed.

TO SERVE 6

½ pound puff pastry (page 200)
1 egg, lightly beaten, for egg wash
¼ cup heavy cream, whipped
½ cup pastry cream (page 247)
2 tablespoons Grand Marnier
½ cup raspberries per serving
1½ cups sauce caramel (page 248)

4. Remove *feuilletées* from the oven and slice them in half horizontally. Place the bottom half of each one on a dessert plate and spread with a spoonful of pastry cream mixture. Arrange the berries on the pastry cream and top with remaining half of the *feuilletée*.

PRESENTATION: Serve the *feuilletées* while hot and carefully surround with sauce.

Pear Tart with Caramel Sauce
Petite Tarte aux Poires avec Sauce Caramel

TO SERVE 6 OR 8

1 pound puff pastry
(page 200)
6 tablespoons almond
cream (page 246)
combined with 2
tablespoons pear
liqueur
1 egg, lightly beaten, for
egg wash
6 or 7 ripe pears, peeled,
halved, cored, and
sliced lengthwise, about
¼ inch thick (or 1½ to
2 cans pear halves in
heavy syrup)
2 tablespoons unsalted
butter, cut into small
pieces
1 cup heavy cream,
whipped
2 cups sauce caramel
(page 248)

The puff pastry should be rolled out as thin as possible to ensure the maximum crispness when cooked. Ripe pears must be used; hard pears will not bake properly. However, canned, well-drained pears may be substituted.

1. Preheat oven to 400°.
2. Roll out the puff pastry ⅛ inch thick and place on a baking sheet. Cut pastry into three or four 6-inch circles, removing scraps of pastry. Refrigerate at least 30 minutes, or until needed.
3. Spread the almond cream to within 1 inch of the edge of each pastry circle. Brush the edges with egg wash.
4. Arrange the pears, like a flower, on top of the almond cream and dot with butter.
5. Bake for 25 minutes.

PRESENTATION: Cut each tart in half and serve warm with whipped cream on one side of the pastry and *sauce caramel* on the other side.

Saint-Honoré with Pears

Saint-Honoré aux Poires

This classic French pastry with pears tastes as good as it looks, and putting it together is as easy as pulling it apart.

To make the shell:

1. Preheat oven to 375°. Roll *pâte sucrée* into a 10-inch circle and place on a baking sheet.
2. Using a pastry bag fitted with a number 6 tip (½-inch plain round), pipe a ½-inch border of *pâte à chou* around the edge of the *pâte sucrée*. Brush the *pâte à chou* with egg wash. Bake for 30 minutes or until the *pâte sucrée* is nicely browned and the *pâte à chou* is dry and firm to the touch. Set aside until needed.
3. On another baking sheet, pipe out remaining *pâte à chou* into 24 small puffs or enough to encircle the pastry. Brush with egg wash and bake approximately 30 minutes. Reserve.
4. Peel, core, and slice the pears into sixths. Place them on a baking sheet lined with baking paper, dot with the butter, and sprinkle with 2 tablespoons sugar. Bake about 30 minutes or until tender. (If pears are not ripe, it is best to poach them or use canned pears.)

To make the crème chibouste:

1. In a medium saucepan, bring the milk and vanilla bean to a boil.
2. In a large mixing bowl, combine the egg yolks and ½ cup sugar. Whisk in the flour. Slowly pour half the hot milk into the egg yolk mixture, whisking all the while. Return to the saucepan and continue to whisk as you bring mixture back to a boil. Remove vanilla bean and reserve this pastry cream in a warm spot.
3. In a saucepan, combine remaining 1⅔ cups sugar and water. Cook over high heat to soft-ball stage (240°). On medium speed of an electric mixer, whip egg whites until stiff. Beat the syrup into the whipped egg whites in a thin stream until stiff peaks are formed.
4. Bring pastry cream back to a boil. Fold hot egg whites into hot pastry cream one third at a time. Fold in the kirsch.

TO SERVE 6

Saint-Honoré:

½ pound pâte sucrée
  (page 199)
½ recipe pâte à chou
  (page 204)
1 egg, lightly beaten, for
  egg wash
4 very ripe pears
1 ounce butter
2 tablespoons sugar

Crème chibouste:

2 cups milk
1 vanilla bean
8 eggs, separated
2 cups plus 2
  tablespoons sugar
½ cup flour
¾ cup water
2 tablespoons kirsch or
  pear eau-de-vie

Caramel:

1 cup sugar
¼ cup water

5. Fill the reserved puffs with *chibouste,* using a number 1 or number 2 pastry tip (small).

To make the caramel:
1. In a saucepan, combine sugar and water. When it is a lovely caramel color, remove from heat. Dip tops of small puffs into caramel and place them on the ring of *pâte à chou.*
2. Arrange the pears on the bottom of the pastry shell. Pipe remaining *chibouste* decoratively over pears, using a large star tip.

NOTE: *Crème chibouste* is nothing other than a hot pastry cream with hot meringue added.

PRESENTATION: Serve at room temperature.

SPECIAL EQUIPMENT:
3 pastry bags with tips number 1 or 2, number 6 (½-inch round), and large star
3 pastry baking sheets
Baking paper
Pastry brush

Candied Grapefruit Peel
Écorce de Pamplemousse Confite

Boiling the peel in several changes of water removes the bitterness and makes it very tender. Orange peel can be prepared in the same way. The skin of the fruit should be thick, not thin and dried out.

1. Trim both ends from the grapefruit and cut it into quarters. Cut away all but ½ inch of the pulp. Slice each quarter into three or four strips.
2. Place the strips of grapefruit in a large deep saucepan with enough cold water to cover by 2 to 3 inches. Over medium heat, bring the grapefruit skins to a boil. Boil for 5 minutes. Drain. Repeat this step three more times.
3. After the final blanching, drain the peels (the pulp will have fallen away) and place them in a large sauté pan. Stir in the sugar. Over very low heat, cook the grapefruit peels for about 1½ hours, stirring occasionally. The sugar will combine with the moisture on the peels to form a very heavy syrup.
4. Add orange liqueur and continue to cook for another 30 minutes.
5. Place the peels on a wire rack to drain.
6. When they are cool enough to handle, roll them in crystallized sugar or dip one end of the candied peel in melted chocolate.

TO MAKE 64 TO 96 PIECES

6 thick-skinned
  grapefruit
1 pound 4 ounces sugar
¼ cup orange liqueur
4 ounces crystallized
  sugar

NOTE: If crystallized sugar is unavailable, raw sugar (obtainable in health-food stores) can be used in its place with very satisfactory results.

PRESENTATION: Serve as a garnish to almost any dessert. Place in small paper cups and serve as a petit four. Use as a decoration on a cake.

VARIATION: Use this same recipe with six or eight thick-skinned oranges. The recipe and procedure are the same as above, except you blanch the peels only three times. The orange flesh will remain with the peel, instead of falling off.

Chocolate Bread Pudding
Gâteau Négresco

This is simple to prepare and the results are always perfect. As delicate as a chocolate soufflé, *gâteau négresco* does not need the meticulous attention a soufflé requires.

TO MAKE TWELVE ½-CUP SERVINGS

Gâteau:

8 slices (5 ounces) challah or brioche
¾ cup heavy cream
6 ounces bittersweet chocolate, cut in pieces
½ cup plus 3 tablespoons butter, at room temperature
5 eggs, separated
¾ cup finely ground almonds
1 cup sugar

Crème Chantilly:

2 cups heavy cream
¼ cup sugar

1. Preheat oven to 350°. Butter twelve ½-cup molds.
2. Combine the challah with the heavy cream and let stand 30 minutes.
3. Melt the chocolate over a *bain-marie*. Let cool and reserve.
4. In a food processor or large mixing bowl, cream the butter. Add egg yolks, almonds, ¾ cup sugar, the soaked bread, and the melted chocolate. Process until well combined.
5. Whip egg whites until soft peaks form. Gradually beat in remaining ¼ cup sugar and continue to beat until stiff and shiny. Fold into the chocolate mixture. Pour into prepared molds and set in a *bain-marie*. Cover loosely with buttered foil, buttered side down.
6. Bake for 45 to 50 minutes, or until set.
7. Whip the heavy cream with the sugar, only to the chantilly stage.

PRESENTATION: Unmold *gâteaux* on a serving platter or tray. Surround with *crème chantilly*.

Chocolate Mousse

Mousse au Chocolat

I prefer using part bittersweet chocolate for mousse because it gives a more intense chocolate flavor and less sweetness.

1. Whisk egg yolks together with ¼ cup sugar.
2. Melt chocolate over a *bain-marie*.
3. Bring cream to a boil and stir it into the melted chocolate.
4. Turn the chocolate mixture into the egg yolks and sugar. Set aside.
5. Whip egg whites and lemon juice until they reach soft peaks. Add remaining ½ cup sugar and continue to whip until whites are stiff and very shiny.
6. Stir one third of the whites into the chocolate mixture to lighten it. Fold in the remaining egg whites, a third at a time.
7. Pour into an 8-cup glass bowl and chill at least six hours or overnight.

4 egg yolks
¾ cup sugar
5 ounces bittersweet
  chocolate
5 ounces unsweetened
  chocolate
½ cup heavy cream
1 cup egg whites (8
  "large" whites)
2 teaspoons lemon juice

NOTE: If the chocolate and egg yolk mixture should tighten, place the mixture back over the *bain-marie,* and vigorously whisk in 3 or 4 tablespoons of the beaten egg whites. The chocolate will smooth out so you can continue with the recipe.

PRESENTATION: Using a large spoon, serve directly from the bowl. Pass whipped cream, if desired. Or spoon the mousse into *tuile* cups and top with whipped cream.

Chocolate Meringue

Meringue à la Mousse au Chocolat

This is a classic presentation that is very effective. The crisp meringue complements the chocolate mousse.

TO SERVE 6 OR 8

1 cup egg whites (8 "large" whites)
A pinch of salt
2 cups sugar
1 recipe chocolate mousse (page 231)
¼ cup cocoa

1. Preheat oven to 325°.
2. Whip the egg whites with salt until they form soft peaks.
3. Whip in the sugar, one fourth at a time. When the egg whites are stiff and shiny, sift in the cocoa. Fold to combine thoroughly.
4. Line a 9-by-14-inch baking sheet with parchment paper. Pour in the meringue and spread evenly with a long-bladed spatula to make a very smooth layer.
5. Bake 1½ hours, or until dry.
6. Cut the meringue to fit into a 9-inch springform pan, using the bottom of the springform as a guide. Fill the pan with mousse. Crush the extra meringue and sprinkle it over the mousse. Dust with cocoa and chill.

PRESENTATION: Serve in wedges, garnished with *crème chantilly* (page 246) or candied grapefruit peel (page 229).

VARIATION: Bake the meringue as small individual cups and use them to hold ice cream or mousse.

SPECIAL EQUIPMENT:
Long-bladed spatula
Parchment paper
9- or 10-inch springform pan

Floating Island

Île Flottante: Oeufs à la Neige

This classic but simple recipe requires all your attention while cooking the egg whites and the *crème anglaise.* In less than 30 minutes you can have a luscious dessert.

1. In a large, wide saucepan, bring the milk and vanilla bean to a simmer.
2. Beat the egg whites until soft peaks form. Gradually beat in ¼ cup sugar and continue beating until stiff. Scoop up several large serving spoonfuls and poach on top of the simmering milk, 3 minutes on each side. Remove with a slotted spoon and place on a platter. Repeat until all the egg whites have been used. Refrigerate until ready to serve.
3. *To make* crème anglaise: Beat egg yolks with 1¼ cups sugar until thick and creamy. Add the milk to the egg yolk mixture and return to the saucepan. Cook, stirring constantly without letting it come to a boil, until mixture thickens noticeably and coats back of spoon. Strain and cool.
4. In a small saucepan, combine the water and remaining ½ cup sugar. Over moderately high heat, cook until sugar has dissolved completely. Continue cooking until syrup turns a light brown (this should take 3 to 4 minutes). Remove saucepan from heat as soon as desired color is reached and immediately pour it over the chilled meringues. (The caramel will have a bitter taste if it darkens too much.)

PRESENTATION: Carefully pour *crème anglaise* into a serving bowl. Arrange meringues on top of *crème anglaise* and sprinkle with almonds. Surround with raspberries.

TO SERVE 8

1 quart milk
1 vanilla bean
8 eggs, separated
2 cups sugar
¼ cup water
½ cup sliced almonds
  (optional)
1 pint raspberries
  (optional)

Glacéed Pears with Champagne Sabayon
Gratin de Poires au Champagne

I prefer Bosc pears because of the flavor and because they retain their texture when poached, but ripe Anjou pears may be substituted. White wine, Marsala, or port may be substituted for the champagne. The sweeter the wine, the less sugar is needed.

TO SERVE 6

3 Bosc pears, peeled, halved, and cored
1 bottle champagne
½ cup sugar
1 vanilla bean
Zest of half a lemon
4 egg yolks

1. In a deep saucepan, combine champagne, sugar, vanilla bean, lemon zest, and pears. Poach pears until tender but still firm.
2. Remove the pears and dry on a towel. Reserve. Reduce the poaching liquid until 1 cup remains.
3. *To make the* sabayon: In a large metal bowl, combine egg yolks and reduced liquid. Set over simmering water and whisk vigorously until the sauce is thick and fluffy (approximately 10 minutes).
4. Preheat broiler.
5. In a gratin dish, arrange the pears and cover with the *sabayon* sauce. Sprinkle with sugar and glaze under the broiler, being careful that the glaze does not burn.

PRESENTATION: Serve directly from gratin dish, warm or cold, with petits fours.

Crêpes with Cheese and Raisins
Crêpes au Fromage Blanc et Raisins

TO SERVE 8 OR 12

1 recipe crêpe batter (page 204)

This is a recipe from my native Austria, and still one of my favorite desserts. The cheese must be dry, like farmer cheese, for the recipe to be successful.

1. Prepare crêpes. Reserve and keep warm.
2. In a food processor, combine sugar and lemon zest and process until lemon zest is minced. Add the cheese, butter, 1 egg, and a pinch of salt. Process until cheese is smooth. With the motor running, add the remaining

eggs through the feed tube, one at a time. Add *crème fraîche* and process just to combine. Transfer to a bowl and stir in raisins and vanilla.
3. *To make the glaze:* Whisk together eggs and sugar. Whisk in heavy cream. Reserve.
4. Preheat oven to 375°. Butter individual gratin dishes.
5. Place approximately ¼ cup filling on each crêpe and roll to enclose. Arrange two or three crêpes in each gratin dish.
6. Pour glaze over crêpes and bake until lightly browned, approximately 30 minutes.

PRESENTATION: Serve in gratin dishes directly from the oven.

SPECIAL EQUIPMENT:
8 to 12 individual oval gratin dishes

Filling:

¾ cup sugar
Chopped zest of 1 lemon
2 cups farmer cheese (a dry cottage cheese)
½ cup unsalted butter
4 eggs
A pinch of salt
¾ cup crème fraîche or sour cream
¾ cup raisins
1 teaspoon vanilla extract

Glaze:

2 eggs
¾ cup sugar
3 cups heavy cream

Pear Soufflé

Soufflé aux Poires

A soufflé for the weight-conscious gourmet. Do not overcook, or it will fall.

1. In a heavy saucepan, place the pears, vanilla bean, and half the fructose. Add water and cook the pears almost to a purée, adding more water if necessary to keep the mixture from burning.
2. Remove the vanilla bean and drain off any excess liquid. Transfer the pears to a food processor and process until smooth. Transfer the purée to a bowl and stir in the pear liqueur and additional fructose, if necessary. Add the egg yolks and combine well. Set aside and reserve.
3. Preheat oven to 450°. Butter individual soufflé dishes lightly and set aside.
4. Beat the egg whites until soft peaks form. Add 1 tablespoon fructose and continue to beat until stiff but not dry.
5. Gently stir one fourth of the beaten egg whites into the pear purée, and fold in the remaining egg whites.

TO SERVE 6

3 pears, peeled, cored, and quartered
1 vanilla bean
Up to ½ cup fructose (adjust according to ripeness of pears)
1 cup water
1 tablespoon pear liqueur
2 egg yolks
1 tablespoon unsalted butter
7 egg whites

6. Fill the soufflé dishes and smooth the tops with a spatula. Run your thumb around the inside edge of each dish. This will form the "hat" on the soufflé, and it will also eliminate the need for a collar.
7. Bake 7 to 8 minutes and serve immediately.

PRESENTATION: Serve one soufflé per person. If calories are not a consideration, the soufflé is delicious served with *crème anglaise* (page 233).

SPECIAL EQUIPMENT: 6 individual ½-cup soufflé dishes

Frozen Strawberry Mousse
Mousse Glacé aux Fraises

If you do not have a candy thermometer, cook the sugar until it starts to bubble and begins to thicken.

TO SERVE 8 OR 10

1½ quarts strawberries, hulled
2 egg whites
½ cup sugar
3 tablespoons water
1 cup heavy cream, whipped
Grand Marnier or kirsch for sauce

1. Reserve eight or ten whole strawberries. Purée the rest in a food processor and chill.
2. Beat the egg whites to soft peaks. Add 2 tablespoons sugar and continue to beat until stiff and shiny.
3. Meanwhile, combine 6 tablespoons sugar and the water. Cook to the soft-ball stage (240°). Slowly pour into egg whites, beating all the while. (This is an Italian meringue.) Continue to beat until whites are cooled.
4. Combine whites with 1½ to 2 cups of the strawberry purée. Fold in the whipped cream. Taste for sweetness, adding more sugar if necessary.
5. Pour into individual molds, or a 5- or 6-cup mold. Freeze overnight.
6. Transfer the mousse to the refrigerator 30 minutes before serving.
7. *To make the sauce:* Strain remaining strawberry purée. Sweeten to taste and perfume with Grand Marnier or kirsch before serving.

PRESENTATION: Unmold mousse onto a plate. Surround with sauce and garnish one whole berry per serving.

SPECIAL EQUIPMENT:
8 or 10 individual 1-cup molds or one 5- or 6-cup mold
Candy thermometer

Coffee-Caramel Mousse

Mousse Café au Lait et Caramel

Do not let the number of steps in this recipe overwhelm you. It is not difficult and the combination of coffee and caramel is delightfully different.

1. In a small saucepan, combine coffee beans and milk and bring to a simmer. Turn off the flame and let steep for 20 to 30 minutes. Strain through cheesecloth and discard beans.
2. In a large saucepan, combine sugar and water. Over moderate heat, cook until golden brown. Remove from heat and pour in ½ cup heavy cream. When bubbles subside, pour in the coffee-flavored milk. Return to low heat, if necessary, to make sure caramel has liquefied. Add gelatin and stir to dissolve. Set aside.
3. In a large bowl, beat egg yolks until thick and lemon-colored. Sift in cornstarch and whisk to dissolve.
4. Whisk some of the hot milk mixture into the egg yolks. Return to saucepan and, over medium heat, cook, stirring frequently, until mixture coats the back of a wooden spoon. *Do not boil.*
5. In a large bowl, combine the rum and vanilla. Pour in the hot liquid and stir to mix well. Chill over ice or refrigerate until custard just begins to set.
6. Lightly oil a 6-cup mold. (Or you may use a 1-quart soufflé dish. Make a waxed-paper collar extending over the top, securing it with tape and string.)
7. Whip the remaining 2 cups heavy cream to chantilly stage and fold it into the custard. Pour the mousse into the prepared mold and chill until set, at least 6 hours.

PRESENTATION: Unmold the mousse onto a serving platter. Cut the ladyfingers as high as the mousse and stick them around the entire edge of the mousse, rounded side out. Cut into wedges and serve. Or simply spoon the mousse directly from the mold into crystal serving glasses. Garnish with unsweetened whipped cream, if desired.

TO SERVE 6 OR 8

5 tablespoons espresso coffee beans, coarsely ground
2¼ cups milk
1 cup minus 1 tablespoon sugar
¼ cup water
2½ cups heavy cream
6 egg yolks
2 teaspoons cornstarch
1½ tablespoons gelatin softened in ¼ cup water
4 tablespoons dark rum
1 teaspoon vanilla extract
½ recipe ladyfingers (page 214)

Vanilla Ice Cream
Glace Vanille

TO MAKE 3 QUARTS

Crème anglaise:

½ gallon milk
2 vanilla beans, split
  lengthwise
2 whole eggs
15 egg yolks
½ pound (1¼ cups)
  sugar

Enrichment:

6 egg yolks
1 cup heavy cream
1 teaspoon vanilla
  extract

Frozen *crème anglaise* is best when eaten the day it is prepared. It can be served with berries, warmed *ganache*, or *sauce caramel.*

To make the crème anglaise:
1. Heat the milk with the vanilla beans slowly in a large saucepan and bring to a boil.
2. Whisk together the whole eggs, egg yolks, and sugar.
3. When the milk is still hot, slowly whisk the milk into the egg mixture. Return to saucepan and cook until mixture lightly coats the back of a spoon.
4. Strain into a bowl and chill.

To enrich and freeze:
1. Whisk the egg yolks and cream. Add the vanilla and stir mixture into the cold *crème anglaise.*
2. Strain and freeze in an ice-cream freezer according to the manufacturer's directions.

PRESENTATION: Serve scoops of ice cream on a chilled plate with fruit or sauce, as desired.

SPECIAL EQUIPMENT:
Ice-cream freezer

Hazelnut Parfait

Parfait Glacé aux Noisettes

Do not add more liqueur than the recipe calls for, or the ice cream will not freeze.

1. *To make the praline:* In a heavy saucepan, combine the sugar and water and cook over moderate heat until it reaches the soft-ball stage (240°). Remove 1 cup of the syrup and let it cool. Reserve. Over moderate heat, continue to cook the remaining syrup until it caramelizes.
2. Place the hazelnuts in a metal bowl, pour the caramelized sugar over them and, using a fork, stir constantly as the caramel cools, to separate the nuts as much as possible. Reserve.
3. In a large metal bowl, combine the egg yolks and the 1 cup reserved syrup. Over simmering water, whisk until thick and creamy. Remove from the heat and continue to beat the mixture a minute longer. Whisk in the hazelnut liqueur and cool over ice.
4. *To finish the parfait:* Whip the cream to soft peaks and fold into the chilled egg yolk mixture.
5. Layer half the parfait into a 4-cup soufflé dish. Sprinkle with half the reserved hazelnut praline and spoon on the remaining parfait. Cover and freeze at least 24 hours.

PRESENTATION: Spoon bitter chocolate sauce onto six serving plates and top with two scoops of the parfait. Garnish with the remaining hazelnuts.

SPECIAL EQUIPMENT:
Candy thermometer

TO SERVE 6

2 cups sugar
2 cups water
1 cup hazelnuts, roasted and peeled (page 218)
8 egg yolks
1 cup heavy cream
3 tablespoons hazelnut liqueur
Bitter chocolate sauce (page 242)

Honey Ice Cream
Glace au Miel

Use natural honey with no special flavor. The preparation is simple, since only the milk requires cooking. This recipe is expandable.

TO MAKE 5 CUPS

4 egg yolks
1¼ cups crème fraîche
1¼ cups milk
1 cup plus 2 tablespoons honey

1. Beat the egg yolks with the *crème fraîche*. Set aside.
2. Bring the milk to a boil, whisk in the honey, and bring the mixture back to a boil. Slowly whisk it into the egg yolk mixture. Strain and refrigerate until cold.
3. Freeze in an ice-cream freezer according to the manufacturer's directions. Store in the freezer compartment of your refrigerator.

PRESENTATION: Place one or two scoops of ice cream on each serving plate. Pass bitter chocolate sauce (page 242) or raspberry sauce (purée 1 cup raspberries, strain through a *chinois* or fine sieve, and add 1 teaspoon lemon juice and sugar to taste).

SPECIAL EQUIPMENT:
Ice-cream freezer

Frozen Grand Marnier Soufflé
Soufflé Glacé Grand Marnier

This soufflé may be prepared days in advance. The Grand Marnier can be replaced by any liqueur of your choice.

1. Beat the egg yolks and sugar until almost white and very fluffy.
2. Boil ½ cup heavy cream and whisk it into the egg yolk mixture. Perfume with 2 tablespoons Grand Marnier.
3. Whip the remaining 1 cup cream until stiff. Whisk in the remaining 2 tablespoons Grand Marnier.
4. Stir one third of the whipped cream into the egg yolk mixture. Gently fold in the remaining whipped cream in two or three batches.
5. Using a loaf pan or 1-quart soufflé dish, fitted with a collar, spoon in one third of the mixture. Cover with soaked ladyfingers. Top with another third of soufflé mixture. Arrange remaining ladyfingers over top and cover with remaining soufflé.
6. Freeze until firm.

PRESENTATION: Unmold loaf onto a serving dish or serve from the soufflé mold. Top with candied orange peel.

TO SERVE 6

4 egg yolks
¾ cup sugar
1½ cups heavy cream
4 tablespoons Grand Marnier or other orange-flavored liqueur
6 stale ladyfingers (page 214) soaked in 6 tablespoons liqueur
3 tablespoons candied orange peel (page 229)

Meringue with Ice Cream
Vacherin

Once the *vacherin* is assembled it can be kept in the freezer for two or three days until ready to serve. Sherbet or another flavor of ice cream may be used in place of the vanilla ice cream.

TO SERVE 8 TO 10

Meringue:

8 egg whites
1¾ cups sugar

Vanilla Ice Cream:

1 quart milk
1 vanilla bean, split
  lengthwise
8 egg yolks
1¾ cups sugar
6 ounces crème de
  marrons (canned)
1 cup heavy cream,
  whipped

Bitter Chocolate Sauce:

8 ounces bittersweet
  chocolate
½ cup heavy cream,
  warmed
2 tablespoons Grand
  Marnier

1. Preheat oven to 150°.
2. Line two baking sheets with parchment paper. Butter and flour the paper.
3. *To make the meringue:* Beat the egg whites until stiff. Gradually add the sugar, continuing to beat until shiny. Spread the meringue over the baking sheets, in two 6-by-12 inch rectangles, and bake for 1½ hours or until the meringue is dry. Cool in a dry area.
4. *To prepare the vanilla ice cream:* In a large saucepan, bring the milk and vanilla bean to a boil. Meanwhile, beat the egg yolks and sugar in a bowl until fluffy. Slowly add the hot milk to the egg yolk mixture.
5. Return the contents of the bowl to the saucepan and cook, stirring constantly, for approximately 10 minutes, or until it coats the back of the spoon. *Do not boil.*
6. Cool and freeze in an ice-cream freezer according to the manufacturer's directions. Reserve in the freezer compartment of your refrigerator.
7. Place one meringue on a serving platter. Spread with the *crème de marrons*. Top with vanilla ice cream and cover with the other meringue.
8. Decorate with whipped cream and transfer to the freezer until needed.
9. *To make the bitter chocolate sauce:* Melt the chocolate over simmering water. Add the warm cream. Flavor with the Grand Marnier.

PRESENTATION: Drizzle bitter chocolate sauce over the *vacherin*. Serve with additional hot sauce.

SPECIAL EQUIPMENT:
Ice-cream freezer

Cantaloupe with Port Wine Sherbet and Raspberries

Melon avec Sorbet au Porto et Framboises

With less sugar than the recipe calls for, this sorbet can be a refreshing appetizer.

TO SERVE 6

1. In a saucepan, combine port, juice of 1½ lemons, water, peppercorns, orange peel, lemon peel, and 1 tablespoon sugar. Bring to a boil and cook for 5 minutes. Strain and cool.
2. Freeze in an ice-cream freezer according to the manufacturer's directions.
3. Purée 1 pint of raspberries in a blender, with the juice of the remaining half a lemon and 2 tablespoons sugar. Strain. Taste and add more sugar if necessary.
4. Cut melons in half and seed.

PRESENTATION: Fill each melon half with two scoops of sherbet. Nap the sherbet lightly with raspberry sauce. Decorate with remaining berries and mint leaves.

SPECIAL EQUIPMENT:
Ice-cream freezer

1 bottle port (fifth)
2 lemons
½ port wine bottle of water
1 level teaspoon green peppercorns
1 strip orange peel (½ inch by 2 inches)
1 strip lemon peel (½ inch by 2 inches)
3 tablespoons sugar
2 pints fresh raspberries
3 ripe cantaloupes
Mint leaves

Melon Sherbet

Sorbet au Melon

As for other fruit sherbets, it is necessary that the melon be very ripe, since the flavor is then at its peak.

TO SERVE 8

3 medium-size honeydew
  melons, peeled and
  seeded
Juice of 2 lemons
Approximately ½ cup
  sugar
Assorted fresh fruits,
  such as whole
  raspberries or
  strawberries and sliced
  kiwi or papaya
  (optional)

1. Cut the melon pulp into small chunks and purée it in a food processor or blender.
2. Add lemon juice and sugar to taste. (If the melons are sweet, less than ½ cup sugar will be needed.)
3. Strain the purée through a fine sieve.
4. Freeze in an ice-cream freezer according to the manufacturer's directions. Store in the freezer compartment of your refrigerator.

PRESENTATION: Place one or two scoops on a serving plate and surround with assorted fruits, if desired.

SPECIAL EQUIPMENT:
Ice-cream freezer

Champagne Pineapple Sherbet

Sorbet d'Ananas et Champagne

If you reduce the amount of sugar in this recipe, the sorbet can be served between the fish and the meat courses.

TO SERVE 6

1 whole ripe pineapple,
  peeled and cored
Approximately ½ cup
  sugar
Juice of 1 lemon
1 half bottle champagne
  (not necessarily
  expensive)

1. Cut the pineapple into small pieces and purée in a food processor or blender. Add sugar and lemon juice to taste and combine well.
2. Transfer the pineapple to a bowl, stir in the champagne, and chill.
3. Freeze in an ice-cream freezer according to the manufacturer's directions.

PRESENTATION: Serve in chilled champagne glasses.

SPECIAL EQUIPMENT:
Ice-cream freezer

Raspberry Sherbet

Sorbet aux Framboises

1. In a food processor or blender, purée raspberries. Stir in sugar and lemon juice and strain through a fine sieve.
2. Freeze in an ice-cream freezer according to the manufacturer's directions.

NOTE: Frozen raspberries may be used, but if berries are sweetened, less sugar will be necessary.

SPECIAL EQUIPMENT:
Ice-cream freezer

TO SERVE 6

2 pounds raspberries
1 cup sugar
juice of 1 medium lemon

Champagne Sherbet

Sorbet Belle de Mai

Any white wine may be substituted for the champagne. If you wish to serve the sorbet between courses, add very little sugar in the second step.

1. Using a vegetable peeler, peel the zest of 1 orange; mince. Cook in 1 tablespoon sugar and 2 tablespoons water until tender and nearly caramelized.
2. Squeeze the remaining oranges and strain the juice. Combine with minced orange zest, champagne, lemon juice, and sugar to taste. Chill until cold.
3. Freeze in an ice-cream freezer according to the manufacturer's directions.

PRESENTATION: Serve in chilled champagne glasses.

SPECIAL EQUIPMENT:
Ice-cream freezer

TO MAKE 1½ QUARTS

6 oranges
1 tablespoon sugar
2 tablespoons water
1 bottle champagne
Juice of 1 lemon
Additional sugar, if
  necessary

Chocolate Chantilly
Chantilly au Chocolat

Use chocolate chantilly to decorate cakes, such as my chocolate cake (page 221) or For Chocolate Lovers Only (page 223).

TO MAKE 2 CUPS

1 cup heavy cream
2 tablespoons sugar
2 tablespoons cocoa

1. With an electric mixer, whip the cream until ribbons form. Beat in the sugar just until the cream holds soft peaks.
2. Sift the cocoa over the cream and fold in gently.

NOTE: Plain *crème chantilly* is prepared exactly the same way. Just omit the chocolate.

Almond Cream
Crème d'Amandes

For small almond tarts, fruit tarts, and especially *Pithiviers.*

TO MAKE 1½ POUNDS

7 ounces almond paste,
  cut into small pieces
½ cup minus 1
  tablespoon sugar
3 ounces unsalted butter,
  cut into small pieces
4 egg yolks

1. In a food processor fitted with the steel blade, combine all the ingredients. Process until smooth. Use as needed. Almond cream will keep up to 3 weeks, refrigerated.

NOTE: To make *Pithiviers* use 1 pound puff pastry (page 200), 1 egg (lightly beaten, for egg wash), and one recipe almond cream. Roll out the puff pastry ⅛ inch thick and cut out one 10-inch circle and one 11-inch circle. Place the smaller circle on a baking sheet and spread it with almond cream, leaving the outer 2 inches of the circle clean. Brush the outer pastry with egg wash and cover with the larger circle and lightly press down. Brush the top with egg wash and make a small hole in the center for steam to escape. Refrigerate for 1 hour. Using a small knife, cut decorative leaves into the top pastry circle (without cutting through it). Bake in a preheated 350° oven for 40 minutes. Serve warm, cut into wedges, with *sauce caramel* (page 248).

Pastry Cream
Crème Pâtissière

An all-purpose pastry cream that can be used to fill pastries such as cream puffs, *feuilletées,* and napoleons. To lighten, fold in whipped cream.

1. In a large saucepan, bring the milk and vanilla bean to a simmer. Turn off the flame, cover the pan, and let steep for 20 minutes. Remove the vanilla bean.
2. In a large mixing bowl, using a wire whisk, whip the egg yolks and sugar until pale lemon in color. Sift in the flour and stir with the whisk.
3. Slowly pour the hot milk into the egg yolk mixture, whisking all the while. Return contents of the bowl to the saucepan and, over medium heat, bring to a boil. Continue to beat with the whisk until the mixture thickens and boils for 1 minute.
4. Transfer the pastry cream to a bowl and dot with butter to avoid crust formation. Chill and use as needed. Pastry cream will keep three to four days, refrigerated.

TO MAKE 5 CUPS

4 cups milk
1 vanilla bean, split lengthwise
12 egg yolks
1⅓ cups sugar
¾ cups unsifted flour
1 teaspoon unsalted butter

Ganache

Ganache is used as a cake filling, cake frosting, or sauce. It will keep, refrigerated, for weeks. Because it hardens when chilled, bring it to room temperature or melt it over simmering water before using.

1. Place chocolate pieces in a medium bowl. Bring cream to a boil and pour it over the chocolate. Let sit for 3 minutes.
2. Using a wire whisk, blend the mixture until smooth and shiny. Cool and use as needed.

TO MAKE 1½ CUPS

¾ pound semisweet chocolate, cut into small pieces
1 cup heavy cream or crème fraîche

Praline

Used in the preparation of many pastries, praline can be stored in airtight containers for weeks.

TO MAKE APPROXIMATELY 9
OUNCES

½ cup sugar
2 tablespoons water
4 ounces shelled
  hazelnuts, with skins
  removed

1. Over a moderate flame, cook the sugar and water to a soft-ball stage (240°) or until the sugar looks white and sandy. Add the hazelnuts.
2. Continue to cook and stir until sugar melts to caramel stage.
3. Pour onto a buttered baking sheet to cool. When cool, break into small pieces.
4. In a food processor, grind the praline to desired consistency. Use as needed.

SPECIAL EQUIPMENT:
Candy thermometer

Sauce Caramel

Serve this sauce with fruit tarts, ice cream, or any dessert you wish.

TO MAKE 2 CUPS

8 ounces sugar
½ cup water
1½ cups heavy cream
3 tablespoons unsalted
  butter at room
  temperature, cut into
  small pieces

1. Combine the sugar and water in a heavy saucepan and cook, over moderate heat, until the sugar turns a light golden brown, which should take 15 to 20 minutes. Do not let the sugar burn.
2. Remove the saucepan from the heat and immediately add the cream, stirring until smooth.
3. Sprinkle the butter pieces over the sauce and let them dissolve. Stir to combine thoroughly.

NOTE: This sauce may also be served cold. It keeps well, covered with plastic wrap, in the refrigerator.

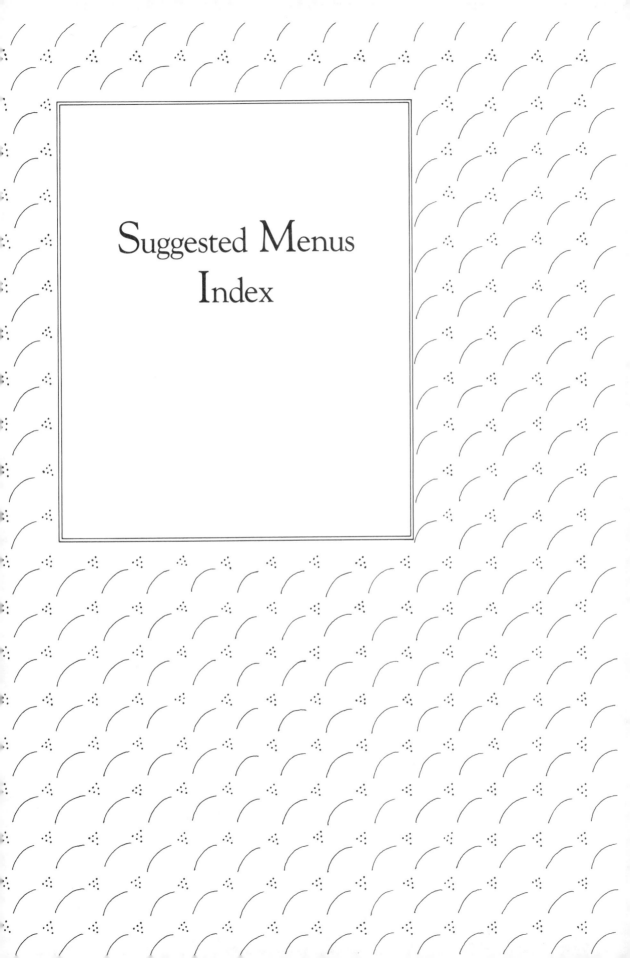

Suggested Menus
Index

Suggested Menus

Planning a menu deserves as much care as the artful preparation of the food. Most essential is viewing the meal as a whole. This overall approach includes considerations such as a general theme (ethnic, seasonal, holiday), the region in which you live (climate, and also availability of ingredients), the season, the number of guests (large numbers exclude elaborate recipes or *à la minute* dishes such as soufflés), your budget, and the range of kitchen equipment available to you.

This comprehensive view also involves more elusive and undefinable elements — personal aesthetics and individual tastes. Some cooks like smooth transitions from one course to the next. I prefer to stimulate and surprise my guests. I attempt to provide contrast by alternating flavors, colors, textures, and occasionally temperatures. Obviously, I try not to serve two fish dishes one after the other, or two similar sauces in close sequence. I am conscious of the balance of the meal as well; if I am serving an elaborate first course, I plan a lighter main course. The nature of my dessert depends on the character of the entire meal. I am never intimidated by tradition; I see no reason not to offer a red wine with fish if my guests and I enjoy it.

I have suggested some menus that you may find interesting to prepare. Most of them have been designed to use the best of the season.

At Ma Maison meat is ordered year-round, but when I cook at home for friends I usually reserve meat dishes for colder seasons (ground steak with Roquefort for a winter lunch). The creamy mushroom soup will impart a warm, cozy tone to your winter lunch, as will the hot pear tart with caramel sauce.

If you enjoy rich desserts such as the marjolaine, remember to offer a small slice; the sherbet served with it tempers the richness and refreshes the palate.

Regarding buffets and cocktail parties, I stress that although guests serve themselves at both, they will be standing at a cocktail party. Bite-size, easily manageable food is necessary. Soup is wonderful for a buffet, but a quiche or pâté is a delicious, practical choice for a stand-up situation.

Like a fine performance, your meal should have a sense of spectacle. This includes attention to table decoration, perhaps flowers, and imaginative lighting, which inspires a lovely mood. If you are short of time, prepare the table the night before; the most rewarding and enjoyable part of the meal should be the company of your good friends.

Bon appétit!

SPRING LUNCH

Asperges Vinaigrette
Asparagus Vinaigrette

Coquilles Saint-Jacques à la Crème
Scallops in Cream Sauce

Vacherin
Meringue with Ice Cream

SPRING DINNER

Soupe d'Écrevisses
Crayfish Soup

Médaillons de Veau à la Moutarde de Meaux
Veal Medallions in Meaux Mustard Sauce

Courgettes au Basilic et Tomates
Zucchini with Basil and Tomatoes

Feuilletée aux Framboises
Raspberries in Puff Pastry

SUMMER LUNCH

Crème d'Avocat Glacée
Cold Avocado Soup

Mille-Feuilles de Saumon
Salmon Napoleon

Concombres à l'Anethe
Cucumbers with Dill

Melon avec Sorbet au Porto et Framboises
Cantaloupe with Port Wine Sherbet and Raspberries

SUMMER DINNER

Salade des Pêcheurs
Fisherman's Salad

Canard aux Pêches et Poivre Vert
Duck with Peaches and Green Peppercorn Sauce

Marjolaine

Sorbet Belle de Mai
Champagne Sherbet

AUTUMN LUNCH

Potage Cressonière
Watercress Soup

Salade de Canard
Duck Salad

Mousse au Chocolat
Chocolate Mousse

AUTUMN DINNER

Pâtes Fraîches aux Truffes
Pasta with Truffles

Côtes d'Agneau Echalotes
Lamb Chops with Cream of Shallots

Champignons aux Fines Herbes
Mushrooms with *Fines Herbes*

Clafoutis aux Kiwis
Kiwi Fruit Tart

WINTER LUNCH

Crème de Champignons
Mushroom Soup

Biftek Haché au Roquefort avec Poivre Vert
Ground Steak with Roquefort Cheese and Green
Peppercorn Sauce

Soufflé Glacé Grand Marnier
Frozen Grand Marnier Soufflé

WINTER DINNER

Mousseline de Brocolis aux Morilles
Mousseline of Broccoli with Mushroom Sauce

Truite en Papillote
Trout with Vegetables Cooked in Foil

Endives Meunière
Braised Endives

Petite Tarte au Poires avec Sauce Caramel
Pear Tart with Caramel Sauce

FOUR SUPPERS

Crêpes Surprise

Bar et Saumon Cru aux Avocats
Bass and Salmon with Avocado

Glace au Miel
Honey Ice Cream

*

Salade d'Épinards
Spinach Salad

Feuilletée de Coquilles Saint-Jacques
Scallops in Puff Pastry

Ile Flottante: Oeufs à la Neige
Floating Island

*

Germiny Glacé
Cold Cream of Sorrel Soup

Saumon au Pistou
Provençal Salmon

Sorbet d'Ananas et Champagne
Champagne Pineapple Sherbet

*

Soupe à l'Oignon
Onion Soup

Petite Salade de Pigeon aux Noix
Pigeon Salad with Walnuts

Soufflé Glacé Grand Marnier
Frozen Grand Marnier Soufflé

ELEGANT BUFFET DINNER

Crème d'Avocat Glacée
Cold Avocado Soup

Artichauts à la Greque
Artichokes à la Greque

Filets de Truite en Chemise
Trout Fillets in Puff Pastry

Coq au Petit Sirah
Chicken in Petit Sirah

Champignons aux Fines Herbes
Mushrooms with *Fines Herbes*

Concombres à l'Aneth
Cucumbers with Dill

Mousse Café au Lait et Caramel
Coffee-Caramel Mousse

Allumettes
Matchsticks

LIGHT BUFFET DINNER

Pâté de Campagne
Country-Style Pâté

Poulet sous Croûte aux Morilles
Chicken Pie with Morels

Tarte Tatin
Apple Tart

COCKTAIL PARTY

Quiche

Saucisson en Brioche au Beurre Truffe
Sausage Wrapped in Brioche with Truffle Butter

Terrine de Poissons
Fish Terrine (cut into bite-size pieces)

Terrine de Canard aux Noisettes et Poivre Vert
Duck Terrine with Hazelnuts and Green Peppercorns

Crevettes au Poivre Rose
Shrimp with Pink Peppercorns

Bar et Saumon Cru aux Avocats
Bass and Salmon with Avocado

Feuilletée aux Framboises
Raspberries in Puff Pastry

Gâteau au Chocolat
Chocolate Cake

THANKSGIVING DINNER

Soupe d'Homard
Lobster Bisque

*Paupiettes de Canard aux Pistaches et Poivre
Vert*
Stuffed Breast of Duck

Galettes de Pommes de Terre
Crisp Potato Flowers

*Salade d'Haricots Verts et Champignons au
Noix*
Green Beans and Mushrooms with Walnut Dressing

Petite Tarte aux Poires avec Sauce Caramel
Pear Tart with Caramel Sauce

HOLIDAY DINNER

Huîtres aux Feuilles de Laitues
Oysters in Lettuce Bundles

Duck Soup and Cheese Ravioli

Pigeon Salmis avec Poires au Vin Rouge
Pigeon with Pears and Red Wine

Gâteau Négresco
Chocolate Bread Pudding

BRUNCH

Gazpacho
Cold Tomato-Vegetable Soup

Oeufs Pochés Toupinel
Poached Eggs Toupinel

or

Oeufs en Cocotte au Saumon et Oseille
Eggs with Salmon and Sorrel

Crêpes au Fromage Blanc et Raisins
Crêpes with Cheese and Raisins

Fresh Fruits and Berries in Season

Sorbet au Melon
Melon Sherbet

Index